The
Educational Technology
Reviews Series

Number eight
Instructional Systems

Educational Technology Publications
Englewood Cliffs, New Jersey 07632

√

Library of Congress Cataloging in Publication Data
Main entry under title:

Instructional systems.

    (Educational technology reviews series, no. 8)
    Articles selected from Educational technology.
    1. Teaching—Addresses, essays, lectures.
2. Curriculum planning—Addresses, essays, lectures.
I. Educational technology. II. Series.
[LB1025.2.I647]   371.3   72-12688
ISBN 0-87778-056-0

Printed in the United States of America.

First Printing: January, 1973.

ABOUT THIS BOOK

This volume contains articles published in recent issues of *Educational Technology* Magazine. The articles were selected from among a larger number of works dealing with the topic of this volume which have been published by the Magazine. The articles herein appeared originally in *Educational Technology* within the past five years.

This volume is to be revised periodically, according to developments in the field, as reflected in the pages of *Educational Technology*.

CONTENTS

Perspectives on the "Instructional System"

Ronald K. Randall
Contributing Editor

In educational innovation, maintenance of the proper perspectives is important, especially as the pressures for change increase and the availability of federal funds lubricates the process. With new instructional products finding their way into salesmen's brochures, and with the "systems approach" being applied to some very narrow sales pitches, only firm and broad perspectives can protect against the danger of "partial" solutions to educational problems — "solutions" which actually create more problems than they solve.

Properly viewed and applied, the "systems approach" can be a useful tool for maintaining the proper perspectives requisite to productive educational innovation and change. But it must be regarded in its very broadest sense and applied to the "whole" of task faced by educational institutions, not just to isolated parts. What is the most useful way of defining the "whole" of the schools' task?

The starting point must be a definition of the objectives sought through the educational process. Where do these objectives, related to curriculum design, come from? How are they interpreted and expressed? What should they consist of? These are questions subject to much controversy.

That objectives relate to changes produced in the pupils — the learners — is certain. The role of the instructional system managed by the schools may most simply be expressed as the achievement of these objectives, the engendering of these changes in the learners.

It is for this reason that the broadest perspective within which to define an "instructional system" must be learner-centered. Specifically, this means that it must avoid being either classroom-centered or even school-centered, for the very obvious reason that it is not only what goes on in the classroom or the school that effects changes in pupils. Jonathan Kozol's book, **Death at an Early Age,** is eloquent testimony to what happens when an educational system fails to appreciate fully the perspective of the pupil.

Recognizing this, a sufficiently broad definition of an instructional system might be phrased as follows:

> An instructional system is that **part** of the learner's environment which is purposely controlled by an instructional institution so as to secure by that learner the attainment of specified learning objectives.

The components of an instructional system defined on the basis of resource categories are:

- **Men,** who interact with the learner in the roles of:
  - Informer
  - Motivator
  - Leader
  - Example
  - Friend
  - Helper
  - Competitor

- **Materials,** which contain and present to the learner information and various forms of meaningful stimuli.

- **Machines,** which aid in the presentation of the materials to the learner and may implement some of the instructional methods employed (in this sense, a textbook is a machine).

- **Master Facilities,** which architecturally house and support the learner, men, materials and machines.
- **Methods,** which prescribe how the men, materials, machines and master facilities are to be employed in interaction with the learner to secure the attainment of the specified learning objectives.

Elements of the learner's environment which are typically not a part of the instructional system (because they are not controlled by the instructional institution) include his:

- **Social Environment,** consisting of his friends, contemporaries, and their social norms.
- **Home Environment,** which is dominantly influential (positively or negatively) in shaping basic values and attitudes.
- **Work Environment,** which may provide his source of income or possible opportunity for employment ambition.
- **Community Environment,** which includes formal and other institutions surrounding these other environments and the instructional institution as well.

There is inevitably a cross-current of influence between the instructional system and the environment it provides to the learner and these other environments not controlled by the instructional system. To the extent that the instructional system is carefully designed to take full advantage of, and encourage, available support from the "external" environments, its effectiveness may be enhanced.

Instructional systems which do not "articulate" the environment they offer the learner with his other environments run the almost inevitable risk of massive failure in achieving their objectives. Such articulation as is possible includes emphasis on:

- **Relevancy,** of curriculum and instructional methods to the value structures and situations confronting the learner in his external environments.
- **Organizational Coordination,** between the instructional institution and other institutions appearing in the external environments.
- **Direct Influence,** on the nature of the external environments, such as is possible through the provision of extra-curricular activities, guidance services to parents, structuring of the employment-seeking processes of the learners, and public statements on relevant social and political issues.
- **Instructional Techniques,** which lead to external encouragement for the learner in his activities within the instructional system.

By way of illustrating this last opportunity, the Behavioral Systems Division of the Westinghouse Learning Corporation has found that by the simple mention of "Mommy" and "Daddy" in a pre-school program, the pupil is encouraged to show off what he has just learned to his parents; this frequently leads to favorable reactions by the parents in the home environment expressed in very personal ways of high meaning to the youngster; these, in turn, encourage the development of an identity of values in the home and school environments and provide stimuli to the pupil to do well at school. While overgeneralization of the applicability of this one technique is dangerous, it does illustrate one way in which available support for the instructional system may be elicited from one important external environment.

Figure 1 is a somewhat surrealistic portrayal of the image of an instructional system resulting from the perspectives noted. In this portrait, those components of the instructional system itself (enclosed within the "Instructional Institution") are viewed in more of a functional than a resource category framework.

The primary men in the system who interact with the learner are identified as "other learners" (who also are present in the external social environment) and the "teacher." Since we are now more interested in the functional role played by each element of the instructional system, it is necessary to associate with the teacher role the impact of teacher training programs.

Similarly, machines and materials are presented as components of the "learning aids," which generalize to represent any inanimate item which aids in the learning process. As portrayed, the mechanical and informational components of a learning aid are not together a complete specification of its instructional role: Needed also is a statement of the manner in which the learning aid is to be used. We are all familiar with examples of learning aids (be they textbooks, instructional television, or computers) which can have very different instructional effects depending solely on how they are employed.

Another factor isolated within the instructional system is the role played by architecture. The current revolution in school architecture expresses clearly the importance of the shape taken by a school's master facilities, and is an indirect commentary on past instructional constraints imposed by the typical classroom layout.

A key point portrayed in this **Figure** is the central role played by the methods used to operate the instructional system, here divided into those relating to the instructional management function and those related to the administrative function. It is only as mediated by the instructional management methods that the other components of the system act to create the "instructional environment" which partially surrounds the learner. Whether it is through

Figure 1

Conceptual Scheme of Learner-Centered Instructional System

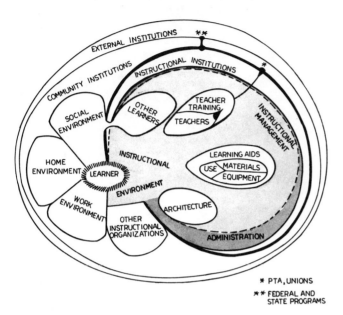

* PTA, UNIONS
** FEDERAL AND
   STATE PROGRAMS

a homeroom teacher or through team teaching, through group instruction or individualized instruction, through adult-led teaching, peer-tutoring, or independent study, the nature of the instructional management methods employed dominates the impact on the learner of the other components of the system. It is for this reason that these other components are imbedded in the all-encompassing instructional management function in the diagram.

With a less immediate, but nonetheless strong, influence on the instructional environment are the methods used in fulfilling the administrative function of the instructional institution. Included here would be student and teacher personnel accounting procedures, budgeting procedures, evaluation procedures, etc. The **Figure** illustrates how, largely through scheduling, assignment and disciplinary functions, the administrative function itself impinges directly on the learner's instructional environment.

Surrounding these other ingredients of the instructional system is the shape of the instructional institution itself. It defines the bounds of the instructional system as here defined, but clearly encloses only a part of the entire environment of the learner. In fact, it even fails to encompass the totality of explicitly instructional elements in the learner's environs, for such other organizations as clubs, boy scouts, summer camp, and the like, also provide the learner with more or less formal instruction.

And, of course, the social, home, and work environments of the learner are not entirely devoid of instructional influences on him, which takes us back to the initial emphasis in this perspective of an instructional system.

Purely political considerations force recognition in this picture of still further outer rings of institutional influences. All of the institutions and environments directly affecting the learner are themselves embedded within community institutions (both formally constituted organizations and social norms), and these, in turn are embedded within larger external institutions, such as state and national governments.

It is interesting to note, as pictured here, how certain institutional relationships bypass "normal" points of contact between elements of the entire learner-centered system. The teachers, for example, are "normally" considered within the framework of the instructional methods which specify the role they are to play, influenced by the administrative function of the instructional institution, and by employment relationships, a part of the instructional institution itself. But the growth of teachers unions, here considered as community institutions, provides a bypass around the instructional institution for one type of special-interest community pressure. Similarly, state and federal programs of aid and opportunity-equalization bypass community institutions in their impact on the instructional institution.

One last perspective is to be noted here, related to the two intertwined functions the instructional system must perform in order to accomplish its objectives. These are the development within the learner of:

- **Motivation** to attain the instructional objectives; and,
- **Mastery** of those objectives themselves.

While it is the latter function which describes the objective of the instructional system itself, it is evident that unless it is able to perform effectively the first function, it will not be able to carry out successfully the second. Conversely, no matter how motivating an instructional presentation may be (e.g., an entertaining film), if its design is not such as to ensure cognitive mastery of the instructional objectives encompassed, it will fail as an instructional vehicle.

The role of the perspectives commented upon here is simply to provide a larger context within which specific instructional techniques, products and proposals can be placed and their relationships to an instructional system's net impact on the learner traced. When this is done consistently, there is less danger of a too narrow appraisal of innovations in the instructional process and a greater likelihood that the wheat can be separated from the chaff in educational innovation. □

A Set of Procedures for the Planning of Instruction

John W. Childs

The purpose of this paper is to describe a specific set of procedures for the planning of instruction.

A flow chart is provided in **Figures 1 to 9.** This is intended to aid the reader in following the sequential decisions, activities and feedback functions of the proposed set of procedures.

Discussion on developmental model

The first activity block in the flow chart is traditional with the education profession. It allows for the inclusion in the developmental process of a number of significant inputs to the design system.

The basic goals and purposes of education, as drawn from the total society, must become a part of the educational enterprise. This initial block suggests that the designer can explicitly recognize the goals of his particular school, its purposes and aims.

Given a reasonably precise set of statements concerning the general goals and purposes of the school, the designer moves to the specification of the behavioral components of each of the goals.

The task of translating the content and experiences of the school into precise statements of behavior is an arduous and lengthy one. In an effort to develop individuals who can do the job of preparing behavioral specifications for something called a course, the author's experience has been that it takes two individuals working together to do a good job. The lone individual is inclined, by the nature of his thinking processes, to miss some significant aspect of the behavior to be learned or the conditions under which it will be learned as he prepares a behavioral specification. When the work is done by a team, the immediacy of feedback concerning missing elements in the specification produces a better behavioral specification in less time.

The meaning of the term "behavioral specification" as used here should be reviewed at this point. The first component of a good behavioral specification is a statement of a learner's observable performance. Examples of some observable performance statements are given below:

Given a map with a printed compass rose of the streets and main buildings surrounding a fictitious school building, the student will be able to answer at least six of ten questions based upon the identification of certain main buildings that would be reached if he followed the ten sets of walking directions from the school (like: walk two blocks west and three blocks north from the school) during a twenty minute period with the map and questions.

At the end of this unit a student will be able to differentiate between the initial sounds of "M" and "B"

There are several ways to construct observable performance statements. These statements are only representative of some behavior areas which may be found within a school.

Dr. Childs is acting director of the Department of Instructional Technology, Wayne State University, Detroit, Michigan.

Figure 1

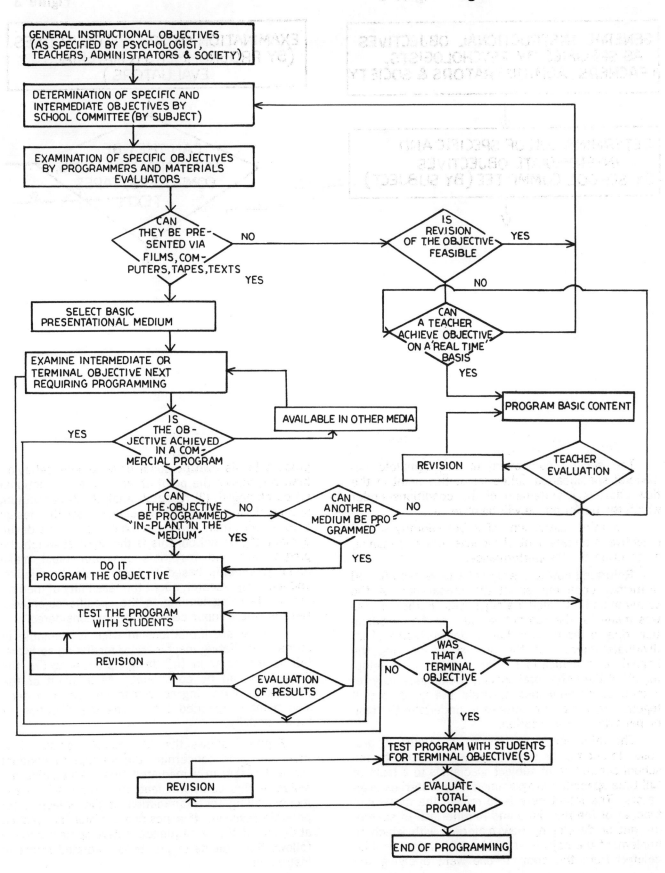

Figure 2

GENERAL INSTRUCTIONAL OBJECTIVES
AS SPECIFIED BY PSYCHOLOGISTS,
TEACHERS, ADMINISTRATORS & SOCIETY

↓

DETERMINATION OF SPECIFIC AND
INTERMEDIATE OBJECTIVES
BY SCHOOL COMMITTEE (BY SUBJECT)

↓

Figure 3

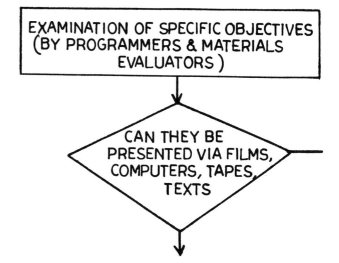

EXAMINATION OF SPECIFIC OBJECTIVES
(BY PROGRAMMERS & MATERIALS
EVALUATORS)

↓

CAN THEY BE
PRESENTED VIA FILMS,
COMPUTERS, TAPES,
TEXTS

↓

The second component of the complete behavioral specification called for at this point in the flow chart is a statement of the conditions under which the performance will be observed.

The third component of a behaviorally stated objective is a statement of the level of performance, or criterion for the performance.

Returning now to the flow chart, we need to add a further comment about the preparation of the terminal and intermediate objectives. Earlier, a case was made for the committee route to the specification, due to the need of having design teams of individuals interact in the process of drafting the behavioral specifications. The logistics of developing all of the behavioral specifications necessary for a total curriculum also suggests the need to pull together teams or committees to undertake the task of behavioral specification.

The third box in our flow chart **(Figure 3)** proposes to submit the specifications developed by the school committee of subject specialists to a team of full-time specialist programmers and materials evaluators. The intent here is to relieve the classroom teacher of the mundane and routine task of searching out or developing new materials with which to implement the objectives. This phase might well be deleted from the chart if one were applying the

process to his own personal development behavior; however, this is the point at which the instructional (1) psychologist, (2) research analyst, (3) curriculum specialist, and (4) media specialist enter the design process with their particular expertise. In the development of instruction, this is the point at which the programmer and materials evaluator must make initial judgments based on experience, knowledge, and learning research about the feasibility of mediating the learning leading to the specific objectives. Here is where input constraints are considered.

If there are limitations in what is available in terms of mediating machinery or mediating software, this is the point in the design process where the limitations can be considered. As a result of the information gathering activity in this block, a decision point is reached concerning the direction of future activity.

Figure 3 shows the "go, no-go" decision that must be made concerning the attempt to conduct the instruction in a mediated form. A negative decision at this point will lead to a sequence in the model calling for examination of the objective for possible revision. If a positive decision is reached at this point, then a sequence of development activity follows that selects or produces mediated forms of instruction.

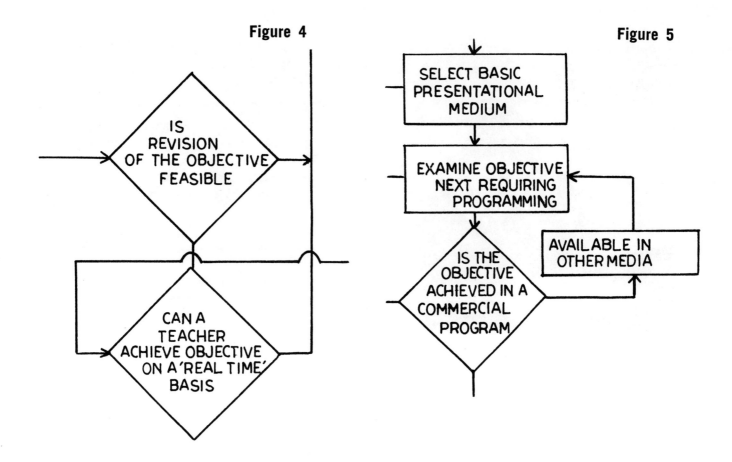

Figure 4

Figure 5

What choices are available if a negative decision chain results from an objective which the design team believes cannot be programmed in a mediated form? It has already been suggested that the first alternative in this situation is the possible revision of the objective; therefore, the first block on the negative chain is one of further decision making on the nature of the objective itself **(Figure 4).**

Two alternatives are available in the flow chart: first, the positive decision for revision and second, the negative decision, which leads to additional decision activity **(Figure 4).** If the design team believes that revision is possible, the proposed revision is fed back to the objective preparation team and a substitute objective is drafted and begins its way through the design process. If the design team believes that no revision is possible, or ascertains from the objective preparation group that no revision is possible, then the next block in the flow chart raises the question of realtime teacher instruction.

Why, in **this** model, was it decided to put the decision for teacher handling of the objective in real-time after the question of other forms of mediation?

If the decision block for teacher handling of the objectives is placed before the mediation question, teacher handling will frequently occur when some other form might do equally well. It is believed that in the end the teacher **can** do just about any instructional task. But should he? Thus, it seems wise to raise the question of mediated individualized instruction first in the flow chart.

Returning to the teacher decision chain **(Figure 4),** two alternative decisions again occur. One, the teacher **can** do it on a real-time basis; or two, the teacher **cannot** do it. In the event that the negative decision is made, the model shows a feedback to the objectives determination block. If the first decision is made for teacher handling, then a move is made to a design sequence which produces or secures the content resources the teacher will need to handle the objective.

A return to the main sequence of the developmental flow chart **(Figure 5),** picks up at the mediation decision block. A positive decision at this point results in a task activity labeled "select the basic presentational medium." This particular block implies the full means for the completion of this task.

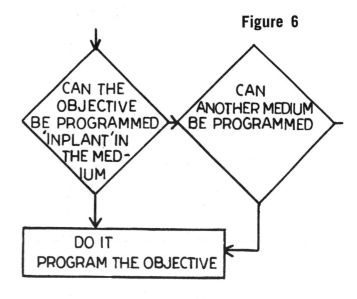

Figure 6

At this date, the media field knows far too little about the decision structure to use in carrying out this task. Some fairly good specifications of the media characteristics exist, but there is no evidence to tie these characteristics to the learning suggested by the specific objectives. Decisions can be made here by considering such things as logistical requirements, ease of preparation of material, visual or audio nature of the learning experience or the availability of the medium. What is needed is a classification structure that will allow the designer to **match the medium to the behavioral objective.**

Two efforts at this type of matching have been

widely distributed. Robert Gagné, in Chapter XI of his book, **The Conditions of Learning,** (Holt, 1965) supplies a chart relating his eight learning types (into which behavioral objectives may be fitted) to the specific medium of communication that may be appropriate for that type of learning.

Leslie J. Briggs wrote of another procedure for achieving this end in the March, 1967, issue of "Audiovisual Instruction" under the title "A Procedure for the Design of Multimedia Instruction." He drew upon the work of Gagné for his learning-type classification, but chose to approach the media

Figure 7

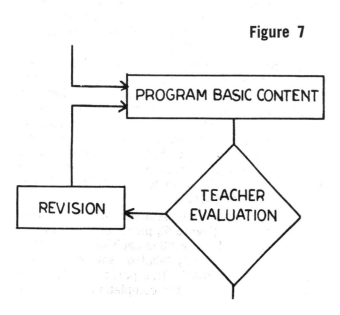

Figure 8

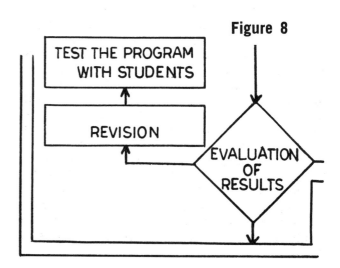

selection process on an overall basis for a series of objectives rather than an objective by objective base. Both Gagné and Briggs indicate a need for considerable additional research on the media-matching variables.

Once the basic presentational medium is selected, further efforts must be conducted to develop the medium in line with the objectives of the mediated sequence **(Figure 5)**. The next activity block on the flow chart indicates this need by suggesting that each objective be taken on for examination of its implications for the design of the instructional material within the selected medium. It results in a decision block in which the designer must answer the question of programming the objective with the design team or selecting the program from a commercially available source.

This decision block is essential to the function of the media specialist. Neither the time nor the funds are available to buy time to create the wheel all over again. If an objective is embodied in the material prepared by an outside agency, then we must make use of the material in order to have the energy and time to create the many resources that do **not** exist.

This decision block has three alternatives: First, a positive response that indicates the objective exists in a mediated form, in which case there is a skip ahead to the trial testing of the mediated form; second, the possibility exists that the objective is met in commercially available form but in a medium other than that selected in the previous sequence. In this case, the feedback is to the medium selection activity to check the appropriateness of altering the medium selection. The third alternative here is a new decision block to determine if the objective can be met through the preparation of a mediated unit in the medium selected within the confines of the design team's development resources.

If a positive decision is made here **(Figure 6)**, then the design team turns over the objective and the specifications for the learning material to the programmer for the medium being used. If the decision is negative, then another design team decision is necessary. At this point, other commercially available media have been ruled out. The remaining decision must be to program in another medium or to feed the objective back for revision or reconsideration of teacher handling.

If the decision is to go back to teacher handling **(Figure 4)**, then we enter again our secondary decision chain. Given that the decision is made to have a teacher handle the objective **(Figure 7)**, the basic program content for the teacher must be prepared along with any additional supplementary materials. An addition to this decision chain (that does not occur in regular teaching patterns as we now know them) is the planned teacher tryout and revi-

sion cycle for the development of teacher handled objectives.

Returning to the main decision chain and the other alternate decision on programming in another medium **(Figure 6)**, the DO IT activity block appears once again.

Perhaps next to the stress placed on objectives in this model of instructional development is the stress placed on the pretesting of materials for their ability to produce the changes in student behavior called for by the objectives. Thus, the activity block following the act of preparing the mediated material in the selected medium is the testing of the mediated instruction with students **(Figure 8)**.

If this phase of instructional development is treated rigorously, and sufficient tests are conducted to "debug" the instruction, it may be expected that the mediated instruction will be adequately developed for a major trial without damaging results to a large segment of the students for which the instruction is designed. This stage of pilot testing and revision should be an integral part of the design team's activity during the preparation of the material to meet each objective.

Figure 9

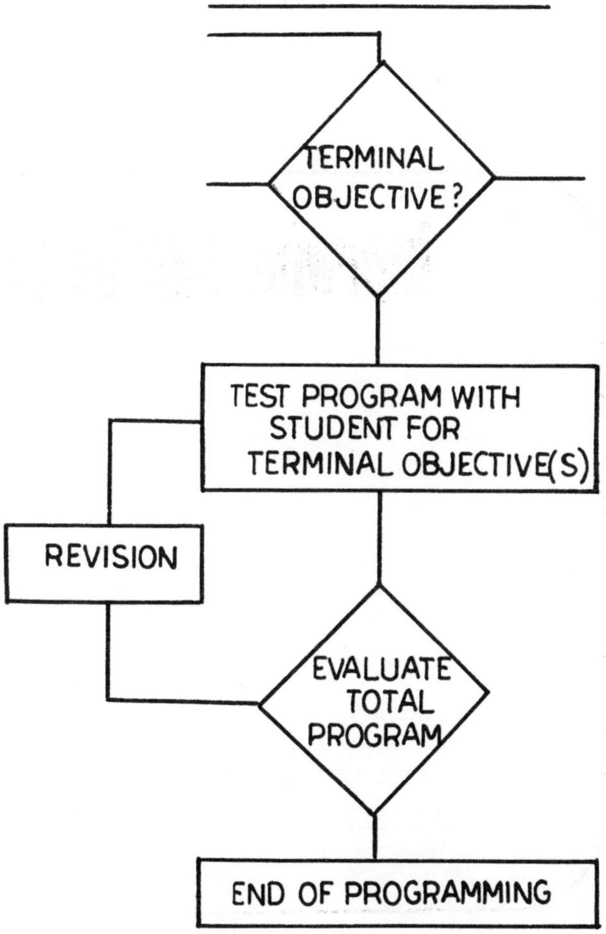

Next **(Figure 9)**, the flow chart leads to the activity block of revision. After enough cycles of pilot evaluation followed by revision, two alternative decisions can be made concerning further activity; **(Figure 9)** the design team may reach a decision to completely recycle to consider other instructional strategies, such as teacher handling. The intent is that the evaluation of the mediated instruction will be satisfactory and thus the design effort will move into another decision situation.

The second alternative will be taken if the objective the team has programmed is a terminal one; hence, the developed mediated instruction will move to full scale testing with a large group of students. This test may result in some revision **(Figure 9)**. A cycle for this activity is shown on the flow chart. Following total program review, the instructional planning comes to an end.

In the event that the objective(s) under design consideration is not a terminal objective at the pilot test point, the system recycles to pick up and carry through a new objective(s) until a terminal one is reached **(Figure 9)**.

Summary

The complex description of the functions depicted by the flow chart can be summarized in a set of procedural steps. The procedural steps are, in essence, the decision activities that must go on in the process of instructional design.

1. Determine general objectives.
2. Determine the behavioral objectives.
3. Specify the learning types for each objective.
4. Determine the feasibility of mediated instruction or teacher-handled instruction: if neither, revise objectives.
5. Select the basic presentational medium.
6. Examine each objective and develop programming specifications.
7. Choose between in-house programming and selecting from commercial sources of mediated programs which meet the objectives.
8. Program the objective in-house.
9. Test the program with students.
10. Revise the mediated program.
11. Evaluate the mediated program with a large student population.
12. Revise and conclude the instructional development sequence for any given set of behavioral objectives. □

10

Components of A Cybernetic Instructional System

M. David Merrill

A system is any group of parts or components working together as a functional unit. All systems include at least three basic elements. The **input** unit provides some process by which material or information is entered into the system. The **processor** acts on the material or information to modify it in some way. The **output** unit consists of some procedure for discharging the results of the process from the system. One useful way to describe the process of learning is to consider the learner as a system.

Learner as a system

The learner system can be subdivided into various components. The senses convert physical energy input into nervous impulses which are transported to the central nervous system.

Perception is a process which interprets the nervous energy and sometimes distorts. the representation of the physical environment as a result of the learner's previous experiences, feelings and attitudes.

Dr. Merrill is visiting assistant professor of educational psychology at Stanford University and research associate at Stanford's Center for Research and Development on Teaching. He is on leave from Brigham Young University.

The memory component is a mechanism for storing a representation of the physical input as modified by the perception component. This unit also involves some mechanism for retrieving the information once it is stored.

The thinking component is a process which enables the learner to manipulate what has been stored by combining, modifying and restructuring the content of memory to produce predictions concerning future physical events in the environment and to represent imaginary stimulation which does not exist in the environment.

The muscles and skeletal system provide the output unit which enables the learner to express the results of the processing conducted by the other components. This expression of behavior represents the output of the system.

The learner system described to this point has been an open loop system, which means that the output of the system has no effect on future input nor on subsequent output. In a **closed loop system** the output is returned to the system and consequently affects future output of the system. Closed loop systems are often referred to as cybernetic systems.

Cybernetic comes from the Greek word **kybernetes,** meaning pilot or governor and **kybernan,** meaning to steer or govern. Cybernetic systems are systems which have some mechanism for controlling or governing themselves.

The most familiar and frequently used example of a cybernetic system is the home heating system. The output is heat, which raises the room temperature. The room temperature is put back into the system by a thermostat which compares it with some preset standard. When the temperature in the room is less than the preset standard, an electrical current starts the furnace. When the room temperature is equal to the present temperature the furnace shuts off. Output from a system which is returned as input to control future output is called **feedback.**

A more accurate description of a learner system is illustrated in Fig. 1. Three kinds of sensory input are indicated. The stimulus situation indicates some physical energy from the environment acting on the senses of the learner and to which, through the process of learning, he develops a reaction or response.

When a learner makes a response, two additional kinds of stimuli are produced. First, the learner feels, sees, hears or in some other way senses the fact that he has made a response. Stimulus input resulting from making some response is called **proprioceptive feedback.**

Second, the response made by the learner usually produces some change in the environment. The stimulus input which indicates to the learner the nature of the change produced in the environment is called **knowledge of results.**

Both of the sensory inputs which result from making a response provide feedback to the learner. This feedback is used by the learner to modify his subsequent responses. The process of response modification as a result of proprioceptive feedback and knowledge of results is called **learning.**

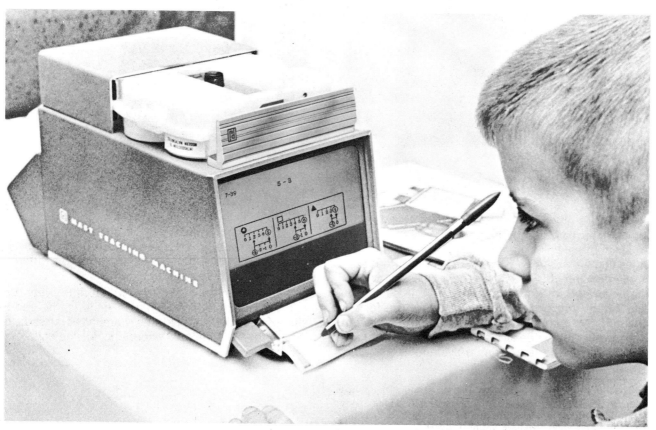

Learning theories are attempts by scientists, who are studying the learning process, to identify the component parts of the learner system and to explain how each of these components operate to produce a modification of responses. While scientists do not always describe their theories in system notation, it is usually possible to make such a translation.

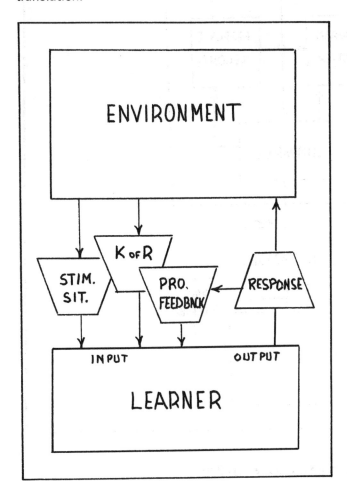

Fig. 1. The learner as a cybernetic system

An instructional system

The discussion to this point has been concerned with the learner system. The description of the environment in relation to the learner system has been ambiguous.

It was established earlier that learning occurs whenever the learner interacts with the environment. **Instruction,** however, involves only interactions with a particular kind of environment and only when there is a deliberate attempt to produce a particular kind of behavior. Instruction represents a subset of all learning situations. An instructional situation requires a particular kind of environment which might be conceptualized as an instructional system.

An instructional system may be any of a number of kinds of environments including classrooms with live teachers, audiovisual presentations, books, machines or any combination of these elements. Like all previously discussed systems, an instructional system also has three major elements.

Outputs of an open instructional system consist primarily of a structured display to the student.

A cybernetic instructional system would also include K of R to the learner and some record of student responses. Inputs to an open instructional system include library material (subject matter content), an indication of learner characteristics and objectives.

A cybernetic instructional system would also include student responses as feedback input. The processor controls the presentation and in a cybernetic system modifies the presentation of the display and/or K of R on the basis of student response correspondence to the objectives.

Fig. 2 illustrates a cybernetic instructional system. The first essential input is the content or material to be presented or displayed to the student. It is convenient to refer to all such material as **library input** and realize that this input may include written material, audiovisual materials of all kinds, programmed instruction frames, diagrams, models, actual events or things, and even information stored in the head of the teacher if the teacher is part of the system.

Perhaps the most important input to an instructional system is the objectives (performance standards) which the system is designed to accomplish.

A third input for a cybernetic instructional system is information concerning the individual characteristics of the students who will interact in the system. This information is essential if the rules for operation of the various components are to be adequate for teaching individuals. This input will be referred to as **learner traits.**

Because this is a cybernetic system, the fourth type of input consists of the feedback from the learner in the form of learner response. Without this feedback input, an instructional system is not able to adjust the presentation to produce the changes in behavior specified by the objectives input.

It should be recognized that in much instruction in schools and elsewhere the input from student response is ignored.

The first essential output from an instructional system is the display to the learner. A **display** can take many forms and does not necessarily infer written material. A given display may be aural, such as a lecture or explanation; visual, such as a picture, movie, model; written, such as a book, frame of programmed instruction, words on the blackboard; tactual, such as an object for the learner to feel; olfactory, such as an odor for the learner to smell; in short, a display is any stimulus situation structured and presented to the learner for the purpose of establishing some response or potential for response.

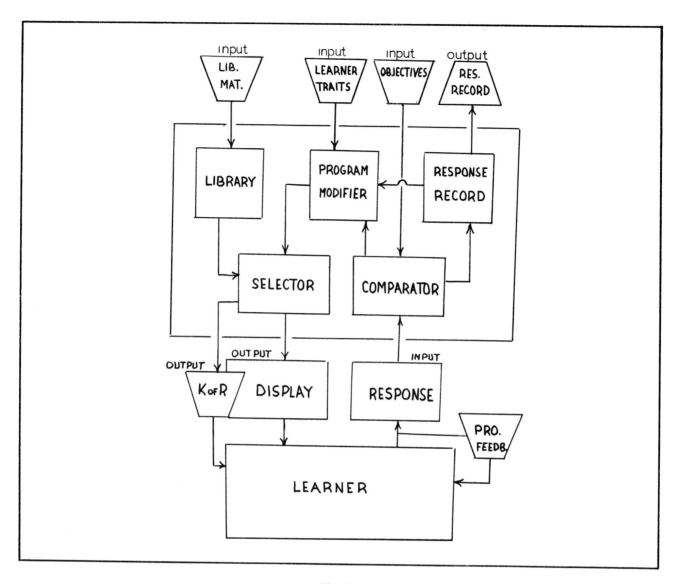

Fig. 2.
Components of cybernetic instructional system

In a cybernetic system a second output presented to the learner is some form of **knowledge of results.** This may be simple information such as right or wrong or may include lengthy demonstrations or explanations of the probable cause of error. The knowledge of results may be immediate or delayed for several hours, days, or longer.

If student response is input to the system, a third type of output which may or may not be used in a particular instructional situation is some **record** of each student's responses. This record may be lengthy and detailed, such as the amount of time required and response chosen on every frame of a machine program or it may be abbreviated, such as the mid-term and final grades in a course.

In an open loop instructional system, the processor is some selection mechanism which presents displays in a linear fashion, one following the other.

Movie or filmstrip presentations are good examples of such an open loop system. Books and other types of presentations may be more or less cybernetic depending on how they are written or on how the learner uses them.

A cybernetic system such as the one illustrated in Fig. 2 is much more flexible. In operation the system must first make some display to the student, who then reacts to the display by making some response. The **comparator** component compares the response with the objective entered into the system.

A record of the comparison and/or the response is recorded in the response record. The results of the comparison are fed to the **selector,** which determines the type of K of R to be presented and to the **modifier,** which makes a decision concerning the adequacy of the presentation and determines if the selection sequence will be altered.

If the student did not make the expected response, the Modifier changes the sequence and indicates that a new sequence is to be followed or that some review sequence is to be introduced to the learner.

If the student made the expected response, control will be returned to the selector, which selects the next display in the sequence from the library and presents it to the student.

Instructional theory

A theory of instruction consists of the identification of the component parts of the instructional system and a description of the principles which are used by the components to select, modify, and present the display and knowledge of results so as to produce particular kinds of responses in the learner.

To be useful, instructional theory must be prescriptive rather than merely descriptive.

Principles specified by such a theory should include rules specifying the display and knowledge of results requirements for producing particular responses (presentation rules); rules specifying the requirements for measuring particular responses and and for comparing responses with objectives (evaluation rules); rules for altering the presentation to adapt to the particular requirements of individual students (individualization rules), and rules indicating modification required when feedback from the student indicates that a particular presentation failed to produce the desired behavior (modification rules).

Since instruction aims at behavior change in some specified direction, the first requirement for establishing an operating instructional system is the identification of the desired outcomes or objectives.

If every objective represents a unique behavior, then the establishment of presentation and evaluation rules becomes a difficult if not impossible task. On the other hand, if objectives can be classified into a finite number of types and an appropriate set of presentation and evaluation rules identified for each type, the task is greatly simplified.

An instructional theory, therefore, requires a classification system for objectives such that for each category in the classification a unique set of presentation and evaluation rules can be identified.

It is anticipated that each presentation and evaluation rule thus identified will require a number of parameters for its specification.

It is further postulated that the function of individualization rules will be to specify the values of the parameters required for individuals with similar relevant characteristics.

If all such rules were known, it would be possible to specify the techniques required to establish any behavior in any individual. Because it is unlikely that all the parameters required by such a theory will be identified in the foreseeable future, it is necessary to specify modification rules so that the system can learn how to teach a particular behavior to a given individual.

This implies that not only must the system modify the instruction for given individuals who fail to attain the objectives but also that it remembers such modifications and implements these same changes when other individuals with similar characteristics are encountered. This leads to a discussion of research strategy with a cybernetic instructional system.

Research on instruction

Perhaps two research strategies can be identified which facilitate the development of an instructional theory. The first approach emphasizes **modification** rules. A program is developed to produce in the learner a specified response or series of responses. As learning proceeds, a record of student responses is accumulated. At given intervals or after a certain number of responses, the record is compared with the performance standards.

If the learner's record does not compare adequately with the performance standards, the presentation rules are modified. After another segment of the presentation, another comparison is made. Modification continues until an adequate procedure is discovered for the particular learner.

If a careful aptitude profile is collected for each student and the individual response records of many students are collected and the strategy changes are carefully identified, then students for whom a given presentation proved effective can be grouped together and their aptitude profiles examined for common elements.

This procedure should yield individualization rules which can subsequently be verified by administering the appropriate strategy to other students who have a similar aptitude profile.

The procedure is generalizable only to the extent that the number of classes of students is small in number and the aptitudes used as a basis for classification are appropriate to other presentations designed to develop similar behaviors in other subject areas.

The value of the strategy changes used is related also to the generalizability of the strategy to other tasks having similar characteristics but teaching different content.

A second research approach might be characterized as a model building or theoretical approach. (It should be noted that the previous approach is not really a sans theory approach, since the number of strategy changes possible and/or the number of aptitude records collected can not be infinite and whatever basis is used for their selection must to some extent reflect theoretical notions.)

In this latter approach a careful analysis is made of the various components of the instructional system, and classification schemes are hypothesized. A given behavioral objective is identified as a member of a particular class of responses. Presentation rules and evaluation rules are hypothesized for each such response class. Individualization rules are postulated and empirically investigated to determine values and qualities for the parameters of the presentation rules.

The emphasis in this approach is on presentation rules rather than modification rules.

This second research technique can proceed at various levels. First, the adequacy of response classification can be checked by comparison of presentation rules. If the presentation rules for one kind of response class are not different from those of another class, there is no value in postulating different response classes.

Second, alternative sets of presentation and evaluation rules can be proposed for a particular behavioral outcome and their relative effectiveness in establishing the desired behavior compared.

Third, various values can be assigned to the parameters of the presentation and evaluation rules and the relative effectiveness compared for different categories of individuals classified on various aptitude measures.

While research on learning is primarily concerned with the identification and description of various components of the learner, research on instruction is primarily concerned with the identification and description of the various components of the instructional system. These two research concerns are closely related but do not represent mirror images.

Learning research often has instructional implications, but understanding the learner system may not be sufficient for prescribing instructional strategies.

Furthermore, a completely adequate description of the learner system is not yet available. But in spite of its absence it is still possible to develop and experimentally validate prescriptive descriptions of an instructional system. □

A Systems Model for Instructional Design and Management

Bruce W. Tuckman and Keith J. Edwards

The purpose of this article is to describe a systems model for the design and management of instruction. The model provides for certain critical features; it proceeds in a systematic fashion; it builds in the feature of relevance; it deals with measurable behaviors; and it specifies the relationships among learnings to be achieved.

The model is broken down into three phases. The first phase, called *analysis*, contains the following three activities in sequence: (1) specification of post-instruction tasks via task analysis, (2) restatement of task as behavioral objectives, and (3) specification of a sequence for behavioral objectives (structural analysis). Following the analysis phase, the *synthesis* phase is undertaken. This phase involves two activities, occurring in parallel: (1) specification of instructional activities, and (2) design of evaluative procedures. The final phase, *operation*, includes two simultaneous activities: (1) carrying out of instructional activities, and (2) the collection of evaluative data. Following these three phases comes a fourth activity, *feedback and iteration*, wherein the data collected during the phase of operation are fed back into the system so that it can be tested, validated and redesigned based on input data. This redesign based on feedback is then followed through to its completion from the point of reentry. The model is shown diagrammatically in Figure 1.

Within this article each activity will be described briefly. Since some of these activities have already been specified in detail in other writings, the purpose here will simply be to refer the reader to these sources. In cases where less detailed writing has been generated, descriptions will include a greater amount of detail.

A. Analysis

1. *The Specification of Tasks Via Task Analysis.*

Task analysis is a procedure by which desired behavioral outcomes are specified in the form of tasks. That is, some final behavioral capacity is analyzed into a series of those tasks that make it up. Task analysis has been most heavily employed in the vocational or occupational field. For example, in considering an occupation such as an electronics technician, one would

Bruce W. Tuckman is professor of education, and Keith J. Edwards is research assistant professor of education at Rutgers University, New Brunswick, New Jersey.

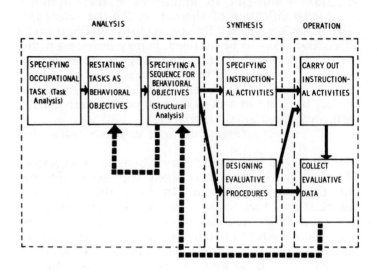

Figure 1

A Systems Model for Instructional Management

attempt to specify the tasks that an electronics technician performs. Similarly, if one wanted to conduct a task analysis of the occupation of secretary, one would take the occupation and analyze it into the tasks that make it up. A task analysis of the secretarial occupation might include such activities as typing a letter, taking messages, preparing and organizing reports, taking dictation, etc. Also, one would be likely to enunciate tasks dealing with interpersonal relations, such as greeting visitors and reflecting the image of the organization. Through the use of such a task analysis, one is able to describe the full range of activities that a person may perform in that occupation.

While task analysis has been traditionally associated with occupations, there is no reason that it cannot be used as a point of departure for instructional material development in any learning area.

The notion that one begins in the design of instruction by specifying the tasks as the goals of instruction represents a departure from the typical techniques used for curriculum development. However, if instruction is seen as a route toward the performance of a wide range of tasks, then it is useful to attempt to identify those tasks in advance so that instructional sequences can be developed which are aimed specifically at the attainment of the tasks. While there are models for task analysis in the vocational areas, models have not been developed in academic, civic or personal-social areas. Thus, the use of the task analysis approach in these areas will represent an attempt to determine how such a task analysis can best proceed.

It is also entirely possible that the specification of academic, civic and personal-social tasks will show generalizability from student to student, school to school and community to community. If such is the case, it should be possible for schools, communities and students to examine a list of tasks in each area and to specify those that are useful for its purposes. Thus, the prespecification of tasks that define an area of interest or activity may provide a highly efficient route to allow for the individualization of goals on the levels of the student, the school and the community. Freedom of selection is difficult to implement if there is not a suitable specification of alternatives. To the extent that task analysis provides for an extensive delineation of alternative tasks to be attained, it may provide a highly useful vehicle for students and program developers in specifying the goals to result from a series of learning experiences. To the extent that students make the choice, they are in a position to uniquely individualize their own educational experience.

2. *The Restatement of Tasks as Behavioral Objectives.*

Much has been written about behavioral objectives. Their use has become increasingly widespread throughout the academic world. In fact, there are now organizations that collect or "bank" and catalogue behavioral objectives making them available for use by any school system or individual teacher.* In addition, much inservice training has been afforded to teachers in the writing of behavioral objectives. However, the role of behavioral objectives in the instructional design and management process has not been clearly spelled out. The purpose of the discussion here is to better specify the place of behavioral objectives in the total sequence of instructional design.

As can be seen from the model shown in Figure 1, behavioral objectives represent neither the beginning nor the end, but merely one step in the total process. By arbitrarily taking the instructional activity that presently constitutes a curriculum and attempting to enunciate behavioral objectives for that instruction, one may be acting to improve the potential of that instruction and the evaluation of performance as a by-product of that instruction. *But* one is not of necessity making that instruction more relevant. Rather than starting with "what is," one needs to consider "what should be" in terms of curriculum and instruction. This is accomplished through the use of a task analysis. Such task analyses provide statements of goals or end-points that are not arbitrary to the instruction being developed, but rather are quite meaningful and relevant in terms of students and their needs. However, in order for the goals identified through task analysis to be suitable building blocks for a systematic curriculum design, it is necessary to put them in a form where they can be used for sequencing, instructional materials design and evaluation. It has been found that the behavioral objective is a useful rendition of the goal statement for the above purposes. Thus, the second step in the process is characterized by an attempt to take the task specified in the task analysis in the first step and to restate these tasks in the form of behavioral objectives.

A behavioral objective, as has been said many times, includes a statement of performance—typically using an action verb, a statement of the conditions under which the performance is to occur, and a statement of the criteria against which the performance is to be evaluated.* By the systematic use of performance language as well as the specification of conditions and criteria, the behavioral objective becomes a useful device for subsequent steps in the instructional management model. However, it is again emphasized that the arbitrary selection of instructional material which is then converted to behavioral objectives is not consistent with the total philosophy of this approach.

3. *Specification of a Sequence for Behavioral Objectives (Structural Analysis).*

Structural analysis, as has been described in detail by Tuckman (1968b), is a technique for specifying the sequential relationships among behavioral objectives. This process is shown in its simplest form in Figure 2. With regard to learning activity as specified by a behavioral objective as a terminal point, one can ask three questions, i.e., (1) what competencies can a learner achieve only after prior achievement of the one in question, (2) what competencies must a learner have already achieved in order to achieve the one in question, and finally, (3) what competencies are reasonably independent of, and therefore can be taught concomitantly with, the one in question?

Figure 2

Specifying a Sequence for Behavioral Objectives

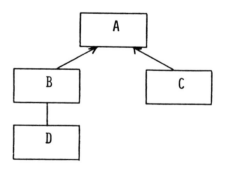

For Example:

(1) What Activities Must This Activity Precede? For B, It Must Precede A.

(2) What Activities Must Precede This Activity? For B, D Must Precede It.

(3) What Activities Can Occur Concomitantly (i.e., Are Parallel)? For B, C Is Parallel.

---

*The Center for the Study of Evaluation at the University of California, Los Angeles, has established the Instructional Objectives Exchange as a depository for behavioral objectives and related evaluation measures (see Popham, 1969).

*The mechanics of writing behavioral objectives have been set forth in various sources including Mager (1962) and Tuckman (1967).

Through the use of this approach, it becomes possible to specify a sequence of instructional objectives which, when put together in the order specified, should maximize movement from entry into instruction to the attainment of some final goal.

The activity of structural analysis is predicated upon the supposition that learning is a sequential process featuring the operation of contingent relationships among the competencies, skills and concepts to be mastered. The establishment of an appropriate sequence, moreover, is one of the essential conditions of learning. The purpose of structural analysis is to attempt to establish, on an *a priori* or hypothetical basis, the contingencies that exist among the competencies to be acquired. This analysis provides the instructional designer or manager with a map to follow in setting forth the order of instructional activities to maximize the probability that each activity will be successful. The instructional manager can then attempt to identify the prerequisites for any set of competencies, with the former serving, in turn, as prerequisites for higher-order competencies. Without this approach, behavioral objectives must be sequenced on some more haphazard and less systematic basis. Ideally, therefore, one would proceed from the restatement of tasks as behavioral objectives to the specification of an order in which these behavioral objectives are to be covered within instruction, this activity being termed structural analysis.

Structural analysis is also highly useful within the evaluation process because it provides a framework into which evaluative data can be fed. The instructional sequence map becomes the vehicle by which individual performance data can be used to assess and improve the instructional process. This function of feedback in structural analysis will be elaborated upon later under the heading of *Feedback and Iteration*.

B. Synthesis

1. *Specification of Instructional Activities.*

The instructional manager is now ready to generate and specify instructional activities. He has already produced a thorough-going analysis of the goals as tasks, as behavioral objectives and as behavioral objectives located in a sequence with their relationships to each other specified. The task remains to design instructional activities which will be aimed at the achievement of these sequenced behavioral objectives. At this point a wide variety of possibilities exists.

It will suffice to simply mention the fact that instructional activity should require some action or participation on the part of the learner, and it should take advantage of multiple instructional alternatives utilizing the full range of media and technology available. Moreover, within the instructional process one should prescribe individual or small group activities where teachers represent one of many instructional resources; and finally and perhaps more importantly, the specification of these instructional activities should be given to the students directly rather than mediated via the teacher. More specifically, the teacher (or manager, or designer) should develop a specification of instructional activities including setting forth textbook pages to be read, other resource books to be examined, films to be watched, audio tapes to be listened to, laboratory experiments to be carried out, shop activities to be carried out, teachers to be spoken to, classmates to be spoken to, etc. This series of instructional activities, relevant to the achievement of an objective, should be given to the student so that he can then, at his own speed and in his own way, go about carrying out the activities in order to guarantee his own competence. Needless to say, this activity must include within it the opportunity for evaluation of not only the student, but also of the instructional process and the instructional materials. This leads to the next step, designing evaluative procedures, which should be carried out at the same time that instructional materials and activities are being produced.

2. *Designing Evaluative Procedures.*

Three types of evaluation are appropriate for discussion here, although, again, none of the three will be dealt with in detail. The first type of evaluation, individual evaluation, is the monitoring of the performance of each individual student as a basis for making decisions about his further progression in a particular sequence or movement on to other sequences. Individually oriented instruction based on the systems model described herein requires reasonably constant monitoring of student performance and instructional prescriptions based on the level of this performance. In order to accomplish this, frequent evaluations must be carried out. Thus, evaluative procedures must be developed in conjunction with the development of instructional activities employing the same behavioral objectives and structural analysis that preceded the development of instructional activities.

The second type of evaluation has been called formative evaluation (Scriven, 1967). Formative evaluation represents an attempt to evaluate the behavioral objectives and their sequencing in order to provide the possibility of improvement in the instructional package. The evaluation is ongoing and occurs concurrently with the instruction. Formative evaluation is distinct from individual evaluation in that the focus is upon the instruction itself rather than the learner. It provides feedback which will help improve the materials as they are being used. Formative evaluation procedures and their relation to structural analysis and behavioral objectives have been set forth in detail by Tuckman (1967).

Finally, a third type of evaluation, called summative evaluation, is the overall evaluation of a final instructional package. Such evaluation does not occur during the development of instructional materials but typically occurs subsequent to their development and refinement. Thus, at some point during the development process, one must begin to think in terms of summative evaluation, but this will more profitably occur late in the developmental process. The design of summative evaluation procedures has been described in considerable detail in Tuckman (1967).

Overall, the process of designing evaluative procedures entails the examination of each behavioral objective incorporated into the sequence and the development of a measurement activity to determine whether the goal as set forth behaviorally has been attained by the student. Thus, in designing evaluative procedures, one attempts not only to measure the success or failure in performance of the terminal objective but to determine relative success and failure of each subordinate or enabling objective which exists in the structure and has been identified as prerequisite to a terminal objective. By measuring performance on each sub-objective and the terminal objective, a detailed evaluation of the instructional package is possible.

If the behavioral objectives have been precisely stated and their sequence properly specified, the task of designing evaluative procedures for either formative or summative program evaluation or for the evaluation of student progress is reasonably simple and straightforward.

C. Operation

1. Carrying Out Instructional Activities.

Little need be said about this step in the process, for it is the one wherein the instruction as set forth in the previous step is now carried out. Since the sequence of instruction has already been determined and the materials or activities which have been designed for the instruction have already been set forth, the process of carrying out instruction is simply to make the instructional activities available to students in the order which has been prespecified.

2. Collecting Evaluative Data.

This activity within the stage of operation, occurring concomitantly with the implementation of instruction, is a reasonably straightforward one. What is entailed is simply applying the evaluative procedures that have been designed to the actual collection of data during the course of instruction. Typically, this takes the form of automatically administering "end-of-unit" or "end-of-sequence" tests by which individual performance on terminal and enabling objectives is measured. This step may also entail measurement of attitudes and interests at various points along the way, or actual observations of behavior. However, evaluation simply follows the procedures which have been established and thus becomes an integral part of the total instructional process.

The more completely evaluative procedures have been designed and programmed into the overall instructional process, the more complete and more useful will be the evaluative data. Most important within this data will be assessments of performance on the terminal objective and each enabling objective, making it possible to determine if a particular competency or skill has been mastered, and if not, where the learning process broke down.

3. Feedback and Iteration.

The step of feedback and iteration is a critical and distinctive feature of the systems model proposed herein. One of the shortcomings of most instruction as it presently occurs is that the results of the instructional process are not systematically collected nor fed back to the designers of instruction in order that these results

can be used to modify instructional activities and their sequencing. That is to say, instruction as we see it today is not self-improving. This is most unfortunate because student performance, as has been suggested above, provides a basis for evaluation not only of the student and his learning capacity, but of the instructional material and program itself. It is uncommon to see the results of student performance pooled across students used as a basis for systematic refinement of instructional activity. Yet, the sum total of students' performance reflects not only their own capacities but also the nature and efficacy of the instructional program.

Thus, while students are evaluated by examining their individual performance, programs can be evaluated by examining data pooled across all students who have had the program. This information, however, can only be used to its greatest effect if some system for the specification of instruction is used to which this data can be related in some meaningful way. The model proposed has incorporated this feature in the steps prior to operation.

One of the critical assumptions made in generating the instruction within this system is the sequential nature of learning characterized by a multiplicity of hypotheses about the contingency relationships between behavioral objectives.* This can be seen by referring again to Figure 2, which reflects a number of hypotheses. The first hypothesis is that "A cannot be mastered unless mastery of B and C precede it." A second hypothesis is that "The mastery of B and C can occur simultaneously." A third hypothesis is that "Mastery of B requires the mastery of D as a precursor," and finally that "Mastery of C has no identifiable precursor."

Each of these hypotheses can be tested with reference to the data which have been collected. If we have systematically measured in the preceding step the ability of students to perform A, B, C and D, we can then determine (for example) whether the majority of students who are able to perform B have already mastered D. We can, in fact, describe four possible outcomes that may occur when one examines the performance of B and D. (These are shown in Figure 3.) We may find, for instance, as we have hypothesized, that individuals who are performing B are also performing D and vice versa. Another possibility is that individuals may succeed in performing D but not B, which is not contradictory to the hypothesis, but leads us to suspect that other prerequisites to B may exist, or that instruction attempting to move students from B to D is insufficient. A third possibility is that certain students are capable of performing B but not D. However, it has been the tendency of educators to blame curricular failures on the students without seriously considering the other two alternatives.

Another possible outcome is that students may succeed on neither B nor D, a finding which is consistent with the hypothesis, but certainly not a

*The rationale and psychological principles concerning the sequential nature of learning have been dealt with in considerable detail by Gagne (1965).

Figure 3

Possible Contingency Outcomes
and Their Implications for Instructional Design

Outcome on superordinate	Outcome on subordinate	Implication for hypothesis	Recommendation for design
correct (+)	correct (+)	support	no change
incorrect (-)	correct (+)	support	look for missing b.o.** improve instruction on super.
incorrect (-)	incorrect (-)	support	look for missing b.o. improve instruction on sub. & super.
correct (+)	incorrect (-)	refute	change sequence

*Superordinate might be **B** in Figure 4 while subordinate would be **D**.
**b.o. behavioral objective; super, superordinate; sub., subordinate.

happy one. It would suggest the improvement of instruction for both *B* and *D.* The fourth possibility clearly contradicts our hypothesis. That is, the possibility that students may fail on *D* but succeed on *B* provides evidence for the refutation of the hypothesis that *D* is a prerequisite for *B.* To the extent that performance data support this last possibility to a greater extent than the preceding three, the instrument designer is encouraged to re-evaluate and subsequently alter the sequence which he has decided upon on an *a priori* basis. Such an alteration in terms of the example given would be to reconsider the relationship between *B* and *D.*

Many alternatives can be considered in the light of the data. If negative alternatives occur frequently enough, instructional designers will be encouraged either to alter the order of the instruction or perhaps to examine the components of the sequence to identify a behavioral objective that has been overlooked. In certain cases improvement of the instructional activities themselves may be necessary in order to increase the likelihood that movement from lower to higher levels in the structure will be achieved.

The characteristics of using performance data describing small bits of student performance and pooling this data across students to examine the structure of the instructional material as prespecified and to alter instruction in accordance with this data is an important and perhaps unique characteristic of this model (as opposed to non-systems oriented models).* The inter-

*The reader is encouraged to examine the work of Walbesser (1969), which describes the uses of this feedback in a more systematic and detailed fashion than has been attempted here. Discussions of this point may also be found in Tuckman (1968a).

active nature of the systems model is depicted by the curriculum development spiral in Figure 4.

The word iteration implies that the instructional activity will be carried out again; that is, the process will be reiterated or repeated. It will not be repeated, however, until the total list of behavioral objectives, the sequence of these objectives and/or the instructional activities for attaining these objectives have been altered in accordance with the evaluative data which have been fed back into the model. When this has occurred, a somewhat modified series of instructional activities will result, sequenced in perhaps a different way than had been originally hypothesized, and featuring perhaps more, perhaps fewer behavioral objectives than originally were made available to students. This repetition of instruction may occur during the next year or semester for a different group of students who will presumably bear similarity to those on whom the first iteration or trial was carried out. In the second iteration, the new group of students will experience the instructional activities, evaluation data will be collected based on their performance, and this data in turn will be fed back into the model. The second trial, or iteration, will then provide for a second testing and refinement of the sequence as prespecified. It is expected that the structure will stand up better the second time around than it did the first. At this point it is conceivable that a third iteration can take place. Every time the instructional materials are used, it can serve as an iteration or trial from which data can be obtained to use for modifying the instruction. A point will be reached when the designers will feel that the model and the design have

Figure 4

The Curriculum Development Spiral
in the Systems Model
for Instructional Management

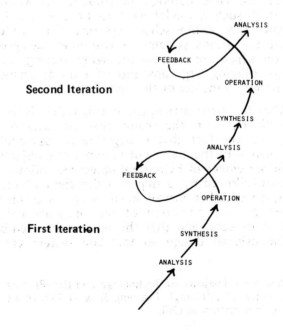

been refined to a point beyond which no further improvements are likely. At this point, the instructional package can be subjected to summative evaluation.

While the evaluative data fed back into the instructional system is the major basis for subsequent refinement, it is not the only one. Those people in charge of curriculum development will need to periodically evaluate the appropriateness of the tasks, objectives and instructional activities in terms of the current social milieu. The changing of technology, the discovery of new principles of learning, or the reorienting of social values are important inputs for the subsequent revision of curricula.

From the above discussion, one should see that there are two somewhat independent concerns in the feedback and iteration phase of the model. The two concerns can be likened to those of internal and external validity in experimental design (Campbell and Stanley, 1969). An externally valid instructional system would be one in which all contingency relationships in the behavioral objectives sequence are valid and the instructional activities are consistent with principles of learning. The external validity of the system will depend on its relevance in the society. Instruction with high internal validity but no external validity, while resulting in efficient learning, is superfluous. On the other hand, instruction which has high external validity but no internal validity is a waste of time and resources. The objective of the instructional manager at each iteration is to strive for both high internal and external instructional validity.

D. Summary

The overall purpose of this article has been to deal briefly with the elements of a systematic model for designing and managing instruction. Considerably more detail would be useful in terms of each of the activities within the model. In addition, little has been said about the manner in which data are to be stored, analyzed and retrieved for large numbers of students, as would be required if such a model were to be used to design instruction for entire school systems. The reader is referred to various systems of computer-managed instruction which are used for managing, storing, retrieving and utilizing large amounts of data as would be necessitated by the use of this approach.*

What has been attempted in this article is to deal most saliently with the major characteristics of the model, i.e., the fact that it begins with task analysis rather than with the statement of behavioral objectives, that the statement of behavioral objectives follows, and is in turn followed by, a step in which these objectives are sequenced, that instructional design is ultimately followed by the operation of the program and the collection of data, and that this data is then fed back into the original design so that the system can be

modified on the basis of its successes and/or failures. This last characteristic may be the most useful and critical feature of the model. ☐

References

Campbell, Donald T. & Stanley, Julian C. *Experimental and Quasi-Experimental Designs for Research.* Chicago, Illinois: Rand-McNally, 1969.

Gagne, Robert M. *The Conditions of Learning.* New York: Holt, Rinehart and Winston, Inc., 1965.

Mager, Robert F. *Preparing Instructional Objectives.* Palo Alto, California: Fearon Publishers, 1962.

Popham, W. James. Objectives and Instruction. A symposium presented at the Annual American Educational Research Association Meeting, Los Angeles, California, February 5-8, 1969.

Scriven, Michael. The Methodology of Evaluation. *Perspectives of Curriculum Evaluation.* American Educational Research Association Curriculum Evaluation Monograph No. 1. Chicago: Rand-McNally, 1967.

Tuckman, Bruce W. *The Development and Testing of an Evaluation Model for Vocational Pilot Programs.* New Brunswick, New Jersey: Rutgers University (Final Report, OE 6-8355), 1967.

Tuckman, Bruce W. An Evaluation Model for Education. Paper presented at the Dallas meeting of the American Vocational Association, 1968. (a)

Tuckman, Bruce W. *Structural Analysis as an Aid to Curriculum Development.* New Brunswick, New Jersey: Rutgers University, Incidental Report No. 1, (OE8-0334), 1968. (b)

Walbesser, Henry H. Curriculum Evaluation. Paper presented at Rutgers University SCOPE Conference, Recent Innovations in Curriculum Design and Instructional Materials, 1969.

---

*The New York Institute of Technology and the IPI Project at the University of Pittsburgh Learning R & D Center are two sources of information on CMI.

Informal Education with Instructional Systems?

Felix F. Kopstein and Robert J. Seidel

In that classic of filmic art, Chaplin's "Modern Times," there is a scene in which the little tramp—momentarily employed as a factory worker—is selected to test an invention. The device is a feeding machine. The machine is brought into the factory; imperiously the "boss" snatches the little tramp from his labors on the assembly line and tells him that he is to be fed by the machine. The inventor seats the little tramp in the machine, which immediately clamps his arms, proceeds to spill all the food into his lap while feeding him and adds insult to injury by frantically wiping his unsullied mouth with a napkin. In the end, Chaplin is freed from the clumsy monster and hurriedly returned to his labors on the assembly line as hungry as before.

This little cinematic gem is a classic indictment of technology's inhumanity. Is it relevant today, and is it relevant to the present topic? The answer to both questions is affirmative. Unfortunately, however, the relevance is most likely misunderstood. The jury may have already rendered its verdict on educational or instructional technology and may not wish to hear evidence that is incompatible with its preconceptions. The defense believes such a verdict to be premature and mistaken.

Incidental Learning and Informal Education

Some years ago there was a lively controversy among the theoretical-experimental psychologists engaged in the study of learning. The issue was the existence of incidental learning—a measurable improvement in performance over time which seemingly came about without overt practice and, more importantly, without reinforcement (see, e.g., Osgood, 1953, Chapter 10). Clearly, such a learning phenomenon, if real, would provide the ideal basis for informal education. Without noticeable effort the informal learner (student) would continue to grow intellectually and the traditional academic processes could be consigned to a richly deserved oblivion.

Despite the pervasive doctrine that all scientific issues can be resolved ultimately through some *experimentum crucis*, few, if any, ever are resolved in this way. In most cases, as Kuhn (1962) has shown, the standing issues are forgotten as the conceptual-theoretical infrastructure is re-thought. In the case of the

Felix F. Kopstein and Robert J. Seidel are with the Human Resources Research Organization, Alexandria, Virginia. Dr. Kopstein is a Contributing Editor.

incidental learning issue, it soon became abundantly evident that whether or not the phenomenon existed (or amounted to an experimental artifact), it could never be regarded as an effective and efficient process of learning. Whatever might be learned incidentally could be acquired deliberately in some small fraction of the incidental learning time and with a far greater reliability. In fact, mounting evidence (Bahrick, 1957; Postman, 1964; McLaughlin, 1965; Wagner, 1968) has shown that the degree of learning that takes place is directly proportional to the degree of intention or motivation to learn the "incidental" material.

Political (social, cultural) revolutions, unlike scientific revolutions, tend to generate more heat than light. Ultimately, however, their doctrines must be able to accommodate within them some unchangeable realities. Presumably, the drive for "informal education" (whatever that much-used term might mean precisely) is a response to rigid academic traditions that no longer satisfy the requirements of a rapidly changing society. Let it be remembered that it is the social institutions that are changing and *not the realities of human learning processes*. It is this confusion which leads to the rejection of a technology that is essential to a strong and effective "informal education."

Learning is desirable, because it expands the individual's range of possibilities for coping with an ever-changing environment. The greater the available options or the number of ways in which the individual can respond to the world—adapt to it, cope with it or solve the problems it poses—the freer he is. However, no one lives forever. Our time for learning is limited and the degree of freedom we can attain through learning thus clearly depends on *the effectiveness and efficiency of the learning process*. This is a reality that "informal education" cannot and must not ignore.

One may ask, is effective and efficient learning compatible with a humane treatment of the learner? Does it not imply unrelenting pressure, rigid procedures, and so on, in the sense of a forcible intellectual feeding akin to Chaplin's experience in "Modern Times"? This danger is ever present, but such an outcome is by no means inevitable.

Instructional Systems

The point has been made many times before (e.g., Seidel, 1969a; McMurrin Commission on Instructional Technology, 1970; Kopstein, 1970; Levien, 1971) and still will need to be repeated many times that neither gadgetry nor technique as such are equivalent to technology. *Predictive* science—whether it be physics or economics, chemistry or psychology, astronomy or sociology—is characterized by its method. Technology is simply *retrodictive* (applied) science, and thus it, too, is characterized by method rather than content. In the popular jargon of today, this method is known as "the systems approach."

At a superficial level the systems approach in the context of instruction is all too well known. There is, first of all, the setting of behavioral objectives, followed by a retrogressive analysis of sub-objectives and the means for attaining them, development of provisions for assuring that all students will demonstrate each specified criterion performance capability, and so forth. At best or at worst, depending on one's biases, the entire process is implemented via a digital computer and the specter of an educational analogy to Chaplin's feeding machine is near at hand. Must it be so necessarily?

Systems and cybernetics are conceptually inextricably intertwined. Originally, cybernetics was characterized as the science of communication and control in animals and machines. Though today the conception of cybernetics is far broader, the original view is not incorrect. Cybernetics still has as a central concern the problems of "steering" a system to a specified (and usually stable) state. In the case of the instructional system, the object is to guide the learning individual through a finite series of transformations from "incompetence" to proficiency. A *properly developed* cybernetic system cannot fail to help the student change from a "can't do" state to a "can do" state. It cannot fail, because therein lies the essence of its own relentless design logic. That inexorable logic demands that the objective be obtained—i.e., that the students have learned—before the system itself attains stability and remains "at rest."

The feeding system demonstrated in "Modern Times" is not a cybernetic one. Indeed it is not a properly designed system, but merely gadgetry gone wild. What were the objectives that its designer might have set for it? Clearly they did not include a specification that its human "client" be transformed from a hungry to a satiated state. Most likely there was no stipulation that the "client" should be able to reject unpalatable nourishment. Nor was the "client" able to contribute guidance toward improving the adaptivity of the system. Most likely, also, no constraint was set that the feeding process should be gentle and in no way injure the "client." The point might be spun out *ad infinitum*, but the parallel will have been noted already.

Properly designed and properly implemented instructional systems (see Kopstein, 1970) are neither incompetent, nor inefficient, nor inhumane. A meaningful instructional system—i.e., one that is not a contradiction in terms—must be beneficially *adaptive* (Stolurow, 1969; Kopstein and Seidel, 1970; Pask, 1969). It must at *all* times adapt to the individual and specific requirements of the learner, who himself must be viewed as an actively striving, information processing, self-(re)organizing system. Above all, the instructional system is the servant of the student and not vice versa. This uniquely adaptive nature makes such a system quite different from the traditional classroom instructional model. If the *adaptive*, individualistic nature is stressed, such a system could be characterized as *informal*. If the requirements for *explicit* aims and for rules to match instructional treatment to specific learner characteristics are stressed, the cybernetic system could be characterized as *formal*. Presumably, in this sense at least, there is no difference between "formal" and "informal" educational systems. Indeed, if such a difference exists at all, it exists in the distinction between *what* is learned and *how* it is learned. The former is a matter of social choice; the latter, a biological given.

There is a movement afoot today which calls for "informal education" without clearly stipulating the dimensions of that phrase. Perhaps the sole clear and univocal message is the rejection of traditional education. What is neglected in such a sweeping rejection is the fact that at least two separable areas for consideration exist. One can reject the methods of traditional instruction including the lock-step, one-room schoolhouse mold into which the student is forced without questioning the objectives or content of such an approach. On the other hand, one can raise objections to the "relevance" of the objectives of traditional education and yet retain the concept of the classroom instructional "system."

If the advocates of informal education reject the uniform mold imposed by traditional education, let them remember that a *properly designed and implemented* instructional system—e.g., CAI—is utterly indifferent about the instructional content it conveys. *What the student learns can be the student's choice,* if the surrounding social and political system is sufficiently permissive to tolerate this. If informal education also rejects the dreary lock-step and pressure for conformity, and if it rejects the tendency in traditional education to have a greater concern for discipline in the classroom than for individual intellectual curiosity (see, e.g., Seidel, 1969b, p. 23), then let it be remembered that a *properly designed and implemented* CAI system is very much concerned with the personalized instructional treatment of the student.

Lest the reader be confused about the general concept of a properly designed and implemented instructional system, being equivalent to CAI, it is by no means the intention of the authors to convey this. It is the case, however, that CAI represents (1) the most advanced form of systematic, personalized instructional systems, and (2) the example for which there exists an abundance of not merely anecdotal but objective and reasonably reliable evidence. As an instance of such an approach without the use of the computer, the reader is referred to Gallup (1969, 1970a, 1970b, 1971). Gallup's personalized instructional system has been in operation now for three years at Lafayette College. While the course attempts to be adaptive to student-controlled pacing, it still requires grades to be given for completion of a given amount of work and it still has the compromise of some classroom attendance. Nevertheless, it is a large step in the direction of an adaptive, individualized instructional system.

Results to date (Gallup, 1970b, p. 6) have been extremely promising:

"... 98 percent positive statements about the course as a whole and its various aspects; ...

"The performance of the students on examinations indicates superior knowledge compared with previous years; ...

"... the number of majors has increased markedly this year."

Elsewhere Seidel (1971, p. 7) dealt with the need for design of proper instructional systems to take into account the allocation of decision-making resources between student and instructional agent.

The key to optimal allocation of learner controls in the instructional decision process requires basic research in human learning to (a) identify those components of strategy selection and use of which students are capable, (b) relate these components to individual characteristics, and (c) determine where program control can or cannot manage the same components. Applying the results to an educational environment, we could then arrive at a cost-effective justification for optimally allocating components of instructional decision-making to students or to a program in an adaptive teaching system. A conflict in meaning between properly designed and implemented CAI systems and "informal" education arises only when "informal" is taken to be equivalent to *incidental* learning.

Facts Versus Fancies

Will the jury hear some evidence? Although the available evidence is drawn solely from CAI, as noted earlier, this is but one example of an adaptive instructional system. Space here does not permit a comprehensive, detailed discussion of available and relevant studies. The best that can be done is to sketch summarily the character of this evidence gleaned from a random browsing in our library. The literature is available for those who want to evaluate pros and cons of the case in detail. So far an overview of that literature suggests that the case *against* is almost entirely based on pre-existing opinions, while the case *for* is backed by data from a host of objective studies.

At least mildly favorable attitudes toward CAI have been reported by Morrison and Adams (1967), Mitzel (1967), Love (1969), Sheldon (1970), Mathis, Smith and Hansen (1970) and many others. Hansen, Dick and Lippert (1968), on the basis of extensive Florida State University field tests of a CAI physics course in 1967 and 1968, report they found "a moderately positive reaction to the [1967] course" which was then in relatively rough form. However, "personal interviews revealed . . . especially important reactions. First, all of the participants indicated a personal feeling of greater concept mastery in comparison with their peers. For example, the participants claimed to be better explainers of homework problems in comparison with dorm-mates who attended the conventional course."

In the 1968 field test, "most students responded that they liked CAI (79 percent); that they would take another course on CAI (73 percent); and that they would recommend CAI physics to another student (79 percent). Ninety-five percent of the students liked the self-pacing aspect of the course, and only 27 percent felt that there was less personal contact with CAI."

This example is quite representative and unquestionably parallels the experience at comparable institutions and for approximately comparable circumstances (e.g., PLATO—University of Illinois, Harvard, SUNY—

Stony Brook, U.S. Naval Academy, etc.). In our own laboratory (HumRRO, 1971) we asked, "How did you feel about being taught by a 'non-human' instructor?" Sixteen of 26 students who answered this question responded in a positive manner; 4 responded negatively; 3 had mixed reactions; and 3 were indifferent. In answer to the question—"Do you feel that there might be reasons why a student might prefer CAI to human classroom instruction?"—twenty of the 24 respondents said "yes." The most frequently given reason was the self-pacing available in CAI; next was *the personal attention given by the computer;* last and equal in frequency was the lack of distractions and competitive pressure and threat found in the classroom. All this is in spite of many shortcomings that we know our still unperfected CAI system to possess.

All the evidence cited so far relates to attitudes of college students or other young adults. However, as nearly as it is possible to determine this, young children, too, like CAI (e.g., informal reports from New York City Project, INDICOM Project and Stanford University). The matter may be most succinctly characterized in Professor Suppes' apocryphal story about the youngster who, one day, brought an apple to his computer terminal. In all specific instances known to us so far, students of all ages tended to prefer being taught "by the computer."

Where does the protest lie? Seemingly not with those who can perhaps be the recipients of improved education, but evidently with those who would be required to change their modus operandi as teachers. To place the issue in proper perspective, let us identify the potential sources of "dehumanization" in the CAI environment. Clearly from the student's vantage point, there are three such possibilities: the channels of interaction between student and instructional material (including the student-station surroundings); the model of instructional interaction; or the instructional materials per se. Considering the latter first, it should be obvious that the materials are as much an extension (amplification, perhaps) of the instructional designer as a text book would be. Consequently, the personality of the author can and likely will appear in the instruction. Obviously, his or her degree of warmth will determine the perception of humane treatment by a student, and this is but one dimension out of many. What should be equally obvious is that this principle applies as well to a text, or classroom lecture, as to instruction at a CAI student-station.

The model of interaction between student and materials may be suggested as a potential source of dehumanization. But frankly this seems absurd. As implied earlier, the most humanizing aspect of CAI is that by definition the adaptive instructional model guarantees *individualization* and treats the student personally, as the sole focus of the instruction. It demands sensitive adaptation to each student and by definition must be—or with progressive development must become—more attentive, understanding and patient than the teacher of 30-odd students in the classroom. At the same time, if the student can be given assurance of confidentiality (anonymity) of results, his feelings of security are likely to be stronger.

The only remaining candidate for dehumanization is the physical setting within which instruction is to take place. Just as in the case of the materials, the personality of the designer is the determinant. If the structural design of the student station (carrel or cubicle) appeals to the student, then a positive personal feeling is likely to result. Providing the student with some control over lighting and a thermostat as, for example, in our CAI environment should add to a feeling of personalization. Clearly, it is a far cry from Chaplin's feeding machine. In fact, we know our students respond favorably.

Perhaps the fears of dehumanization come then not from the student but from the other side of the instructional coin. Who but the traditionalist teacher is most threatened? Why is this the case? For one thing, it is very demanding to prepare instructional materials properly for CAI. For another, direct "eyeball to eyeball" interaction with students is gone. The feedback is not direct and subjective, but indirect and objective. Finally, there is the overriding premise, explicit or implicit, that the "teacher will be replaced by a machine." This misconception, which ignores changing roles in a new type of instructional model, nevertheless could be the crux of the matter.

Exactly in contrast to CAI, traditional teaching does not accept the responsibility for student failure. Programmed instruction and CAI assume that the instruction has failed if performance falls off. They explicitly provide for updating and change of materials and interaction when this occurs. By contrast, the traditional teacher hides in the "bell shaped curve" and other normative statistics.

At another level, the question becomes meaningless. The "free schoolers" and other recent critics (e.g., Silberman, 1970; Illich, 1971) have already denied both the "relevance" or the humanism of the current model of education—without any thought of the computer. The very dimensions are being questioned—the teacher, the classroom, the school, etc. A computer in this context would make no difference in degree of humanism, since the learning setting has already been accused of being devoid of humane considerations for the student.

A Computer-Based Learning Center

If there are still some lingering doubts, let us sketch the *realistic* possibilities for informal education offered by a computer-based "Learning Center." To begin with, that Learning Center (LC) can be a community resource. It can be there for members of the community to use if and when they see fit without artificial prerequisites and academic red tape. It will be there, "willing and able" to compete on equal terms for the individual's time and attention against fun and games or any other potential activities. It will be used because each user *prefers* to learn and not because he is *coerced* into learning.

The LC will be there to serve the student's intellectual curiosity at all times. It can await his pleasure and convenience; it need not demand that the student "meet the class" at the convenience of the class

or the teacher. It need not demand that the student maintain a pace of progress other than the one with which he feels comfortable. It can allow him the luxury of browsing among the possibilities of knowledge. It can let him set his own learning goals. It can offer a complete and varied "menu." Like the library, it is indifferent to the nature and direction of intellectual inquiry; unlike the library, it "cares" profoundly about the quality and ease of that endeavor.

The instructional system implemented through the computer and interacting with the student through a terminal located within the LC will seek only to satisfy the student. There need be no competitive examinations and there are to be no grades. This is to be primarily a cooperative enterprise. By contrast with traditional educational practice, it is in the student's best interest to reveal, not to conceal, his ignorance to the system. This system has no need to compare him to a "norm." Its sole "desire" is to remedy the ignorance—to adapt its instructional presentation to the momentary needs of the student so as to render him capable and informed. It needs to evaluate him only against his own professed learning objectives.

The system is guaranteed to be objective. If properly implemented, it will be indifferent to irrelevancies such as race, sex, personal appearance and intelligence—within limits, cultural background, and so forth. It can be infinitely patient, and it is certain to be untiring. It is assuredly consistent from day to day in following an optimal, rational and scientifically based instructional strategy. It is bound to be unvarying in maintaining its instructional efforts at the highest level of which it is capable; and it will consistently improve and only improve its own capabilities, so long as it is backed by coherent research and development programs.

Conclusion

If these characterizations are dismissed as utopian (see, e.g., Oettinger and Marks, 1969), this dismissal must ignore the indisputable fact that each and every one of them follows as a direct implication from the premises of an advanced CAI system design. It is like the denial of the possibility of flight, because no one had ever flown before (and many had tried and crashed). It is like the denial of the possibility of a manned lunar landing, because no one had yet developed the requisite propulsion systems, guidance systems and life support systems, and because early space vehicles tended to blow up on the launch pad. Advanced instructional systems have a greater reality today than either of these technological developments did in their early stages, and their ultimate benefit for mankind is likely to be vastly more far-reaching and profound.

Clearly, the question posed in the title is to be answered not by "why not?" but by "how else?" The enormous potential that cybernetic instructional systems possess cannot but benefit mankind unless these systems are grossly misused or deliberately turned to evil purposes. ☐

References

Bahrick, H.P. Incidental Learning at Five Stages of Intentional Learning. *Journal of Experimental Psychology,* 1957, *54,* 259-261.

Gallup, H.F. Individualized Instruction in Introductory Psychology. In Sheppard, W.C. (Ed.) *Proceedings of the Conference on Instructional Innovations in Undergraduate Education.* Eugene, Oregon: University of Oregon, 1969.

Gallup, H.F. Report on Psychology 1, 2 to the Curriculum Committee, Easton, Pa.: Lafayette College, February, 1970. (a)

Gallup, H.F. Individualized Instruction in an Introductory Psychology Course. Paper presented at EPA, April, 1970. (b)

Gallup, H.F. Problems in the Implementation of a Course in Personalized Instruction. Paper presented at "Personalized Instruction," a symposium in honor of Fred Keller, APA Meeting, September 6, 1971.

Hansen, D.N., Walter Dick & H.T. Lippert. Research and Implementation of Collegiate Instruction via Computer Assisted Instruction. *Technical Report No. 3.* Tallahassee, Fla.: CAI Center, Florida State University, 1968.

HumRRO. Technical Progress Report to National Science Foundation. Alexandria, Va.: HumRRO, Office of Computing Activities, 1971.

Illich, Ivan. *Deschooling Society.* New York: Harper and Row, 1971.

Kopstein, F.F. Why CAI Must Fail! *Educational Technology,* 1970, *10* (3), 51-53.

Kopstein, F.F. & R.J. Seidel. The Computer as Adaptive Instructional Decision Maker. *Professional Paper 1-70.* Alexandria, Va.: HumRRO, 1970.

Kuhn, T.S. *Structure of Scientific Revolutions.* Chicago, Ill.: University of Chicago Press, 1962.

Levien, R.E. National Institute of Education: Preliminary Plan for the Proposed Institute. Publication R-657-HEW, Santa Monica, California: Rand Corporation, 1971.

Love, W.P. Individual versus Paired Learning of an Abstract Algebra Presented by Computer-Assisted Instruction. *Technical Report No. 5.* Tallahassee, Fla.: CAI Center, Florida State University, 1969.

Mathis, A., T. Smith & D. Hansen. College Students' Attitudes Towards Computer-Assisted Instruction. *Journal of Educational Psychology,* 1970, *61,* 46-51.

Mitzel, H.E. The Development and Presentation of Four College Courses by Computer Teleprocessing. Final Report, Contract No. OE 4-16-010, University Park, Pa.: Pennsylvania State University, 1967.

Morrison, H.W. & E.N. Adams. Pilot Study of a CAI Laboratory in German. *Report RC 1974.* Yorktown Heights, N.Y.: IBM Watson Research Center, 1967.

McLaughlin, B. "Intentional" and "Incidental" Learning in Human Subjects: The Role of Instructions to Learn and Motivation. *Psychological Bulletin,* 1965, *63,* 359-376.

McMurrin Commission on Instructional Technology. To Improve Learning: A Report to the President and the Congress of the United States. Washington, D.C.: U.S. Government Printing Office, 1970 (40-715-0).

Oettinger, A.E. & S. Marks. *Run, Computer, Run: The Mythology of Educational Innovation.* Cambridge, Mass.: Harvard University Press, 1969.

Osgood, C.E. *Method and Theory in Experimental Psychology.* New York: Oxford University Press, 1953.

Pask, G. Computer Assisted Learning and Teaching. Paper prepared for British National Council for Educational Technology, 1969.

Postman, L. Short-Term Memory and Incidental Learning. In A.W. Melton (Ed.) *Categories of Human Learning.* New York: Academic Press, 1964, 145-201.

Seidel, R.J. Theories and Strategies Related to Measurement in Individualized Instruction. *Professional Paper 2-71,* Alexandria, Va.: HumRRO, 1971.

Seidel, R.J. Computers in Education: The Copernican Revolution in Education Systems. *Computers and Automation,* 1969, *18* (3), 24-29. (a)

Seidel, R.J. Is CAI Cost/Effective? The Right Question at the Wrong Time. *Educational Technology,* 1969, *9* (5), 21-23. (b)

Sheldon, J.W. Computer Assisted Instruction in Engineering Dynamics. *Tech. Memo No. 18.* Tallahassee, Fla.: CAI Center, Florida State University, 1970.

Silberman, C.E. *Crisis in the Classroom.* New York: Random House, 1970.

Stolurow, L.M. Some Factors in the Design of Systems for Computer-Assisted Instruction. In R.C. Atkinson & H.A. Wilson (Eds.) *Computer-Assisted Instruction: A Book of Readings.* New York: Academic Press, 1969.

Wagner, H. Incidental Versus Intentional Learning of Paired-Associates. Unpublished doctoral dissertation, New York University, 1968.

DESIGNING SIMULATION SYSTEMS

PAUL A. TWELKER

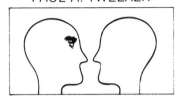

The purpose of this paper is to outline the approach to designing instructional simulation systems developed at Teaching Research. Detailed step-by-step explanations are beyond the scope of the present paper. They are available elsewhere (Crawford and Twelker, 1969). However, the 13 phases of simulation design will be summarized, and an effort will be made to expose the vital decision points that confront the designer as he develops simulation experiences.

A rationale for the design of instructional simulation systems

In designing an instructional simulation system, or any instructional system, for that matter, it is useful to think of a gap — the difference between where the learner is before instruction and after instruction. Before instruction, we assume that he lacks some knowledge or skill necessary to perform satisfactorily in an operational situation. After instruction, we assume that he possesses these.

Our problem is to specify the learning conditions necessary to bridge the gap between the learner's initial repertoire and final criterion repertoire.

How best are these instructional conditions specified? Are there instructional methods effective in all kinds of learning activities? To be certain, there are some general rules of thumb that seem to hold in a variety of conditions, such as the provision for proper feedback, active participation, spaced practice, and so forth. Yet, it is clear that these guides do not lead us far enough down the road of instructional specification to be of much help at this stage in our technology. Too many decisions must be made in the course of specifying instructional conditions that cannot be answered by examining past research, theory, or intuition. Decisions must be made in the best manner possible,

and this requirement has in large part prompted the approach to be discussed below. This approach may be summarized as: (1) determining what shall be taught; (2) determining how best it might be taught; (3) validating the system.

The word "system" used above has a special connotation, and points up the fact that a simulation experience should not be conceived of as an isolated experience taken out of the context of the over-all instruction. The term "simulation system" infers that the simulation component of the system is accompanied by other "non-simulation" components. The components describe what curricular units precede, accompany and follow the actual simulation exercise. Also, the word "system" denotes an inter-related set of components ranging from media and manuals to student learning materials.

Specific steps in designing instructional simulation systems*

Step 1. Define instructional problem

Before one can improve instruction, he must step back and examine in broad terms what preceded his decision to develop a new instructional system, and what might follow if his intentions were realized. What condition has motivated his tampering with the status quo — why does he believe that intervention can improve the conditions? What is the problem? What are the proposed solutions to the problem? What information led to the definition of this problem? In addition to defining the problem, the designer should make a thorough analysis of the context in which the system is to operate.

Step 2. Describe the operational educational system

Why analyze the operational system? What is suitable for one set of objectives taught in a given

Paul A. Twelker is director of the Simulation Systems Program, Teaching Research, Oregon State System of Higher Education, Monmouth.

*The 13 steps are summarized in **Figure 1**.

environment may not be effective for the same objectives taught in a different environment that has different constraints placed upon it. For example, an excellent instructional system that is designed for teaching one child at a time may not be appropriate for teaching two or more simultaneously. The constraints of the system in which the designer expects to operate must be described. In analyzing the operational system, the designer must define:

Learners for whom the system is being designed (target group)

Number of personnel available to him on the project (manpower)

Supporting equipment (machines)

Personnel scheduling, available curriculum material, description of course limits, and developmental time (procedures and materials)

Administrative limits (management)

Facilities (setting)

Money available for the ongoing system and money available for developing the new system (funds)

Instructional philosophy or orientation that guides the system as well as the designer (educational orientation).

In summary, the designer should examine any element that he feels helps him to define the problem more clearly and to propose appropriate solutions.

Step 3. Relate the operational system to the problem

The inputs identified above must be related to each other. It makes little sense to think of an educational problem in isolation to the context in which it is found. This relating of the initially identified problem with the system may cause the designer to redefine or restructure the problem. In some cases, the designer will face the choice of delimiting his interests and choosing certain aspects of the problems he has identified. This is based on the assumption that the more one knows about the system, the more problems will be perceived.

Step 4. Specify objectives in behavioral terms

There has been some confusion regarding the "hows" of specifying behavioral objectives, whether they be enabling or terminal. Enabling objectives state in precise terms the specific knowledge/skills the student must learn in order to arrive at the terminal performance. Terminal objectives state in precise terms the behavior that the learner is expected to exhibit after instruction.

Where do objectives come from? Typically, the designer might begin by examining the unique key words, phrases, concepts, definitions and rules

Figure 1

Steps in the Design of an Instructional Simulation System

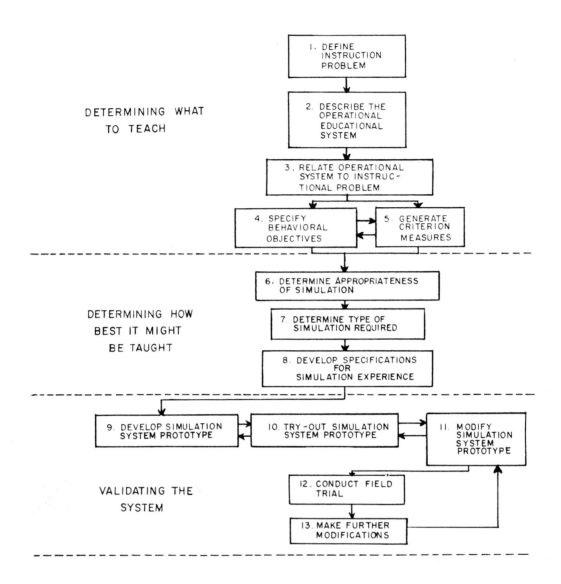

DETERMINING WHAT
TO TEACH

1. DEFINE INSTRUCTION PROBLEM

2. DESCRIBE THE OPERATIONAL EDUCATIONAL SYSTEM

3. RELATE OPERATIONAL SYSTEM TO INSTRUCTIONAL PROBLEM

4. SPECIFY BEHAVIORAL OBJECTIVES

5. GENERATE CRITERION MEASURES

DETERMINING HOW
BEST IT MIGHT
BE TAUGHT

6. DETERMINE APPROPRIATENESS OF SIMULATION

7. DETERMINE TYPE OF SIMULATION REQUIRED

8. DEVELOP SPECIFICATIONS FOR SIMULATION EXPERIENCE

9. DEVELOP SIMULATION SYSTEM PROTOTYPE

10. TRY-OUT SIMULATION SYSTEM PROTOTYPE

11. MODIFY SIMULATION SYSTEM PROTOTYPE

VALIDATING THE
SYSTEM

12. CONDUCT FIELD TRIAL

13. MAKE FURTHER MODIFICATIONS

that he frequently uses in the instructional unit. He looks at their natural sequence. That is, he analyzes a set of key concepts or definitions to see which are requisite for learning other key ideas. He constructs a hierarchy of principles that tell him in what order these principles should be taught. Basically, this analysis is used in the context of specifying what to teach, and requires the designer to choose some performance (that may or may not end up to be a terminal performance) and to successively ask the following question: "What kind of capability would an individual have to possess if he were able to perform this objective successfully, were we to give him only instructions to do?"

Where else does the designer look for objectives? He may check the final exams he has been giving, and attempt to assess the degree to which they really tap the skills desired on the part of the student. He sees if there are some life-like settings that could be developed that might more closely approximate the real skill that is being taught and tested. Perhaps a case study, filmed situation, or taped dialogue would be a better assessment tool. The designer actually generates specifications for some of these tests. Then he asks the question, "Does that behavior satisfy me that the knowledge skills have been taught?" The designer infers knowledge from performance.

Figure 2

Graphical Relationship Between
Reality, Models and Simulations

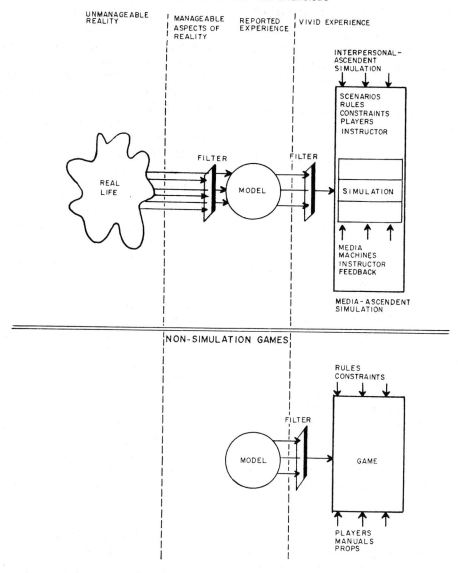

SIMULATION GAMES AND EXERCISES

UNMANAGEABLE REALITY | MANAGEABLE ASPECTS OF REALITY | REPORTED EXPERIENCE | VIVID EXPERIENCE

INTERPERSONAL-ASCENDENT SIMULATION

SCENARIOS
RULES
CONSTRAINTS
PLAYERS
INSTRUCTOR

REAL LIFE

FILTER

MODEL

FILTER

SIMULATION

MEDIA
MACHINES
INSTRUCTOR
FEEDBACK

MEDIA-ASCENDENT SIMULATION

NON-SIMULATION GAMES

RULES
CONSTRAINTS

FILTER

MODEL

GAME

PLAYERS
MANUALS
PROPS

One other point should be emphasized. Educational objectives may be thought of as either stated (intentional), or unstated (unintentional). Stated objectives are those determined by the designer to be important and relevent to his problem. Unstated objectives are those which are not verbalized by the designer, but which may be just as appropriate as those stated. In designing instructional simulation experiences, where vivid experience rather than reported experience is the keynote, it is especially important that unstated objectives are considered. For example, extreme competition in a simulation game may produce the desired stated objectives, but at the risk of promoting dishonesty, thus not fulfilling an unstated objective regarding proper interpersonal behavior.

Step 5. Generate criterion measures

Simultaneous with determining behavioral objectives is the development of criterion measures. These take two forms: (1) terminal performance measures and (2) enabling performance measures. The measures for assessing terminal performance determine whether or not the stated outcome behaviors were acquired by the learner as a result of the instructional experience. The measures for assessing enabling performance determine whether or not prerequisite behavior, necessary for adequate performance on the terminal objectives, has been acquired during instruction. Again, the designer should pay some attention to generating measurement instruments for unstated objectives.

Step 6. Determine appropriateness of simulation

Simulation has several advantages over more conventional forms of instruction, although the cost may be higher. Seven possibilities in which simulation may offer a useful and cost-justifiable alternative are:

1. Simulations are appropriate when objectives emphasize emotional or attitudinal outcomes.
2. Simulations integrate affective and cognitive behavior.
3. Simulations initiate sustained learner activity and motivation.
4. When the objective is to represent a social or man-machine system in such a way that the learner must interact with it, the system will react to the learner's moves, and the learner can discover the effects of alternative decisions.
5. Simulation, in which a high degree of commitment may be introduced, is useful when emphasis is upon incorporation of the behavior desired within the personal domain of the learner.
6. Simulations provide an interest-sustaining mode that is particularly useful for exercising behavior, particularly under a variety of contexts.
7. Simulation is a most powerful means of placing a learner into a desired "set" or "perceptual frame" to sensitize and direct him.

On the other hand, there are some arguments against the use of simulation:

1. Simulation is not so efficient when it comes to the acquisition of cognitive knowledge as measured by typical tests.
2. Simulation may cost more than conventional types of instruction.
3. More information can be presented in less time by more traditional means of instruction.
4. Simulations, particularly the learning game variety, often introduce considerable changes in classroom noise level, physical movement and teacher role that are highly suspect to some instructors.
5. Simulations are often difficult to evaluate because of the human processes that are modeled.

Step 7. Determine type of simulation required

If a decision has been reached to consider the use of simulation, the next set of decisions relate to the kind, or the attributes, of the simulation to be designed. The three major possibilities are: interpersonal-ascendent simulation, machine/media-ascendent simulation and non-simulation games.

Interpersonal-ascendent simulation refers to the role playing and decision making, player-interacting simulations as typically found in such games as Consumer, Crisis and Manchester. Interactions between learners carry a large share of the instructional burden.

Machine- or media-ascendent simulations are characterized by the instructional burden being carried largely by media (for example, slide-tapes, films, programmed instruction, computer output, and so forth). Examples include flight trainers, systems trainers, such as weapons systems simulators used by the military for submarine crew training, computer-based business games and classroom simulation (Twelker, 1967; Cruickshank et al., 1967).

The third category, of non-simulation games, is included, despite its non-sequiter label, largely because of the number of learning games that are being developed that do not simulate a model of reality. Such games include the Nova game, Wff'n'-Proof, On-sets and Equations. These games certainly bring some of the advantages of simulation games to instruction, but do not simulate any social or physical system. Yet, they do provide involvement on the part of the learner in the application of concepts and principles drawn from formal disciplines.

Table 1 presents the advantages of each type of simulation technique. It should be noted that the advantages listed are relative advantages and do not preclude the possibility of one or another type of simulation being adequate in any given situation.

Step 8. Develop specifications for simulation experience

A common error that novice simulation designers make is to assume that the simulation exercise represents reality per se. They fail to realize that the simulation is not based on reality directly, but on a model or theory of reality. In other words, the model is a representation that is in some way removed from reality.

It might be appropriate to say that a simulation will be only as good as the model on which it is based. The model is usually stated in general terms, and includes many variables that may be deleted or altered in the simulation. Thus, the simulation is a representation of the model, but not an exact image. Changes have occurred. It behooves the simulation designer to construct or use the best

Table 1
Advantages of Each Type of Simulation

	Type of Technique		
Factor	Interpersonal Ascen-dent Simulation	Machine/Media Ascendent Simulation	Non-simulation Game
1. Control (reproducibility) desired	Questionable	Good	Difficult
2. Control (planned variation) desired	Questionable	Very Good	Good
3. Input must be machine mediated, e.g., visual stimuli required	Not easily adopted	Appropriate	Not easily adopted
4. Psychomotor and perceptual learning involved	Questionable	Very Good	Questionable
5. Learners possess low entry skills & limited response repertories that prevent an inter-personal-ascendent simulation from functioning	Limited value	Useful	Questionable
6. Teacher control over class required	Not so good	Very Good	Fair
7. Simple and inexpensive technique desired	Good	Not easily done	Very good
8. Interaction between learners required	Very good	Possible but costly	Good
9. Burden of simulation experience on learner required	Good	Possible	Possible
10. Model that emphasizes human interaction involved	Very good	Not easily done	Questionable
11. Individual differences must be considered but expensive to implement	Good	Not easily done	Good
12. Feedback must be easily designed into system	Good	Sometimes costly and difficult	Good
13. Feedback must come from peers	Good	Difficult	Good
14. Easy development process required	Sometimes difficult	Sometimes difficult	Very good
15. Insertion into curriculum must be easy	Sometimes difficult	Sometimes difficult	Very good
16. Must be generally acceptable	Sometimes difficult	Good	Very good
17. Few learners involved	Limited	Good	Very good
18. Learning objectives congruent or identical to standard course objectives	Limited	Good	Very good

fitting model he can so that he subsequently builds a fair chance of representing the relevant aspects of reality adequately. If the model is not a good representation of reality; that is, if it distorts reality or omits relevant aspects of reality, and the simulation designer does not recognize this, the simulation has little chance of instructing learners in the appropriate behavior. The relationship between reality, the model and the simulation are graphically presented in **Figure 2.**

Step 9. Develop simulation system prototype

At this point, a good share of the work of simulation system design has been accomplished, and the "fun" of building the system begins. The main task is that of translating instructional "blueprints" into prototype. The more complete and thought out the blueprints, the faster and easier the development.

Step 10. Tryout simulation system prototype

An empirical tryout of this system is mandatory. The tryout is limited in nature. If possible, small groups of learners, or even one learner at a time if appropriate, are taken through the system by the designer. Close monitoring of the learners is undertaken. Analysis of the system is not limited to this. Learners may be requested to verbalize problems with the materials, and suggest alternate strategies. It should be noted that the limited tryout of a system such as a simulation game may look quite different from a tryout of the media-ascendent simulation. Videotaping of simulation game prototypes is an extremely effective way to capture activity for later analysis with a select group of learners sitting with the designers. Sometimes, a simulation may be tried out on colleagues before using learners that represent the target group so that responsible criticism may be obtained.

Step 11. Modify the simulation system prototype

Three major decisions are made during this step: (1) If the system seems appropriate for obtaining the stated objectives, how can it be improved? (2) If the system does not seem to be appropriate for obtaining the stated objectives, how can it be changed? (3) If the system does not seem appropriate for obtaining the stated objectives, should it be discarded in favor of a non-simulation system?

Step 12. Conduct field trial

The field trial serves to aid the designer in determining if his newly developed system is capable of standing by itself, that is, being used in the field under operational conditions by members of a target population. Designers often neglect this crucial step, reasoning that "since I was successful in using the system, everyone else can use it now." The safest thing a designer could do is subject his system to a trial under field conditions. When this is done, the designer may wish to collect data concerning the stated outcomes as well as the unstated outcomes. In some cases, the designer might consider securing the services of a third-part evaluation team to conduct the field trial.

Step 13. Make further modifications to the system deemed appropriate from field trial evidence

When this point is reached, it is hoped that few "bugs" are found in the system as detected during the field trial. If the previous steps have been executed in excellent manner, the field trial will indicate improvement, not major changes. At this time, the designer may also begin investigating ways to disseminate his system.

A final word

Sarane Boocock and E. O. Schild state in their book on **Simulation Games** that "simulation design is not only not a science, it is hardly a craft, but rather an 'art' in the sense that we have no explicit rules to transmit" (Boocock and Schild, 1968, p. 266). Others have made essentially the same statement of media-ascendent simulation. This position cannot be argued. Further, the guidelines offered above certainly are one step in the right direction as meaningful research directions may be specified in the context of the development of simulation exercises. □

References

Boocock, Sarane S. & Schild, E. O. (Eds.). **Simulation Games in Learning.** Beverly Hills, California: Sage Pub., Inc., 1968.

Crawford, Jack & Twelker, Paul A. The Design of Instructional Simulation Systems. In Paul A. Twelker (Ed.), **Instructional Simulation: A Research Development and Dissemination Activity.** Monmouth, Oregon: Teaching Research Division, Oregon State System of Higher Education, February, 1969. (U.S. Office of Education Final Report, Project No. 7-I-045).

Cruickshank, Donald R., Broadbent, Frank W. & Bubb, Roy L. **Teaching Problems Laboratory.** Chicago: Science Research Associates, Inc., 1967.

Twelker, Paul A. Classroom Simulation and Teacher Preparation. **The School Review,** 1967, 197-204.

The Use of a Common Experiential Referent in Instructional System Design

Lawrence T. Alexander and Stephen L. Yelon

When people work together designing instructional systems, they invariably encounter communication difficulties. This is usually because, coming from different backgrounds and having different ways of approaching the task, they tend to view problems differently. Often each employs a different vocabulary, or technical language, derived from his particular area of training or competence, which also impedes communication of ideas.

A typical example of such a group might be a team composed of a psychologist, a teacher, an educational technologist and a media specialist working together to produce an instructional system which achieves stated instructional objectives; that is, to produce a product or to implement a design plan to meet prescribed output specifications.

The purpose of this paper is to describe a technique that the authors have employed in a variety of system design tasks. It has been found to facilitate communication among members of the design team, has speeded up the design, development and production processes, and has increased the mutual satisfaction of the team members with the ultimate product.

One of the authors was a member of a team responsible for designing a laboratory model of a computerized terminal Air Traffic Control system for research on problems of man-computer interaction (Alexander and Cooperband, 1964). The design team was composed of psychologists, physicists, engineers, mathematicians, computer programmers and air traffic controllers.

Two of the basic design problems this team had to solve were: which functions to assign to the human controller and which to the computer and how to ensure efficient communication between the two. The team members soon found that they needed some common language by which they could exchange ideas and work out the performance implications of the various design suggestions.

To meet this need, a set of engineering drawings of instrument panels was prepared. This simple schematic model served as a representation of the functional interface between the man and the computer. More to the point, however, was the discovery that it provided a common task language, or framework, by which the team members could communicate unambiguously: a Common Experiential Referent (CER). As such, it facilitated the design process by focusing discussion and making visible the implications and ramifications of each design suggestion (Alexander, et al., 1962).

Another of the authors was designing a programmed instructional unit for use in his college course. Since the unit involved the use of motion picture films, the instructor required the consultation of film media specialists. When film design meetings were held, communication difficulties immediately arose; the instructor did not know the film makers' jargon and they were not acquainted with the course subject matter vocabulary. Consequently, no common understanding could be achieved of the instructor's expectations regarding the characteristics of the final film products or of the author's intent regarding their use in the total system.

In order to facilitate communication, it was decided to employ a videotape recording technique. Live subjects were used to demonstrate the behavior required, and the recorded "scenes" were immediately played back and viewed on a TV monitor. Modifications and corrections were made, and the "scene" was "shot" again. Each replay brought the product closer to the final desired result; the film maker was able to translate the verbal instructions of the instructor into a visual product, and the instructor was able to see exactly what the final

Lawrence T. Alexander is professor and assistant director of Learning Services at Michigan State University, East Lansing.

Stephen L. Yelon is assistant professor of education, Michigan State University.

Figure 1. Stages in the instructional system design process.

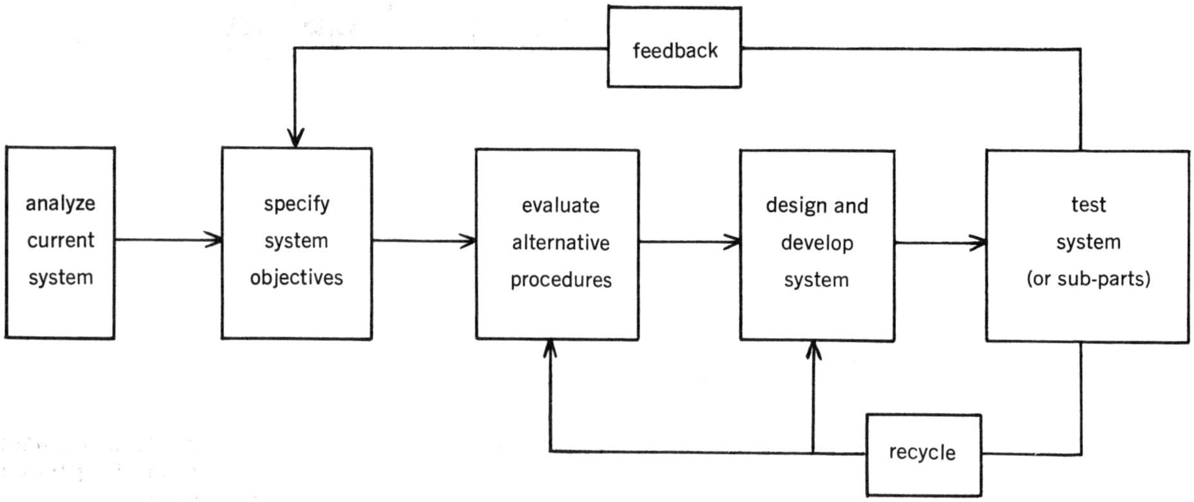

product would be like. In the design of this instructional system the videotape served as a dynamic script: a task-related common experiential referent for effective communication.

In a college training program for graduate teaching assistants, the participants taught regularly scheduled courses in an experimental classroom and learned to identify classroom problems and explore alternative solutions to them. They practiced organizing and presenting subject matter, identifying and discriminating among cues that indicate student learning progress, and modifying their instructional behavior contingent upon the nature of these cues.

When the trainees met with their professor, they found it difficult to verbalize and communicate the exact nature of the problems they were having. This difficulty was removed when the class session was videotaped, and a portion of the video tape, showing the problem, was reviewed. Thus, the participants had a common referent to use as a basis for discussion and analysis.

CER principles

These examples illustrate some of the situations in which a CER has been used successfully to facilitate communication among a group of people. What general principles can be derived from these examples that might assist the reader to decide when and how to use a CER? In what kind of situations can a CER be used most efficiently? What functions may it perform? What characteristics should it have?

We have found that a CER is most useful when the following conditions prevail: (1) a team of two or more people are working on a common task that requires the creation or design of a new product; (2) a language is not available by which the team members can communicate their ideas unambiguously, and (3) if an unambiguous language is available, e.g., mathematics, and the participants are not skilled in its use.

When a group of people are working on a task that involves creating or designing a new product, they do more than communicate a set of facts. Such a task requires a multitude of design decisions based on careful consideration of, and choice among, a variety of alternatives; and communication entails a mutual groping for new ideas, clarification of hazy relationships, and examination of tentative suggestions.

It is obvious that the decision process will be impeded if the team members have no common frame of reference or language for mutual interaction. Problems arise when a team member assumes erroneously that he has stated an argument unambiguously when, in fact, each listener interprets the message in a different way.

Thus, efficient decision making is replaced with something analogous to a multi-faceted psychological projective test — each person interprets the "inkblot" in his own way. Under these conditions, the team cannot make maximal use of the resources of each member. If the team tries to increase its efficiency by subdividing the total task and assigning the sub-tasks to different members, it usually turns out that the sub-products do not fit together or do not meet the expectations of the other members.

How can CER assist communication among members of a design team? This question can be answered by a consideration of the instructional system design process and the communication requirements it imposes on the team members. In discussing this question, we shall rely upon an analysis of the computer as a communication device, by Licklider and Taylor (1968).

The design of any instructional system involves going through a series of stages that include: analysis and description of problems in the current sytem; statement of system objectives; consideration and evaluation of alternative procedures for attaining the objectives; consideration and evaluation of alternative procedures for attaining the objectives; design and development, and test (Yelon, 1969). These steps are shown in **Figure 1.**

The recycle loops indicate that for all but the simplest systems, the design process usually requires iteration through the stages several times as the ideas of the designers become progressively more concrete, and their predictions about the operations of the system are substantiated by empirical test. The feedback loop indicates that all tests of system operations are evaluated in terms of the criteria stated in the system objectives.

Anyone who has been a member of a design team can recall the difficulty in getting started. This is because each individual brings to the meeting a different conception, a different mental model, of the nature of the task, its objectives, the way the members are to work together, and what each shall contribute. (As we have said before, if the team members have different backgrounds, they are also likely to bring different languages.)

In order to have any creative mutual exchange of ideas and reach agreement regarding the many design decisions that must be made, the individual models must be compared and brought into some degree of accord. In order to create new ideas, it is necessary for the team members to engage in cooperative modeling. Indeed, Licklider and Taylor say that communication **is** cooperative modeling.

When people communicate face to face, they bring their models out into the open so that they can be sure they are talking about the same thing. They draw pictures, sketch diagrams, or make outlines. Such externalized models can be seen by all members. Each serves as a common framework and focus for discussion.

Our experience indicates that a CER performs this function. It can serve as a model of the system and at the same time as a common frame of reference against which individual models can be compared. It can provide a "physical vehicle" that can be molded and shaped by each member because it is accessible to all. It provides a medium whereby new ideas may be tested, complex relationships made explicit, and consequences of design alternatives explored.

We found that a CER should have physical and functional characteristics corresponding as closely as possible to the final system, and it should be

manipulatable so that it can be used to model most of the decisions that have to be made at each stage of the design process. An example of this correspondence in one of the illustrations at the beginning of this article is the use of videotape as a model for a final film product.

We have found also that a physical CER, e.g., a diagram, a drawing, or a piece of equipment, provides a more unambiguous medium of communication, more concrete than an abstract model that uses language. Mathematics is a language which, of course, is a possible exception. In addition, the CER should be cheap and easy to build and modify.

The high-speed, large-storage-capacity digital computer is potentially the most flexible and useful CER for system design. But, at present, high cost, unavailability of suitable programs and lack of experience of most designers of instructional systems make the kind of CER we have described an immediately available and viable alternative.

In summary:

1. A Common Experiential Referent (CER) is useful when a team composed of people with different backgrounds is engaged in designing a new instructional system.
2. A CER provides a common frame of reference and medium of communication about the design task when an unambiguous language is not available or when all team members are not equally facile in its use.
3. A CER should be a physical model of the system.
4. A CER should be able to represent most of the important characteristics and functions of the finished system and especially the behavior of any people.
5. The CER should be manipulatable and dynamic so that it can be modified as new ideas are adopted.
6. The CER should be less expensive to build and modify than the final system. □

References

Alexander, L. T. & Cooperband, A. S. Schematic Simulation: A Technique for the Design and Development of a Complex System. **Human Factors,** 1964, 6, 87-92.

Alexander, L. T., Kepner, C. H. & Tregoe, B. B. The Effectiveness of Knowledge of Results in a Military System Training Program. **J. Applied Psychol.,** 1962, 46, 202-211.

Licklider, J. C. R. & Taylor, R. W. The Computer as a Communication Device. **Science and Technology,** April, 1968, 21-31.

Yelon, S. L. Toward the Application of Systems Analysis to Counselor Education. **Educational Technology,** March, 1969.

The God of Complexity

John W. Loughary
Contributing Editor

One claimed advantage of a Sabbatical year is that it provides an opportunity to "get away from it all." While this expectation may be realized by some, it is not a foregone conclusion for all. At least I can report that my wife and I spent the last three months of our "away from it all year" teaching our children. Six, altogether, and if you use grade level as a frame of reference we were responsible for grades one, three, four, six, seven and ten. Even though occasionally there are signs of brightness — even brief flashes of precociousness — there is not really an intellectual giant in the bunch. There are the well organized, the plodders, the sometimes goof-offs, the inspirationalists, the fast readers and even

the dyslexic. There are those who can make a workbook or project last seemingly forever, and those who are still bugging you at bedtime for more to do. Suffice it to say, that everything considered, it's hardly what you would call "getting away from it all."

The only reason for reporting this and what follows in these pages is that for the last ten or so years I've been an educator involved primarily in the educational systems movement, and during the past year I think that I discovered, or more accurately, **experienced** something which may be of value to others with the same interest and commitments.

But, first, to complete the perspective, it should be said that I have tried to keep in touch with those things in which I was actively engaged some eight or nine months ago. This has included thinking about the educational systems and technology that I have either observed or helped develop, as well as following developments of the last year as reported in **Educational Technology** and other publications.

All of this has led me to wonder increasingly why is it that so many educational systems incorporating modern technology fail to come up to expectations? The answer cannot be a simple one. But at least part of it may have to do with complexity. Many of the emerging education systems are **SO** complex. Is such a condition of educational systems necessary? There is no question but what education — and learning — increases in complexity each month, or even week, as society propels itself further into the space and computer age. But is teaching — and learning — all **THAT** complex? It seems almost, as one reviews the work of educational technologists, that many of them worship the god of technology — up to and including the practice of periodically offering human (learner) sacrifices to their idol.

Anti-technology? I think not. Perhaps it is that technology is not infrequently confused with clarity of purpose and specificity of objectives. It is true that the lack of such qualities characterizes most educational efforts even today, but it is likewise erroneous to think that simply because something is complex, it is **ipso facto** scientific, i.e., clear, purposeful and maximally effective. The experience I am about to describe suggests the opposite. That is, that **the more clear and specific the objectives, the less complex an instructional-learning system needs to be.**

Off to a warmer climate

After spending the winter in England, where father put the children in English schools and concentrated on "his own" work, two things became extremely clear. One was the need for sun and a warmer climate, and the other was for some attention to the children's basic skills. English culture be damned — neither we nor they wanted them to be "held back a year" when we returned to the States. The then obvious answer was a cross-country trip to Portugal; and two days after arriving in a small fishing village, school for the six grades was in operation. The Instructional Materials Center, at least the initially defined one, was transported in a medium size suitcase. It consisted of three modern math (and that's a cause I someday want to question to the children's basic skills. English culture and their accompanying workbooks, a world geography text and two high school level correspondence courses. There were a few other texts, and of course ruled paper, boxes of pencils, pens, and, fortunately, a couple sets of felt tipped pens. What developed during the next three months might aptly be described as Felt Tipped Pen Educational Technology.

This, as noted above, was what we perceived as the initial set of instructional materials, and within a week its inadequacies were woefully apparent. We brought many other books and items with us, and nearly each day several of these were moved permanently to the dining room (our physical plant — and even that expanded eventually). A few examples should suffice. The **World Almanac** and **Websters Pocket Dictionary** became basic references for all except the first grade. Ambitious, and to the students, meaningful projects were completed with these as references. The cry for supplementary sources was heard immediately, but there were none. Except the **Europa Touring** books, the **PanAm World Travelers Guide,** Michener's **Iberia** and **Hawaii,** numerous paperbacks and, of course, travel brochures. The travel books were adequate sources of comparative measurement systems, and the foreign language phrase books became language labs. The cassette tape recorder, taken along as a source of entertainment, became a precision tool for the student with reading difficulties. The American checkbook and bank statements served well as a record keeping practice set, and the small store across the street provided a "living laboratory" for all kinds of cross-cultural experiences.

The kitchen, with cooking projects, served to teach a little chemistry. Being starred at by the local natives . . . and then talking about it . . . helped to learn a little about prejudice. Watching the fishermen's children dig through garbage cans for bread as the weekenders from Lisbon arrived with their maids in their Mercedes limousines taught something about poverty and social systems.

Complaints about the lack of TV disappeared within the first week, and it's surprising how even small children can learn to tune a Volkswagon AM receiver to pick up American news and music. **Newsweek** and the **Herald Tribune,** read only occasionally, if at all, by the older grades in England, became sought after (and sometimes fought over) sources of information regarding current events. Comic books and "Charlie Brown" and "Dennis the Menace" paperbacks helped a dyslexic 13-year-old read with meaning and enjoyment (man! just READ) for the first time; and, for lack of nothing better to do, two others tackled books "far too difficult for them" — and parents had that rare experience of watching their children discover the joy of reading.

Saved by technology

But, with all of this, we would have been doomed to ignorance without technological resources. It was our good fortune to bring several sets of felt tipped colored pens with us, as I noted. On a lecture trip to Germany, I brought back another half dozen sets. These, using the cardboard backs of tablets, were used to construct games, both for amusement and teaching. The biting technology of the felt tipped pen applied to sheets of ruled paper resulted in instructional materials which attacked learning deficiencies discovered minutes or even seconds before. The learner who takes the same hard hitting technology in his fist and applies it directly to the printing or map in the textbook seems to experience a sense of relationship and awareness to what he is studying that doesn't happen when the same materials are treated as educational paraphernalia not to be soiled.

A monitoring system

Without thinking about it very much in advance, we discovered that we had a fairly sensitive, if not complex, monitoring system for our school. In fact, it was usually impossible to be unaware of what each pupil was achieving or was not achieving. Sometimes, it was painfully obvious. But this being the case, the simplest thing to do was manufacture on the spot, or conjur up immediately, materials or procedures designed to serve the specific need of students at the time. In short, we had a sensitive means of observing pupil behavior, a manageable set of instructional materials, specific objectives, and we certainly were not burdened with complexity, i.e., the necessity to understand complex systems ourselves before using them in instruction.

We had, of course, several other things going in our favor, including extremely cooperative pupils, a small N and few other pre-occupations. These will never be discounted; but, nevertheless, the comparison between the simple educational endeavor we were maintaining and the tremendously complex educational systems being mounted in the U.S., both of which are concerned with essentially the same substantive materials and behaviors, was impossible to ignore.

And so, in my own thinking, at least, I was back to square one. Why do so many technologically oriented educational systems fall short of their expectations? Is it in part a function of the complexity of so much technology? I think so.

Serving the god of technology frequently leads one to lose sight of the simple objective(s) which were the initial concern. "System for system's sake"

is a catch phrase, and an over-simplification, and thus I abhor it. Nevertheless, it suggests something of the negative aspects of educational technology.

Consider several examples: with all of its positive values, the modern math sometimes goes around the barn four times to teach the pupil that to divide fractions you simply invert and multiply; and confuses many students during the trip. Ask a few, if you doubt it. The complex conceptualizations of educational systems presented in a number of the current journals could be described in two or three paragraphs, if the authors would be less concerned with complexity and more with clarity. And flexible scheduling may not always necessitate a computer. There are times when a teacher can simply send three pupils to the hallway and another three to the breezeway while she works with the rest. Not always, but the concept can be applied at times without technological complexity.

Few classroom teachers probably will read this paper, and I suppose that this is to my advantage as an author. For, if they did, they would simply suggest that it took **me** 15 years to discover what is very apparent to any elementary school teacher worth his or her salt. And that's probably true. At the same time, no one can question the dependency of education on technology in the decades to come. Education's contribution to man's peaceful survival, often summed up as "individualized instruction," simply **cannot be made** without the extensive use of technology.

Keeping designers honest

Not everyone can haul their children off to a fishing village in Portugal or some such place and get back to the basics, nor should they. EDUCATION is complex — more than most of us realize; but specific acts of teaching and learning by themselves are not that complex. And certainly the systems which we design to aid teaching and learning should never be so complex that they, in fact, inhibit the very behaviors that they are designed to generate. My plea, of course, is not just to keep it simple. As there is no inherent virtue in complexity, there is none in simplicity. It is instead a matter of function, of workableness, of energy expended **vs.** results achieved.

For myself, I will now practice more diligently something which I have frequently preached. Never design an instructional system without involving — as partners — students and teachers who will use the system. They tend to keep you honest.   □

Individualized Instructional Systems for Vocational Education

J. William Ullery

During the early 1960's a growing concern was being expressed among educators over the apparent inability of the public schools to apply newly developed educational technology. It was during this time that behavioral objectives, individualized instruction, systems development techniques, new methods of curriculum evaluation, curricular organizations based on hierarchies of skills and knowledges, and other popular themes were also gaining a hearing within the professional literature.

Out of such concerns grew Project ABLE—a unique developmental effort which involved a local school system and a major research organization in a joint contract with the U.S. Office of Education. The initiators of the project included Robert M. Gagne of the American Institutes for Research (presently professor at Florida State University), Robert E. Pruitt, who at the time was superintendent of the Quincy, Massachusetts Public Schools (now director of the Division of Comprehensive and Vocational Education Research, U.S. Office of Education) and Maurice J. Daly, assistant superintendent of schools in Quincy, Massachusetts. The major activities were centered in the local school system in an attempt to involve students, teachers, administrators, school board members and others within the community. The first five-year contract was recently completed, with continuation presently being sponsored by Quincy. However, a coordinated effort of national scope has been under consideration by 21 of the largest school systems in the country. It now appears that the early efforts of Project ABLE may well be of some significance to all engaged in vocational and technical education.

Project ABLE is a "systems" approach to occupational education. It was intended to base development upon a unique combination of the most effective features of modern educational technology. This included an appropriate use of the state-of-the-arts in vocational-technical education, drawing on some of the best existing methods. However, it was felt that the operational instructional systems must be within the financial capabilities of most vocational-technical schools. Thus, the characteristics of the ABLE approach should find wide acceptance among vocational and technical educators. Based upon widespread reactions

J. William Ullery is project director of Project ABLE and a research scientist for American Institutes for Research.

from around the country, a "model" may well emerge. If the research was appropriately conducted, such should be the outcome. Here, it would be important to point out that the features of ABLE are not unique to the Quincy-AIR project. The "bandwagon" has a rapidly proliferating list of advocates and practitioners.

The chart, "Do You Have An Instructional System?" (Figure 1), portrays the major requirements of a learner-centered system, such as that described in the following sections. It is doubtful that many public schools have programs at the operational stage of a truly individualized instructional "system." However, rapid progress toward such goals is taking place. Figure 2 plots the learner activity process within an individualized instructional system. Note the flexibility available to each school, teacher and student in the choice of instruction (methods and materials) available through the student-instructor contract options. Such an approach may well be the only effective means of meeting the problems associated with the wide variance in individual learning styles and preferences while maintaining local control over the instructional process.

Below are listed a number of characteristics of a modern instructional system which should typify, in the opinion of many scientists and educators, all of vocational and technical education. Project ABLE has attempted to work within such a design in the establishment of demonstration programs.

Characteristics

Individualized instruction—each student

Enters chosen job family program at a level corresponding to his previous experience and knowledge.

Is guided to learning experiences consistent with goals agreed upon by him and his instructor.

Learns at a rate based on his own ability by using self-instructional materials and techniques.

Has greater flexibility in allowing for a change of program with fewer penalties.

Experiences successes in learning—there are no failures. Some students simply take longer than others to accomplish goals.

New roles for teachers and students

The teacher is more able to perform as a diagnostician, tutor and manager of learning.

The instructor is free to assist the individual student with accomplishment of the student's goals and in accordance with his needs.

Students participate in the selection of learning materials for a variety of educational media.

Each student is required to be actively involved in not only the learning process, but also in his evaluation and program management.

There is student and teacher involvement in program development and testing.

Figure 1

DO YOU HAVE A LEARNER–CENTERED INSTRUCTIONAL SYSTEM FOR VOCATIONAL AND TECHNICAL EDUCATION?

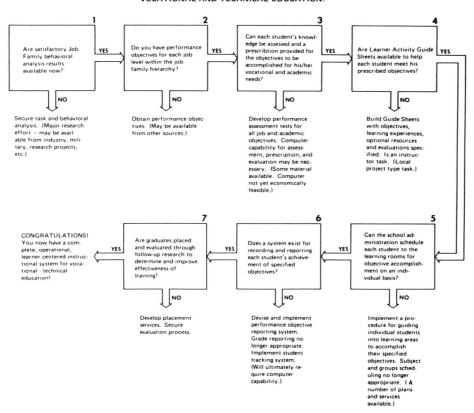

Job-based instructional units

Detailed job analyses are used to determine needed skills.

Jobs are organized into clusters and skill families.

Brief performance evaluation tests and learning activity guides are developed for each task within the occupational family.

New methods of sequencing instruction by job levels and hierarchies of skills and knowledges are used.

Clearly stated performance objectives are based on a scientific task analysis.

The focus is on job *entry* level skills and knowledges by job levels within a family cluster.

There are *no* age or grade level restrictions to programs organized by job levels.

Units are activity- and job-oriented rather than classroom- or theory-oriented.

At whatever point the student chooses to leave he does so with job-related proficiencies.

Students know the standards of performance and the nature of all evaluation.

Students know exactly where to concentrate remedial study.

Flexibility

Better integration of cooperative work-study programs.

Use of existing or new course materials possible.

Programs of study which can be easily modified to fit the unique needs of any school system or student.

Changes more easily accomplished with technological advances in job family (evaluation and management plan).

Student advancement by job levels (not grade levels) with multiple entry and exit points.

Performance evaluation

Provides self-evaluation tools, preventing premature formal testing, while saving teacher time and student embarrassment.

Standards are derived from a task analysis.

Test structure informs student where to concentrate any remedial study.

Students are permitted to skip instructional units by simply demonstrating an adequate level of knowledge and skill.

Occupational readiness certification specifies skills of graduates.

Testing procedures provide students with immediate "knowledge of results."

Figure 2

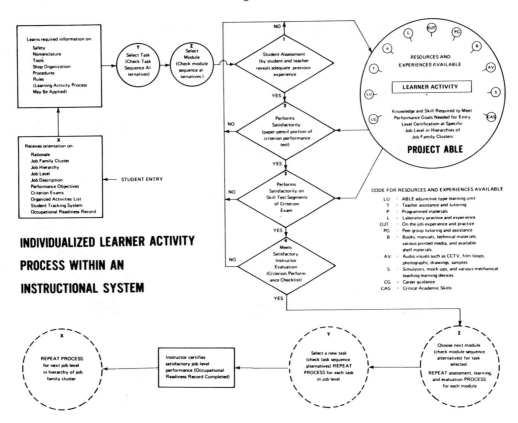

INDIVIDUALIZED LEARNER ACTIVITY PROCESS WITHIN AN INSTRUCTIONAL SYSTEM

Some Anticipated Benefits

Students build self-confidence through successful learning experiences (especially important for slow learners).

Fewer discipline problems (50 percent fewer in one instance).

Fewer dropouts.

Greater flexibility for students desiring a change of program of study.

Marketable job-related skills for every student.

Greater dignity for the student; no failures combined with a joint student-teacher learning effort in objective accomplishment.

Evaluation methods (student, teacher, program) economical and simple for students, teachers, and administrators.

Minimal instructor training to operate system with emphasis and focus on inservice training.

Systems techniques and better management with quality control throughout the developmental process and ongoing operation.

Reduction of clerical chores for teachers.

More easily adapted to new school-wide flexible scheduling systems.

Efficiency and cost savings in equipment and supplies because of the detailed specification of instructional objectives.

Ability to specify to publishers precise instructional objectives for better learning material development.

Instructional Example

1. A student enters the study of a particular job family in light of his present skills and interests.

2. He is provided with a brief activity guide for each job task giving him
   a. a clear statement of what he should be able to do;
   b. a suggested guide to optional learning experiences (also method, media, materials, etc.);
   c. self-evaluation aids to check his own progress.

3. He follows the guide, obtaining from the teacher counsel and advice as necessary. Team approaches, where students help each other, are frequently used. He does *not* work in a vacuum all alone.

4. When he feels competent to perform the unit task requirements, he goes to the teacher who evaluates his task performance and knowledges according to a guide provided to both student and teacher. (There are no secret test items; the student is told at the outset what abilities he will have to demonstrate.) If the student has had job experience and can demonstrate the required level of skills and knowledges, he can bypass most of the instruction and move rapidly to more advanced tasks.

5. If he demonstrates competence, the student and teacher select the next task to be learned. In view of his experience and interests, he may shift goals within a job family or even change job families. The modules are short and related to job tasks providing flexibility for such changes at any time.

6. The student moves along as rapidly as *he* is ABLE, not in lock-step with other students. He moves at a pace at which he can be successful.

Figure 3

FLOW CHART OF INSTRUCTIONAL SYSTEM DEVELOPMENT PROCESS

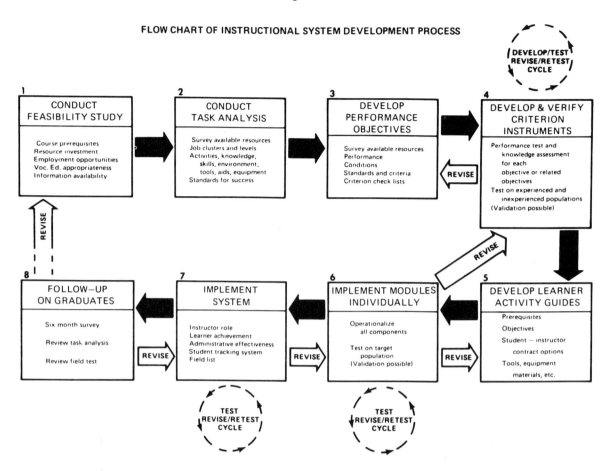

Technical Development

A number of technical reports on ABLE are available through ERIC or the American Institutes for Research, 135 N. Bellefield Avenue, Pittsburgh, Pennsylvania 15213, or the Quincy Public Schools, at cost of printing. One such document, "Management and Evaluation Plan for Instructional Systems Development for Vocational-Technical Education," was recently released. A brief review of the goals and objectives of the project is included in the report. A review of the literature is provided for the purpose of defining and clarifying the rationale for the plan. Major emphasis in the manual is given to formative evaluative procedures drawing on student performance data as the primary source of corrective feedback. The system is designed around an interactive process with the major goal of continuous program and product improvement. It is felt that such an approach would provide a regenerative element with self-renewal and updating taking place as a result of the evaluation, validation and follow-up activities. It is shown how test/revise/retest cycles can and should be perpetuated for as long as the program is in operation. Figure 3, the "Flow Chart of Instructional Systems Development Process," illustrates the general approach.

The primary evaluation instruments for ABLE have been derived from job and task descriptions and the subsequent specification of behaviorally stated performance objectives. This entails a detailed breakdown of the task activities and an identification of the "critical incidents" which are then translated into criterion checklist instruments. Criterion instruments, called "performance evaluation modules," are also developed from the task descriptions for the purpose of structuring replicable and reliable assessment situations. The performance evaluation modules are further refined to permit effective class management. While such instruments incorporate objective paper-pencil items on related knowledge, the emphasis is on the more important "hands-on," or practical performance, skill test activities. Self-scoring response and feedback techniques with numerous simulators, mock-ups, samples and other aids are emphasized in recognition of the critical role such devices play in a functional instructional system.

The entire developmental effort has been characterized by a system approach centered around successive tryouts and systematic testing. Procedures for the design and application of developmental and evaluative instruments have been developed in considerable detail. Sample materials are included in the previously mentioned report, along with flow charts, work sheets and various systems control documents. Management procedures are defined and the entire process is carefully documented. A plan for summative evaluation is outlined and guidelines are suggested for appropriate application. Sample instruments for both formative and summative evaluation are included. □

A Basic Operational Learning System

Harold Bergquist

The paramount contemporary goal of vanguard schools is the organization of a learning system which provides financially feasible and educationally effective individualized instruction. Tragically, most of these schools are waiting for federal government or private industry funding to accomplish the goal. This article describes the successful efforts of a small (12,000-student) and poor ($2,600 per pupil tax base) school district to independently fund, organize and implement an individualized curriculum within the context of a learning system.

It is contended that all learning systems result from organization of personnel, materials, equipment and space. Time, another factor of learning, is a dependent variable which can be utilized economically or squandered as a result of such learning systems organization.

Since a learning system is created primarily to facilitate learner progression through a curriculum, curriculum development is an essential first step to the establishment of the paramount goal identified in the first sentence of this article. Such a curriculum must "fit" the learning system, or, perhaps, the learning system must "fit" the curriculum; the point is moot.

The Grand Forks School District Curriculum is based on behavioral objectives. It encompasses all major subject areas in a kindergarten through grade 12 sequence. At this writing, nearly 3000 behavioral objectives have been identified and a contract (learning package) has been developed for each. The curriculum is dynamic in that its numeration system permits the addition of behavioral objectives, with accompanying contracts, at any point in the presently utilized sequence of behavioral objectives.

An examination of the Grand Forks School District Curriculum format illustrates its several dimensions.

Contract Number:
General Content Description:
Prerequisite: (If any.)
Behavioral Objective:
Sample Test Item:
Learning Area Taxonomy:
Pretest: (oral, written, demonstration)
Instruction Experiences:
  1.
  2.
  3.
  4.
  5.
  6.
  7.
  8. Check Test (suggested)
  9.
  10.
  11.
Posttest:

This listing should be multimedia and its extensiveness is usually closely correlated to the potential of the contract to provide for individual differences.

Readers should note that the diagnostic and prescriptive activities of quality teaching are promoted by pretests, prerequisite identification and the suggestion of a variety of learning experiences. In addition, the progression of a student through a series of behavioral objectives enhances the ability of professional instructors to more precisely report the individual learner's achievement, more conducive modes of learning and subject interest areas. Such knowledge is vital to future instructors of the learner and is of interest to parents.

The curriculum promotes the individualization of instruction through three characteristics.

1. Learner interest is identified and served. The instructor and the learner have extensive opportunities to select behavioral objectives which satisfy and further develop student interests.

2. Unique learner pacing is promoted. Since the curriculum is organized into small units (behavioral objectives), the pace with which a learner moves is not a critical concern. Hence, some students may, for example, progress through several years of mathematics while peers progress at a more moderate rate.

3. Learner proficiency in the various modes of learning—visual, auditory, tactile, etc.—can be applied positively. A contract normally includes learning experiences which are based on a variety of learning modes. while

The Grand Forks School District Learning System and Curriculum is formally operational in 13 "Islands of Continuous Progress" within the District. These "Islands" provide instruction to 2500 students in all subject areas.

This system, too, is comprised of personnel, materials, equipment and facilities. Each "Island" has a differentiated staff (*personnel*) which includes as many as 11 employed adults.

Each "Island" has a variety of learning *materials* which are identified as learning experiences in the curriculum contracts. These materials are representative of the highest quality of commercially prepared materials. Various locally produced materials also are available.

Equipment for the "Islands" varies with the needs of the students instructed in the "Islands." This equipment includes visual projectors, study carrels, dial access systems and video tape equipment.

Funds for materials and equipment utilized in the Grand Forks School District Learning System were limited to an initial capitalization of $50.00 per student, in addition to the regular annual district-wide materials

Harold Bergquist is assistant superintendent-instruction at Grand Forks, North Dakota.

and equipment expenditures per pupil. This initial capitalization is judged adequate.

The system is thought to function best in open flexible *space* which is acoustically treated. Several "Islands" were implemented in facilities which were originally built to such specifications. The variety of remodeling efforts in older facilities obviously defies description in this article. Significantly, facilities design is the least important of the factors, and it represents a small cost when compared to personnel cost.

The Grand Forks Learning System is an operating model. Implementation of such a model is within the financial means of nearly every school district in the United States. In rural areas, several school districts could cooperate to implement one such Learning System.

Much educator time is presently utilized to design hypothetical models for systems learning. Unfortunately, most school districts cannot afford these models; furthermore, school personnel are not available to function in the most grandiose schemes, if the needed EDP hardware were to be assembled.

The Grand Forks Learning system may have similarly unpublicized sister systems located throughout the nation promoting individualized instruction, dynamic curriculum development and inservice staff growth. As the cost of EDP hardware is reduced and as these systems continue to effect savings in personnel and instructional efficiency, additional EDP hardware will be utilized to upgrade these systems to more closely approximate the futuristic learning models of computer managed instruction (CMI) and computer assisted instruction (CAI). Meanwhile, "back at the ranch," without malice or envy (theorists are essential to progress), we will continue to perfect functional systems which serve learners *today*. □

Developing a Methodology for Designing Systems of Instruction

Polly Carpenter

The Problem
Many new ways of teaching and much instructional technology have been developed and validated for their contributions to effective instruction, yet these innovations have seen little implementation in existing teaching institutions. One of the prime reasons for this is that the designers of instruction, even when they are not also burdened with the task of classroom teaching, are not sufficiently familiar with the new systems to plan their implementation or must rely for planning and design on their intuition and judgment. These are shaped largely by their familiarity with existing facilities, equipment, operating practices and materials, and by available personnel. Innovations in the process of instruction at a teaching institution arise primarily from the efforts of a few people who believe that some particular strategy of instruction or application of new instructional technology will be more effective than methods already in use. If such people succeed in convincing school personnel of the merits of their position, they must either go through a lengthy design process with very little to assist them besides their own convictions, or they must effect the change through trial and error. Inevitably they cannot have had firsthand experience with a variety of alternatives. More effective or less expensive instruction may result, but there is no assurance that it is as effective as it could be, no assurance that other strategies could not be used along with the one of primary interest to improve efficiency, no assurance that more desirable combinations of techniques, operating procedures, materials and equipment have not been overlooked.

No single designer or design team can have had enough firsthand experience to know all possible alternatives or to choose wisely among them. The objective of some current Rand research is to correct this situation, at least in part, by developing methodologies for the design of systems for instruction. These design methodologies will assure that promising alternatives are not overlooked, thereby pointing the way to improved instructional systems in a wide range of situations.

The Approach
This article describes some Rand work* directed toward improving the effectiveness of instruction,

*This work is sponsored by the U.S. Air Force with the assistance of Headquarters USAF, Headquarters Air Training Command, Chanute and Lowry Technical Schools and the Air Force Human Resources Laboratory.

Polly Carpenter is with the System Sciences Department, The Rand Corporation, Santa Monica, California.

whether it be in the classroom, shop, laboratory or in the field, by facilitating the implementation of innovations in actual school situations. The work focuses on the development of methodologies for planning and designing systems for teaching a course defined in terms of a set of learning objectives. These methodologies will provide planners with tools that will make it easier for them to design new instructional systems, and will help assure that their designs are comprehensive, coherent and appropriate to their needs. The process could take a matter of a few weeks or perhaps even a few days, rather than taking, say, several months to a year—as it does at present. This will allow planners to consider several possible alternative ways to conduct a particular course so that they may choose the way that is most promising.

In short, we are working out a process for instructional system design. This process has certain inputs and outputs. A description of the outputs will illustrate the direction of our efforts in specific terms. The outputs are the following characteristics of an instructional system: course length; student flow, as a function of time during the course; and the time-dependent requirements for resources, such as facilities, materials, instructors and support personnel (see Figure 1). These outputs will be related to the inputs, which we characterize in three general areas: the teaching institution, learners for whom the course of study is intended and the course objectives.

The design process relates outputs to inputs so that the outputs will be acceptable to the teaching institution, and the instructional system they describe will teach the course of study to the designated learners. We are now in the process of identifying the steps in the design process, determining their sequence and discovering their interrelationships. This has never before been done in a systematic way, to our knowledge; it is a challenging and exciting pioneering effort.

The first step is to characterize the learners in terms that will affect the way the course will be taught (Step 1, Figure 2). For example, some learners may have already had experience in the particular field in which they will be studying. If the percentage of such learners changes with the time of year, this will also be included in the analysis.

The second step, we believe, is to state general policy (Step 2, Figure 2). *Policy*, as used here, means such things as the nature of the objectives of the institution. Many institutions have input-oriented objectives; some have output-oriented objectives. An input-oriented institution might be, for example, a labor union which requires that every union member have taken a certain number of weeks of a specific kind of vocational course. Most military and industrial training, however, is output-oriented. Industry and the military want a man who has particular skills and knowledge; if the amount of input required to get that same output can be reduced, so much the better.

General policy also requires a statement of whether the school wants a standard or a diverse output. If the learners are fairly homogeneous, this question is not very important, but if they are heterogeneous, it is. (The

Air Training Command tries to produce standard graduates in the technical center, although no one really believes that all airmen are exactly the same when they have finished a technical course.) Another aspect of general policy has to do with the way in which the school relates to those institutions that use its graduates and those that supply its students.

The third step, the Lesson Analysis, is denoted in Step 3a (Figure 3) because it is interrelated with the next step. This analysis is a branching questionnaire that guides the user in providing a detailed description of the course of study. First, it typifies each lesson in "system-oriented" terms such as whether the instruction must be given in a classroom or in a laboratory, whether it requires special equipment, or whether it requires a monitor to ensure student safety. For example, if the students are learning how to take good pictures, the instruction would require special equipment, namely, a camera. If the students are learning only how a camera operates, the instruction might take place entirely in a classroom with only visual aids to show how the camera operates.

As used here, a strategy of instruction has two dimensions. For each type of instruction identified in the Lesson Analysis, it specifies: (1) whether a person or medium will be teaching and (2) how students will interact with this teaching. Answers to these two questions specify a teaching method. The strategy also permits specification of details of the use of media or people for each type of instruction, such as the level of skill the people should have. The user is assisted in finding his way through the logic tree by a time-shared computer program accompanied by a manual that presents the pros and cons of the decisions to be made at each point.

The Lesson Analysis also characterizes each lesson's requirements for communication media. We have focused on communication media because a communication medium can carry the burden of classroom instruction and therefore can provide alternatives to teachers under expectedly heavy student loads or in cases where high-quality teachers are scarce. The selection of appropriate communication media for instruction is an extremely difficult process; we believe that we can provide systematic guidance in this area.* However, the design methodology does *not* specify that communication media must be used for every lesson even though the Lesson Analysis describes possible requirements for communication media. Another process allows the *user* to specify whether or not he will use media. This process is a logic tree that assists the user in specification of strategies of instruction, Step 3b, which interacts closely with the Lesson Analysis (see Figure 3). At the same time, the framework for this specification is provided by the statement of general policy as well as by indirect input from the teaching institution.

*Rudy Bretz. *A Taxonomy of Communication Media.* Englewood Cliffs: Educational Technology Publications, 1971.

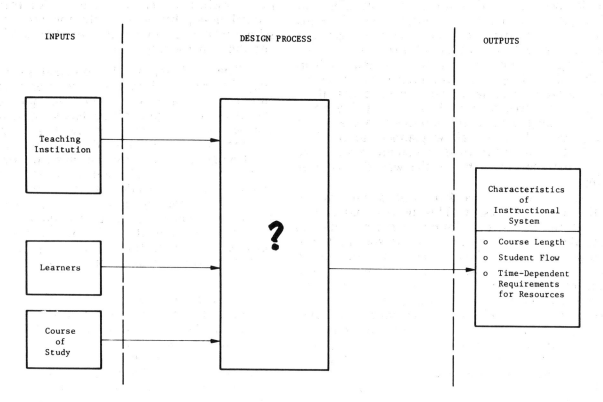

Figure 1

Framework of the Design Process

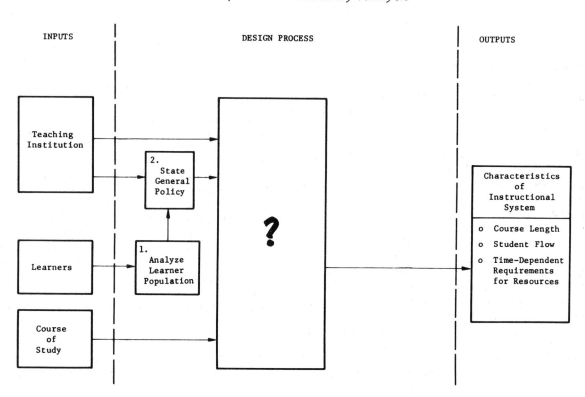

Figure 2

First Steps in the Preliminary Analysis

Figure 3

Preliminary Analyses: Setting the Stage

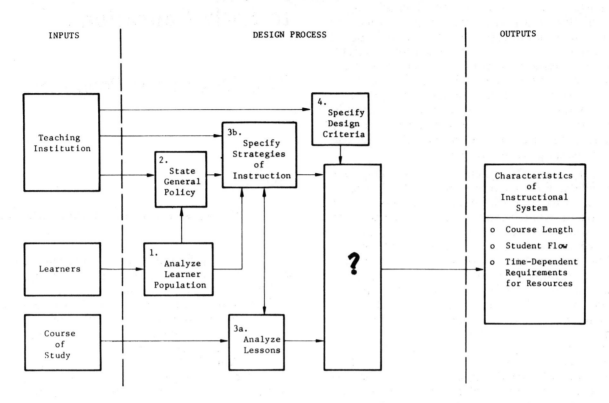

Figure 4

The Design Process as a System of Interrelated Elements

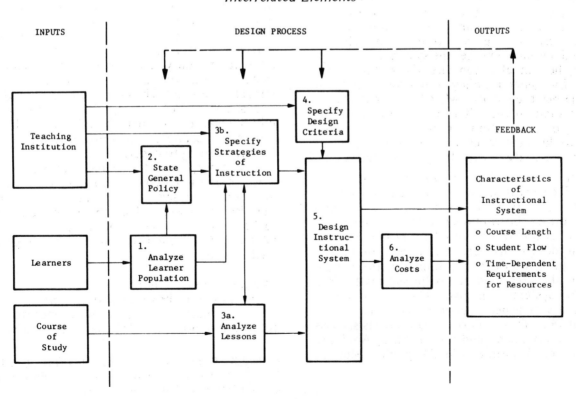

49

Step 4, Figure 3, establishes a set of design criteria, input from the teaching institution. They will be of the following sorts: least cost, shortest course length, graduation of the most students per unit time, or maximum use of communication media. The user would assign each criterion an order of importance or a weight.

Once the criteria have been specified, the actual system design can begin (Step 5, Figure 4). The direct inputs to the design will be the strategies of instruction, the Lesson Analysis and the design criteria. Characteristics of the learner population, the stated general policy and the general features of the course of study also enter into the design process indirectly.

At present, we see the design process as having four main components: First, each learning event is linked to the strategy of instruction that has been chosen for that particular type of event. Second, student flow through the course is simulated by a flow and scheduling model. Third, a set of criteria is used to select specific media systems. (The Lesson Analysis only identifies the class of media [for example, motion-visual] that might be used for a particular lesson. What precise form the media system should take [for example, silent film] will be specified by the strategies of instruction and other criteria which are being developed.) Fourth, a set of criteria is used to assign personnel. Although there will be instances where a certain number of people will be required to carry out a particular task, such as monitoring for safety, other personnel requirements will be harder to identify—such as determining the number of students that can feasibly be assigned to a teacher in a classroom. This component still has to be worked out. The final step will be a cost analysis to determine the time-dependent dollar requirements for the system.

As noted above, the outputs of the design process will be: course length, student flow and time-dependent requirements for resources; all are useful for the planner. He can then compare the requirements for resources with resources he expects to be available to the school, to determine whether the system is economically feasible; he can also compare the outputs with requirements for general policy and other inputs to determine whether they satisfy what he wanted. If not, he can change some of the initial specifications such as the strategies of instruction or the design criteria. Possibly he would want to change the learner population, the course of study or even the general policy.

Although these tools compose a closely interrelated set of elements in system design, several are useful in their own right. For example, the decision process for setting instructional strategy contains a comprehensive checklist of considerations in instructional system design that can be used without the computer program if so desired. Similarly, the Lesson Analysis helps the user look at his subject matter in a methodical and systematic manner. The work has been directed toward very general applications so that it will be of use not only to Air Force organizations such as the Air Training Command and the Air Force Academy but to educational institutions in the public sector as well. □

A Systems Approach to Early Education:

The Discovery Program

Ronald K. Parker and David C. Whitney

The Discovery Program is a comprehensive educational system designed to enhance the learning of preschool children through involvement of both the children and their parents. From October 1969 to September 1970 the Discovery Program successfully involved more than 1,700 preschool children and their families in nine Discovery Centers operated by Universal Education Corporation (UEC) in five northeastern states: New York, New Jersey, Pennsylvania, Connecticut and Massachusetts. These children ranged in age from two to six years, with the median age 3.7 years. Most of the children were from middle-income families, who paid tuition for the program. Approximately 1,000 low income children will receive a modification of the Discovery Program in day care centers in Pennsylvania during 1971 [see article by Richard Ney].

In recent years much emphasis has been placed on innovative approaches to curricula for early education, but with little discussion of the total context in which the curricula exist. Viewed from a broad perspective, a curriculum represents the core of a complex set of interacting subsystems that must function together smoothly for the curriculum to have its maximum impact on a child. The curriculum may be thought of as one subsystem of a comprehensive system that determines what the learner should learn, while the other subsystems create an environment that makes it possible for the learning to occur.

The purpose of this article is to describe the central features of the Discovery Program from the perspective of a comprehensive early education system. In doing so, the discussion will include three overviews: (1) conceptualization of the curriculum; (2) interacting components; and (3) modification of the program through feedback information.

The Conceptualization of the Discovery Program Curriculum

The Discovery Program was conceptualized on the following hypotheses: (1) that, quantitatively, the bulk

Ronald K. Parker is with the Graduate Center, City University of New York. **David C. Whitney** is with the Educational Systems Division, Universal Education Corporation.

of learning for preschool children has always taken place and is likely to continue to take place in the home environment rather than in structured institutional environments; (2) that, qualitatively, most learning among preschool children has been of a haphazard or unplanned nature, largely dependent on the quality of the home environment; and (3) that, if dramatic changes are to be brought about in both the quantity and quality of preschool learning, the focus of the early education program must be on the family, rather than merely on the child. In other words, the educational program must work cooperatively with the parents, as well as with the child, if it is to be effective.

One important consequence of these hypotheses is that the curriculum and the interacting subsystems must be described in terms that have positive connotations and are understandable to parents who play an important role in implementing the curriculum. The label "Discovery Program" was selected because it has a positive connotation among the lay public and because it describes one effective method by which young children acquire new information.

From a professional standpoint, we are aware of both the positive and negative connotations of the term "Discovery." Ausubel's (1968, pp. 467-504) brilliant discussion of discovery-learning, noting the lack of solid empirical support for this approach for school age children, leaves little doubt in our minds that discovery-learning per se does not have the widespread applicability that some of its early advocates supposed (Hendrix, 1961; see also Chambers, 1971). It does seem, however, that what has been called *guided* discovery-learning" has important implications for preschool curricula. Structured discovery methods that lead the learner to a desired generalization through the use of carefully organized materials and experiences have some demonstrated empirical validity (Beberman, 1958; Gagne & Brown, 1961).

In addition to the applications that discovery-learning principles have in some parts of the Discovery Program, there are many other salient features of this curriculum conceptualization that will be discussed under the following headings: (1) behavioral orientation and objectives; (2) learning and development; (3) instruction and development; (4) motivation and development; (5) continuous education; (6) continual evaluation of skills and concept acquisition; and (7) accountability.

Behavioral Orientation and Objectives

The field of early education is filled with dedicated individuals who want to help children by focusing on the whole child without ever clearly identifying their specific educational objectives, specifying the program to attain those objectives, and determining whether the objectives have been attained. It is easy to fault the thousands of applied preschool programs that not only have failed to identify their educational objectives but also have never even considered what their specific objectives are or should be. The distressing fact in the 1970's is that so many of the "research" preschool programs have not identified their specific educational objectives or made explicit their educational programs.

A recent overview (Parker, Ambron, Danielson, Halbrook & Levine, 1970) of the literature surveying the preschool programs for three-, four- and five-year-old children concluded "...that most programs do not have an operational statement of their curriculum. Literally hundreds of programs were reviewed for this paper that did not have any written curriculum" (p. 120). Without a written curriculum, one would hardly expect to find behavioral objectives in these programs.

The Discovery Program has carefully defined its behavioral objectives in order to avoid some of the ambiguities that characterize most preschool programs. Three somewhat incompatible criteria guided the selection of the behavioral objectives: (1) the objectives should present a comprehensive view of child development; (2) the list of objectives should be manageable; and (3) each objective should be easily understood by learning staff members and parents. The criterion of comprehensiveness has been met by insuring that behavioral objectives were selected across all areas of child behavior, including cognitive, linguistic, affective, motivational, social and physical development.

The current list includes more than 1,800 key behavioral objectives, representing the combined efforts of our staff and consultants to enumerate those key skills and concepts that are thought to lead a child to future success in school and in life. After the behavioral objectives were identified, they were classified into thematic skill areas and then organized into a comprehensive taxonomy of behavioral objectives for early education. The term "skill area" in this context may be defined as a cluster of behavioral objectives that have been grouped together for thematic and conceptual clarity. Obviously, some of these skill area groupings are more arbitrary than others. The 43 skill areas in the Discovery Program are presented below.

Lifetime Skill Areas

A.	Creativity	E.	Understanding the World
B.	Reasoning		
C.	Perception	F.	Communication
D.	Work and Study Skills	G.	Self-Confidence
		H.	Initiative

Basic Learning Skill Areas

1.	Observing	19.	Understanding Rules
2.	Listening	20.	Tasting and Smelling
3.	Expanding Vocabulary	21.	Finger Dexterity
4.	Improving Memory	22.	Drawing and Design
5.	Recognizing Characteristics	23.	Making and Building
6.	Classifying	24.	Using Tools
7.	Solving Problems	25.	Knowing the Alphabet
8.	Predicting and Testing	26.	Relations with Others
9.	Touching	27.	Self-Care and Safety
10.	Understanding Shapes	28.	Understanding "What?"
11.	Knowing Color	29.	Understanding "Where?"
12.	Speaking	30.	Understanding "When?"
13.	Following Directions	31.	Understanding "Why?"
14.	Counting	32.	Understanding "How?"
15.	Understanding Numbers	33.	Understanding "Who?"
16.	Telling Time	34.	Making Sounds and Music
17.	Measuring	35.	Physical Coordination
18.	Sticking to a Task		

Recognizing the need for a unified taxonomy of behavioral objectives that does not present a fragmented picture of a child, we have attempted to integrate the skill areas with one another by coding them in such a way that a specific behavioral objective may be included in more than one skill area and be internally cross-referenced. For example, in the skill area 1.00 OBSERVING, the sub-skill "1.01 Understands the words *same* and *different*," also carries the cross-reference "equals 5.03." Within the skill area 5.00 RECOGNIZING CHARACTERISTICS, the sub-skill "5.03 Understands *same* and *different*" carries the cross-reference "equals 1.01."

To establish the interrelationships among behavioral objectives across skill areas is an extremely difficult task. The most inviting error is to begin thinking as a faculty psychologist and divide the child into self-contained parts. While such an approach might simplify the task of developing a comprehensive taxonomy of preschool objectives, it would violate the integrity of the organism and lead to an over-simplified conceptualization of the program. For example, even the binary division of a child's behavior into "mental" and "motor" skills on the Bayley Scales (1969) possesses many dangers, because any sample of behavior does not clearly fall into only one of these categories. With full awareness, therefore, of the inherent risks in specifying distinct skill areas, we have continued to work out the complex relationships across skill areas in the belief that the logical and conceptual clarity gained from this approach is worth the risks. Lastly, we feel that we are only beginning the task of a sophisticated taxonomy of behavioral objectives for preschool children. As Bloom, Krathwohl and others have discovered, to develop a taxonomy of behavioral objectives is a time-consuming, expensive and difficult task.

Learning and Development

Several key assumptions about learning and development guide the Discovery Program: (1) normative developmental data provide important leads for preschool educational programming; (2) principles of learning, such as task analysis of objectives, successive approximation, learning sets, overlearning, transfer, generalization and reinforcement, must be embedded in the educational programming; and (3) mixed age grouping of children enhances the opportunities for individualized learning experiences.

Instruction and Development

Several explicit theoretical assumptions about instructional materials and experiences guide the Discovery Program: (1) concrete sensory experiences are important for maximum development; (2) multimedia materials are important in promoting maximum learning; (3) educational diagnosis is important in providing the "match" between a child's developmental level and planned learning experiences; and (4) differentiated staffing provides the best use of staff resources.

Motivation and Development

The challenge in planning a well-designed educational program and environment is to capitalize on a child's general motivation in order to attain certain important behavioral objectives without interfering with his curiosity and exploration. The Discovery Program has employed five techniques successfully: (1) allow the child time to self-select his own activities after each planned activity; (2) plan the total environment so carefully that no matter what materials he self-selects they can be used to achieve specific behavioral objectives; (3) allow children of different ages to work together; (4) provide planned learning experiences with high-interest value designed to stimulate a child to work with the materials to achieve specific behavioral objectives; and (5) apply contingent social reinforcement to shape and strengthen particular behaviors. During a two-hour Discovery Session, five planned activities are alternated with Discovery Time in which a child is free to self-select any play materials in the Center. The learning staff initiates the planned activities, but they do not force a child to participate.

Continuous Education

The limited contact time between any child and the typical preschool program makes it imperative that the child's parents be involved in his early education and development. Additionally, as early education programs begin earlier and earlier, it is advisable to work with the parent during the first two years of life. Gordon (1970), Levenstein (1969), Weikart (1969) and Nimnicht (1969) are among those who have included parent education and/or home visitation in early education programs.

This program was designed around parental involvement in order to involve the major figures in the child's life more deeply in his development and to provide the child with a continuous educational experience that extends beyond the visits to the Discovery Center. The program provides for parent involvement with Take-Home Materials that include: (1) weekly materials answering questions about various facets of child development; (2) suggested daily activities at home appropriate to a child's development; (3) specific learning materials, such as worksheets and educational toys; (4) parent instructions for use of the materials with the child at a range of ability levels; and (5) a parent observation form to summarize and report strengths or weaknesses of the Take-Home Materials and the week's activities.

Continual Evaluation of Skill and Concept Acquisition

On a regular basis the learning staff observes and evaluates the child's skill acquisition. A complete record of all observations and learning activities is kept for each child to assure proper planning and appropriate continuity of experiences for the child. The staff obtains needed detail by talking with the child and by watching him at play. One of the prime ingredients in staff development is the training of staff members to observe and listen to the child in order to guide him to activities that will help him build his abilities from his existing level of skills and concepts.

Curriculum Focus

The Discovery developmental programs (cognitive, language, affective, motivational, social and physical) are interlaced to represent as closely as possible the interactions that occur in real-life situations. These programs move away from standard classroom educational techniques in which one area of the curriculum is assigned to a specific period within the schedule and another curriculum area to another period. [See Whitney and Parker (1971) for a thorough discussion of the Discovery developmental programs.]

Accountability

Because the Discovery Program is designed around behavioral objectives, the system can be held accountable as to whether or not the children attain the established objectives. A parent can readily understand the step-by-step approach to learning within each skill area, because the objectives are clearly stated in lay terminology. Thus, the parent can readily determine whether the immediate objectives are being met. Because parents are free to withdraw their children from the Discovery Program at any time, the system must be constantly accountable to the parents in terms of the results with the individual child. We feel that, because it is so easy for a parent to withdraw from the program, we have been exceedingly fortunate in achieving an average weekly retention rate of more than 96 percent of the parents and children remaining in the program—this despite the many withdrawals caused by families moving to other communities among a highly mobile population.

The Interacting Subsystems of the Discovery Program

The design of the Discovery Program includes consideration of its subsystems, requirements and design of facilities, programs and services, staff requirements, staff development and fiscal planning. In addition, the interaction and relationships among the people, places and programs have been taken into account in the planning. The subsystems include: *People*—the parents, the child, the staff, the administration and the community; *Places*—physical facilities and locations for Discovery Centers, homes, schools and other community institutions; *Programs*—cognitive growth, language development, socialization and social development, values and motivations, emotional adjustment, physical development, and special services to meet individual, family and community needs.

The Interacting Human Subsystems

Parents. In the Discovery Program's conceptualization of its curriculum, the parents play the key role in facilitating the child's development. The program, first, focuses on parent education in the broad area of child development, and, second, supplies the parent with the necessary materials and toys to provide a continuing educational experience in terms of helping the child attain specific behavioral objectives. This orientation is dictated not only by common sense, but through recognition that high quality and economical early education programs can be successfully delivered only with parent involvement.

To help motivate the parents' involvement, interactions were designed with all the other subsystems. For example, consider the parents' interactions with the learning staff. During a Discovery Session, a member of the staff discusses with the parents the activities being conducted in the Center that day and indicates why they are important. While a Discovery Session is in progress, the parents watch the child interact with the staff either directly or over closed-circuit TV; this provides two benefits to the program—(1) the learning staff members constantly perform at their best because they are under close scrutiny from the parents, and (2) the learning staff members serve as role models for the parents, and (2) the learning staff members serve as role models for the parents on how to interact with the child. At the end of a Discovery Session, a member of the staff demonstrates the Take-Home Materials to the parents and answers questions the parents may have. In addition, members of the staff have conferences with parents to report on individual achievements of the child and to suggest individualized approaches to meet the needs of the child.

The Child. The interactions of the child with the other subsystems have been designed to motivate the child to succeed. For example, both staff and parents are encouraged to reinforce the child's positive accomplishments and to refrain from criticizing his failures. The planned activities at the Discovery Center and the suggested activities to be accomplished at home are designed to be fun and entertaining, with their educational objectives being attained incidentally, so far as the child is concerned.

The planned activities *must* be entertaining and motivating, because the child has the prerogative to join or reject each activity. Alternating with the planned group activities, the child has the repeated opportunity in "Discovery Time" to select materials and activities that appeal to his individual interests. The child participates in the planned activities as part of a learning group of no more than 12 children. Two staff members are assigned to each learning group in an adult-child ratio of 1:6, thus insuring that there is ample opportunity for individualized interaction with each child.

Learning Staff. The learning staff of each Discovery Center is composed of a Learning Director, Learning Advisors and Learning Aides. The term "teacher" is consciously avoided in the belief that the conventional connotation of the word "teacher" is antithetical to the learning environment of the Discovery Program. The learning staff organizes the environment and presents interesting activities that stimulate a child to use materials and concepts. The staff members diagnose a child's strengths and weaknesses, guiding him to discover relationships and concepts through careful verbal probes and demonstrations designed to help him acquire specified behavioral objectives.

The qualifications and job descriptions of the members of the learning staff are in brief: (1) *Learning Director*: A teacher with five years of experience and a degree in early education. Her specific responsibilities include: (a) staff supervision and training; (b) Discovery Program administration and (c) relations with parents. (2) *Learning Advisor*: A teacher with two or three years experience and a degree in early education. The primary responsibility of a Learning Advisor is to interact with the children to assist them in the learning process. Specific responsibilities include: (a) conduct of the Discovery Program sessions; (b) guiding children to meet individual learning needs; (c) insuring accuracy of child records; and (d) relations with parents. (3) *Learning Aide*: A man or woman, who is specially trained in observing and working with children using Discovery Program techniques and procedures. He or she is responsible for recording observations as to each child's achievements and assists the Learning Advisor in implementing a Discovery Session with a particular learning group of children.

Educational Consultants. Each Discovery Center is assigned a Ph.D. educational-school psychologist who functions (1) as a consultant to the parents, (2) as a consultant to the Center's staff, and (3) as an arm of the research program. Routine consultation is provided free to the parents in the form of brief individual conferences and regular group conferences.

Personnel Development. Probably the most critical aspect of implementing any preschool program is a good training program for the staff. Weikart (1969) has suggested that staff training and other noncurriculum concerns may have more to do with the success or failure of a program than its curriculum content. The learning staff members are trained through a four-step procedure: (1) thorough familiarization with the Learning Staff Handbook; (2) assignment to a fully operating Discovery Center for preservice training; (3) placement in a continuing training program using videotape training materials; and (4) field monitoring by staff development personnel using the Learning Staff Inventory.

Research Staff. The research staff is comprised of a director of research, four Ph.D. psychologists, a M.S. statistician, and several consultants. The research focus is on data storage and retrieval, and evaluation of the program.

Center Administration Staff. The Center Director is responsible for fiscal management of the Center, demonstrating the Discovery Program to prospective enrollees, scheduling new learning groups, and in general operating the Discovery Center. He is assisted by a Registrar, who enrolls new children into the program and is responsible for the flow of recorded information between the Center and UEC headquarters.

UEC Operations Staff. A national operations staff administers the operation of the Centers, providing logistical support with materials, and monitoring the operation of each Center.

UEC Educational Systems Division Staff. A highly-trained staff develops, produces, evaluates and acquires materials and equipment for the Discovery Program. All instructional materials used within the program are developed and produced by this staff. On the other hand, most of the learning materials, such as educational toys, have been acquired from other producers after these materials have been evaluated and tested with children. This Division administers the staff development program for the learning staffs of the Centers. In addition, the Division produces many of the audiovisual materials used in the Discovery Program, including TV tapes, slide/sound shows, filmstrips and audio tapes.

The Interacting Materials and Equipment Subsystems

Many of the interactions within the Discovery Program system are stimulated by the manipulation of materials and equipment. Special attention is given to determine the best use of each of these components to insure that it fulfills its purpose. All of the ideas, procedures, assumptions and programs discussed in the section on the conceptualization of the curriculum are considered important components which interact with the total educational system. Additionally, the three major types of materials and equipment which were designed to interact with one another include: (1) instructional materials; (2) learning equipment and materials, includings books, educational toys and equipment used directly in learning processes; and (3) the physical environment of the Discovery Center.

Instructional Materials. The instructional materials comprise more than 2,300 pages and include printed handbooks, notebooks and booklets that contain the specific instructional information about the Discovery Program.

The Learning Staff Handbook. The learning staff handbook includes all of the policies and procedures needed to understand and implement the Discovery Program. Its 15 chapters serve as the basic handbook for the learning staff, and include: (1) the basic principles of the Discovery Program; (2) the detailed responsibilities of each member of the learning staff; (3) the uses of the various handbooks, booklets, notebooks and report forms of the program; and (4) suggestions concerning the best methods of interacting with children and parents.

The Child Development Chart contains the taxonomy of over 1,800 behavioral objectives classified into skill areas and coded numerically across each skill area. Earlier we discussed the criteria for selection of these objectives and the organization of the objectives into a taxonomy.

The Learning Materials Handbook includes: (1) a picture of each learning material used in the Discovery Center; (2) a brief discussion of the way to use the material; and (3) a list of behavioral objectives that may be addressed using this particular material. This handbook is used extensively by the learning staff to help them understand the flexible uses of the learning materials, and to relate each material to the total objectives of the Discovery Program.

The Learning Group Notebook. Separate 16- to 32-page Learning Group Notebooks serve as guides for the learning staff in conducting specific sessions. Each notebook is a guide for the learning staff in conducting a specific Discovery Session. Each includes: (1) a table of contents; (2) answers to queries from the staff about policy procedures; (3) an outline of the planned activities, locations and materials for the entire session; (4) separate pages of step-by-step instructions for conducting each of the planned activities; (5) a set of behavioral objectives for each planned activity, with space for the Learning Aide to record observations of each child's achievements, and (6) a Session Research Form to be filled out by the Learning Advisor and sent to UEC headquarters at the conclusion of the session.

Use of these notebooks insures a measure of uniform quality control in the presentation of each session at all preschool sites.

The Parent Suggestion Notebook. A separate 24- to 36-page Parent Suggestion Notebook also is prepared and printed for each of the numbered sessions of the Discovery Program. Each notebook is a guide to parents and is given to a parent to take home at the end of a session. Each notebook contains: (1) a description of each of the planned activities presented in the session and an explanation of its importance in terms of its behavioral objectives; (2) answers to questions about child development that have been asked by the parents; (3) a list of suggested Home Discovery Activities that may be used with the child during the forthcoming week; (4) a weekly planning calendar on which the parent may schedule various suggested activities with the child throughout the week; (5) instructions for the use of workbook material which has been given to the child to reinforce skills or concepts presented during the Discovery Session; (6) step-by-step instructions for activities to be conducted with the child at a range of ability levels from early, to middle, to advanced, utilizing the educational materials or toys that have been given to the child at the end of the session; and (7) a Parent Observation Form for the parent to fill out and return to the Discovery Center, reporting on the week's activities at home.

Parent Report Letters are sent each month to parents with children enrolled in the Discovery Program. These letters detail each of the behavioral objectives achieved by the child during the month and provide suggestions as to ways the parent can help reinforce these skills and concepts. To handle the large volume of letters, a computerized information retrieval system was designed. Separate paragraphs were written for each of the behavioral objectives in the Child Development Chart, and these paragraphs have been stored in the computer. A letter is compiled by the computer when a child's account number and code numbers of the behavioral objectives the child has attained are given to the computer. The computer also stores the data on each individual child for use in research evaluation.

Retail Material Booklets have been prepared for each of the educational toys and games that are available for purchase by the parents at the Discovery Center. Each booklet contains a picture of the materials, a description, and a series of early, middle and advanced level activities to engage the child in achieving various behavioral objectives. The content of these booklets is similar to that of the Parent Suggestion Notebooks, and encourages parent-child interaction with the learning materials.

Learning Equipment and Materials. Most learning activities center around 600 different learning materials that have been evaluated and tested for use in the program. Each item of educational material has been selected for effective interaction with a young child, and much care was taken in choosing the objects and equipment. The furniture and room arrangement are designed to promote learning by taking into consideration the children's needs and the requirements of different activities. Each toy, book, slide projector,

microscope, television set, concept builder, or set of creative materials is carefully evaluated both for its role in learning and for its quality.

The following are examples of educational materials and equipment that have been developed and are used in the Discovery Centers: (1) a multimedia system which is housed in a single compact unit provides audio tapes, films and slides; (2) a Portable TV Studio on Wheels, complete with its own TV camera, TV tape recorder and viewing screen that can be used by the children themselves in producing cooperative TV shows; (3) a "Chatterbox" device that enables children to freely select printed cards showing letters, words and numbers which the machine reads aloud to them; (4) a learning device that enables a child to press buttons to respond to programmed slide/sound materials in learning the alphabet, beginning reading, beginning spelling and beginning arithmetic; (5) a closed-circuit TV system designed to provide the parents and Center Director with unlimited opportunities to make unobtrusive observations of the staff and children during a session; (6) a computer terminal is hooked up to a computer on a time-sharing arrangement to provide programs from simple letter matching and identification to reading and math programs; (7) educational TV tapes designed around the program's objectives that use puppets to introduce new concepts and processes in a dramatic manner to stimulate and motivate young children; and (8) slide/sound programs that assist children in understanding concepts of the world around them, such as the microscopic world that can be seen through magnifying glasses.

The Take-Home Materials in the Discovery Program are given to the child at the end of each Discovery Session to take home and keep. Each of these materials is accompanied by Suggestions to Parents and a Parent Observation form to be used in reporting back to the Center on the child's use of the material. The crux of the Discovery Program is the parent-child use of the Take-Home Materials.

Physical Environment of the
Discovery Center

The Discovery Center environment was carefully planned to implement the educational philosophy and behavioral objectives of the program. The learning materials are grouped in 16 activity centers of related material, including a reading corner, a listening post, a science library, a number corner, a store, an office and a music corner. Each center is colorfully decorated and is comfortably furnished and air-conditioned to provide year-round temperature control.

Modification of the Program
Through Feedback Information

To insure continual improvement of the Discovery Program based on its usage by staff, parents and children, several feedback loops were built into the program: (1) weekly reports by the Learning Director of each Discovery Center containing statistical data on child attendance as well as specific parent and staff comments about the successes and failures of specific activities, materials and equipment; (2) daily session reports filled out by a Learning Advisor each time a session is conducted, so that data are accumulated as to the success of each activity in each session in terms of length of time an activity held the interest of the children involved, and learning staff suggestions for the improvement of the activities in the specific session; (3) child profile forms sent into UEC Headquarters on each individual child, enumerating the skills and skill levels accomplished each month by each child; and (4) weekly reports by each parent detailing the accomplishments of the child in using Take-Home Learning materials and the parent's suggestions for improvements in the activities and the materials.

In the first 11 months of operation, more than 164,000 items of information were recorded and analyzed from these feedback loops. Information derived from this feedback system enabled the Educational Systems Division staff to produce, print and distribute the first revision of the program in March 1970, only six months after the first version of the program had begun to be used.

In sum, the interacting subsystems provide sensitive feedback, which results in a large data base that makes rapid and precise modifications of any facet of the curriculum possible and feasible. ☐

References

Ausubel, D.P. *Educational Psychology: A Cognitive View.* New York: Holt, Rinehart and Winston, Inc., 1968.

Bayley, N. Mental and Motor Development Scales. New York: Psychological Corp., 1969.

Beberman, M. *An Emerging Program of Secondary School Mathematics.* Cambridge, Massachusetts: Harvard University Press, 1958.

Chambers, D.W. Putting Down the Discovery Learning Hypothesis. *Educational Technology.* (In press.)

Gagne, R.M. & Brown, L.T. Some Factors in the Programming of Conceptual Material. *Journal of Experimental Psychology, 62,* 312-313, 1961.

Gordon, I.J. *Reaching the Child Through Parent Education.* Institute for Development of Human Resources, College of Education, University of Florida, 1970.

Hendrix, G. Learning by Discovery. *Mathematics Teacher, 54,* 290-299, 1961.

Levenstein, P. *Cognitive Growth in Preschoolers Through Verbal Interaction with Mothers.* Mimeo., 1969.

Nimnicht, G. *Toy Lending Library.* Far West Regional Educational Laboratory, 1969.

Parker, R.K., Ambron, S., Danielson, G.I., Halbrook, M.C. & Levine, J.A. *Overview of Cognitive and Language Programs for 3-, 4- and 5-year-old Children.* The City University of New York, 1970.

Weikart, D.P. *Comparative Study of Three Preschool Curricula.* Paper presented at the biennial meeting of the Society for Research in Child Development, 1969.

Whitney, D.C. & Parker, R.K. A Comprehensive Approach to Early Education: The Discovery Program. In Parker, R.K. (Ed.) *Conceptualizations of Preschool Curricula.* Boston: Allyn and Bacon, 1971 (in press).

Developing Instructional Modules for Individualized Learning

Joe Lars Klingstedt

An instructional module (IM) is a planned series of learning activities designed to help the learner accomplish certain specific objectives. Most IMs are designed so that the learner can work through most, if not all, of the learning activities on his own and at his own pace. Although minor differences in definition exist in the literature, one point is generally accepted by all of the authorities: *an IM individualizes instruction.*

The concept of individualizing instruction has gained widespread acceptance among professional educators. Many new techniques and devices have been developed which aid and promote this trend. Among these are microteaching, computer assisted instruction, single concept film loops, slide-tape presentations, programmed instruction, and many more. In addition to the traditional approach of using assigned reading materials, the IM provides alternate instructional routes which may include one or more of the above-mentioned techniques or devices.

As one tackles the job of developing IMs for use by learners, he should have a clear understanding of the underlying purpose. Put simply, the purpose of an IM is to individualize instruction so the learner will be able to:

1. Identify the objectives.
2. Progess at his own rate in his own learning style.
3. Identify his strengths and weaknesses.
4. Recycle when objectives have not been achieved.

Once the purpose has been internalized, it becomes clear that a procedure for achieving it is necessary. Although there are several possible approaches, the one which has proven most effective for the author involves six steps.

Step one. The first step in developing an IM is to state its objective or objectives. These are the behaviors toward which the learner works. An objective should be stated in specific terms so that the learner knows exactly what he is expected to be able to do upon completion of the IM. In addition to being stated in specific terms, the objective should describe the desired behavior, and it should be stated from the learner's—not the teacher's—point of view. Depending upon the type of objective, it might also include some special condition under which the behavior is to be demonstrated, for example, " . . . in five minutes with the use of the textbook."

To further illustrate, let us suppose that one wanted to write an IM which would help the learner understand the instructional module concept. The objectives might be as follows: upon completion of this IM, the learner will be able to (1) describe from memory, in writing, the purpose of an IM, and (2) list and describe from memory, in writing, the scope and sequence of the various parts of an IM. Both of these objectives are stated from the learner's point of view. They are both specific in that they state the learner is to be able to *describe* and *list* certain things. In addition, the desired behavior is specified ("in writing"), and a condition ("from memory") is included.

Joe Lars Klingstedt *is at the University of Texas at El Paso.*

There are many excellent sources to which the reader can turn for help when writing specific objectives. If there remains any doubt concerning ability to state objectives in specific terms, select and read one of the references included at the end of this article.

Step two. The second step in the preparation of an IM is to design and include a pretest. The function of the pretest is to determine "where the learner is." If the learner has already achieved the objectives of the IM, he may not need to proceed through the instructional activities, unless it is done for enrichment or reinforcement. Work for its own sake has no place in the IM concept. Both the learner and the instructor normally will be more successful if valuable time is not wasted covering material which has already been internalized. The pretest can be thought of as both descriptive and prescriptive. It is descriptive in the sense that it provides data which help the learner and the instructor determine the student's knowledge, attitudes and skills which relate to the instruction about to be undertaken. It is prescriptive in that, armed with the factual data, a more intelligent prescription can be made concerning future instruction. It can answer such questions as: Is the learner ready to proceed through the IM? Should the learner undertake certain remedial programs before continuing with the module? Is the learner able to skip the module entirely, based on demonstration of ability to perform the desired behaviors, and proceed to more advanced learning?

A pretest for the objectives stated in the previous example might consist of having the learner state, in writing, the purpose of an IM, and select, from a prepared list, the words which describe the parts of an IM. Furthermore, it could be stated that the learner is to indicate the order in which the parts should appear in an IM.

The pretest should be followed by a form which would allow the learner to evaluate the appropriateness of his responses.

Step three. After the objectives have been stated in specific terms, and the pretest has been designed, it is necessary to develop the rationale for the IM. This third step involves establishing the *value* of the module. The rationale indicates to the learner why it is desirable to achieve the stated objectives of the IM. The consequences both of achieving and not achieving the objectives should be pointed out explicitly. When the learner sees that the consequences of achieving the objectives are important, both now and in the future, he will, in all probability, value the objectives.

Assuming that the learner has read and understood the objectives and has taken the pretest and discovered that he does not possess the desired behaviors, what makes him want to continue through the IM? He may do it just because the instructor says that it is necessary, especially if he is concerned with his grade in the course, but we all realize that the transfer value of this kind of learning is very limited indeed. The learner must *value* what he is about to learn if it is to "stick." It is not good enough to be content in the assumption that he will see the value later. He will have forgotten what was included in the IM by that time.

Step four. Providing instructional alternatives is the fourth step in the process of developing an IM. These instructional alternatives form the heart of the IM.

Because the purpose of an IM is to individualize instruction so the learner will be able to identify the objectives, progress at his own rate in his own learning style, identify his strengths and weaknesses, and recycle when objectives have not been achieved, it is necessary to have instructional *options* in order for the learner to be able to select the most appropriate route to follow toward the accomplishment of the objectives of the IM. No one type of instruction is best suited to everyone, any more than one size shoe fits everyone. In order to provide for different learning styles, the designer of an IM might include such things as

readings, filmstrips, seminars, slide-tape presentations, computer assisted instruction or programmed instruction. Although most of the instructional alternatives will involve only the learner, some of them may include the instructor.

An example of an instructional alternative for the hypothetical IM which has been discussed might be to have the learner select and read certain articles from the literature on instructional module design. Another possibility would be to make available a slide-tape on the IM concept. Still another alternative would be to conduct a seminar-type discussion with the learner and other students who are working on the IM, concerning the purpose and the scope and sequence of an IM.

Step five. The fifth step is to design a posttest to measure the learner's achievement of the objectives of the IM. If the objectives have been stated properly, it is very easy to write the posttest. The posttest may be similar, even identical, to the portion of the pretest which measures the desired performance ability.

Because the learner takes the posttest any time he feels ready, the instructor may desire to develop parallel forms of the posttest in order to validate competencies. When the learner does not reach an acceptable level of competency on the posttest, he should be instructed to recycle himself and select another instructional alternative.

By way of illustration, a posttest for our mythical IM might be to have the learner describe, in 80 words or less (in writing), the purpose of an IM; list, in the proper sequential order, the various parts of an IM; and describe, from memory, in writing, each of the parts of an IM.

As was the case with the pretest, the posttest should be followed by a form which would allow the learner to evaluate the appropriateness of his responses.

Step six. The final step in developing an IM is to include a resources section. This section should include references to all of the materials and equipment necessary to complete the IM. Such things as readings, special equipment, films, filmstrips, flow charts and slide-tapes should be listed in this section of the IM.

Summary

There are numerous ways in which an IM can be utilized. A whole course of instruction can be completed through the use of IMs, or they can be used to enrich an already existing course. Each IM is a small curriculum package which has been designed with the individual needs of students in mind. The instructional module concept is a promising alternative to the traditional "textbook" approach to instruction. □

References

Armstrong, Robert J. *et al. The Development and Evaluation of Behavioral Objectives.* Belmont, California: Wadsworth Publishing Company, Inc., 1970.

Gronlund, Norman E. *Stating Behavioral Objectives for Classroom Instruction.* London: Collier-Macmillan, Limited, 1970.

Kapfer, Philip G. & Ovard, Glen F. *Preparing and Using Individualized Learning Packages for Ungraded, Continuous Progress Education.* Englewood Cliffs, New Jersey: Educational Technology Publications, 1971.

Mager, Robert F. *Analyzing Performance Objectives or "You Really Oughta Wanna."* Belmont, California: Fearon Publishers, 1970.

.... *Developing Attitude Toward Learning.* Palo Alto, California: Fearon Publishers, 1968.

.... *Preparing Instructional Objectives.* Palo Alto, California: Fearon Publishers, 1962.

A Cybernetic Modification Scheme for an Instructional System

Mical C. Clark and
M. David Merrill

In his paper, "How Can Instruction Be Adapted to Individual Differences?," Cronbach (1967) suggested at least five procedures that are or can be used to individualize instruction. The first is to eliminate from further schooling those students who seem not to profit from the experience. Second, one should assume that certain learnings were necessary for every student and have students continue to study a given topic until mastery. The third is to modify the goals of instruction to match the needs of the individual so that different individuals learn different things. Fourth, remedial loops should be appended to a fixed instructional program so that a student unable to grasp a particular skill from the main track is branched into a remedial sequence and then back into the main track. The fifth is to teach different pupils by different methods with the intent of reaching a common goal. In some form all of these procedures are used in our present school system in an attempt to meet the needs of individual learners.

Cronbach indicated that psychologically the most interesting technique is the fifth, teaching different students by different methods. This procedure poses some difficult questions: How does one decide which student should receive which method? How does one alter methods to meet the needs of individual students? What dimensions can be maniuplated to alter instructional method? Which of these dimensions make a difference and which have little or no effect on instructional efficiency or effectiveness? This article proposes a cybernetic (self-correcting or self-changing) procedure for manipulating instructional displays, so that after a period of time the instructional procedure used is optimum for a given individual. The procedure described fits Cronbach's fifth category in that a fixed goal is assumed and an instructional method is adjusted so that each student can attain the goal as efficiently and effectively as possible.

In his article, "Components of a Cybernetic Instructional System," Merrill (1968) identifies three processing components. The selector consists of those rules for a particular kind of behavior (see Merrill, 1971) which state (1) the type of stimulus display needed, (2) the psychological conditions necessary to establish the behavior, and (3) the most appropriate media to use to present the display to the student. The *Comparator*

consists of those rules for a particular kind of behavior which state (1) the type of stimulus display needed, (2) the psychological conditions necessary to adequately observe the behavior, and (3) the criterion of acceptable performance. The *Program Modifier* consists of those rules for a particular kind of behavior which indicate ways that the stimulus display can be modified under a situation where the student is unable to acquire the desired behavior from the initially selected displays. This suggests a procedure for implementing the third component.

This instructional model makes a number of assumptions. First, the psychological conditions necessary to establish or observe a particular kind of behavior do not vary with individuals. That is, a condition necessary for one individual is necessary for all individuals. A corollary of this assumption is that if a condition appropriate for a given kind of behavior is not present during the display, the behavior acquired or observed will be different from that which was intended. Second, a given condition may be implemented with a number of different specific stimulus displays and these displays may differ on a number of dimensions. Individual students will respond differentially to different values on these stimulus dimensions.

Based on the above assumptions, the following postulates seem warranted: If a modification procedure consists of changing the psychological conditions under which a particular kind of behavior is promoted or observed, then the individualization which is taking place consists of a variation of the third type identified by Cronbach; that is, the goals are being modified rather than the instructional method. Program modification in which the instructional method is changed (Cronbach's type 5 individualization) consists of maintaining the appropriate psychological conditions but modifying the dimensions of the stimulus display which do not change these basic conditions.

A given condition can be defined by a set of parameters[1] whose values[2] can vary, thus specifying specific instances of the condition. A given stimulus display can be defined by two sets of parameters: one set are those parameters which define the necessary psychological conditions for the type of behavior being taught; and the other set are those parameters which are content-specific, which define aspects of the stimulus display that are unique to the subject matter or particular display but which are not part of the necessary psychological conditions. Setting values for each of the parameters in these two sets defines a particular stimulus display.

Individualization by modification of instructional procedure (Cronbach's type 5) is accomplished by changing the parameter values of those parameters that define a given psychological condition or by changing the values and/or the parameters which define the content-specific conditions of a particular display.

Mical C. Clark is with the Department of Education, Arizona State University, Tempe. M. David Merrill is director of instructional research, Brigham Young University, Provo, Utah.

---

1. Parameter is defined as a characteristic element or constant factor which helps define a particular psychological condition.

2. Values do not refer, in this context, to philosophy but to quantities, amounts, categories or some other position on some type of metric scale.

Parameters for Classification Behavior:
An Example

The application of the notion of parameter value modification to a particular kind of behavior for a concrete example may help clarify the above.

Merrill (1971) defined classification behavior as follows:

> ... when a student is able to correctly identify the class membership of a previously unencountered object or event or a previously unencountered representation of some object or event.

The behavior specified is the student's ability to indicate class membership. This can be accomplished in a number of ways; e.g., distinguishing a member from a nonmember, checking yes or no for a list of instances, sorting instances into piles representing different categories, matching category name with the instance, etc. Recognizing or reciting the definition or list of attributes for the class is *not* the appropriate behavior.

This definition suggests that a necessary condition to observe an instance of classification behavior is that unencountered instances and non-instances of one or more concept classes must be presented to the student for identification. This condition is defined by the following parameters.

Parameter 1: Ratio of Instances to Non-Instances

Some students may perform better when asked to pick out the single instance from a set containing several non-instances, while another student might perform better if asked to pick out the non-instance from a set containing several instances.

Parameter 2: Number of Simultaneous Classes

Classification behavior can deal with a single class having the student indicate members and all others as nonmembers or it can deal with several classes at the same time, having the student label each instance as a member of A, B, C or none. Students differ in the number of simultaneous classes they can handle at one time.

Parameter 3: Representation of Referent

Classification behavior is involved, whether the student is asked to categorize actual events/objects or representations of events/objects. A scale from the referent (actual event/object) to simulation/model to picture (motion/still) to verbal description can be used to represent a given referent. Some students may do better with more literal representation, while others respond best to abstract representation.

Parameter 4: Type of Question Asked

Identification can be accomplished by using several types of questions (as indicated above). Some students probably respond better to one type, while others prefer another.

Parameter 5: Discrimination Required

Instances of a given class can be very clear in that

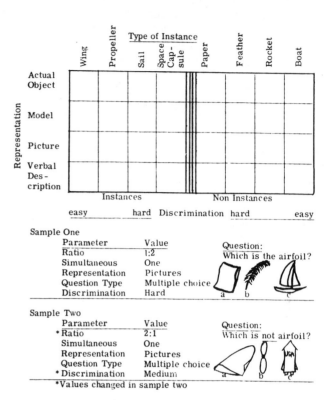

Figure 1

Concept Airfoil Potential Parameter Values

identification of relevant attributes is relatively easy, while other instances may be much more difficult in that their attributes closely resemble members of other classes. Students differ in their ability to make fine discriminations of this type.

The above parameters do not necessarily represent a comprehensive list, but they do enable us to specify the characteristics of a given display designed to assess classification behavior. Note that the conditions and parameters specified do not deal with promoting acquisition of classification behavior, but rather with observation of the behavior. A similar set of conditions and parameters could be identified for behavioral acquisition.

For illustrative purposes, assume the concept to be taught is "Airfoil." The behavioral objective might be stated as follows: Presented objects which are airfoils and those often confused as airfoils, the student will be able to correctly indicate examples of airfoils. The statement of the objective has arbitrarily set the value of Parameter 2, the number of simultaneous classes, to a single class. Possible values for the remaining parameters are illustrated in Figure 1. In Sample One a value is indicated for each parameter and the resulting display for the student is shown. Sample Two illustrates the change in the question when two parameter values are changed.

Technical Modification Model

The proposed modification scheme allows the parameter values to be set differently for each individual in accordance with his own aptitudes. It also allows the parameter values to change as the individual's aptitudes (interests, acquired knowledge, etc.) change. Hence, the modification scheme provides a dynamic process for utilizing aptitude information.

The system requires that parameter values all be scaled from 0 to 1.0. Discrete variables fall into the same range. In other words, parameter values can be designated in any way (randomly or at group means, etc.). For example, a parameter consisting of four categories might be mapped into a scale where category A was 0 - .25; B was .26 - .50, etc.

Once the system begins to operate, parameter values for a given individual are always changing. After every learner response, parameter values are reset. The operators used to change parameter values are given in Table 1. Operator A will result in the parameter value to be increased. Operator B will decrease the parameter value. After every response, one of the operators will be applied.

The selection of the operator to be applied is made independently for each parameter. The selection is according to a "win-stay; lose-shift" strategy. Either operator may be applied after the first learner response. From then on, the selection of the operator is determined by the operator used previously *and* by the correctness of the previous response. After a correct response, the same operator is to be used as was used on the previous trial (win-stay). After an incorrect response, the operator that was not used on the previous trial is to be used (lose-shift).

This model provides a method to maximize correct responding by the learner. It monitors performance, and its dynamic property makes it always try to do better. A change in parameter values results in changes in the content, organization and sequencing of instructional displays. This model changes parameter values so that the values tend to oscillate around an "ideal value" for the individual where correct responding is maximized. The band of oscillation is made narrower by decreasing the value of θ in the operators as a function of number of trials (as n gets larger, θ gets smaller).

If all of the parameter values were to be modified simultaneously, the changes could all be confounded and a few very salient parameters could mask inhibitory changes in other parameters. Thus, parameters must be modified at least somewhat independently of one another. Modifying one at a time provides independence, but optimization of instructional presentation would be incredibly slow. Thus, a sampling scheme must be used to allow a subset of parameters to be manipulated simultaneously, but to constantly change the members in the subset so that confounding of changes is effectively eliminated.

The instructional paradigm for each kind of behavior (Merrill, 1971) has many parameters associated with it. The sampling scheme then calls for a few (say three) of these parameters to be sampled whenever an objective requiring that paradigm is being taught. The values of those three parameters are then modified in accordance with the above rules. If the learner response is correct, those modified three values are returned to the system, and another three parameters are selected for modification. If the learner response is incorrect, the same three parameters are remodified in accordance with the above rules. At all times sampling is done with replacement and with a consideration of the saliency (or relative importance) of each parameter. An estimate of the saliency value for each parameter can be derived either logically or empirically.

The instructional system requires that:

1. All parameters must always have a value.
2. A given parameter can have different values as it is associated with paradigms for different kinds of behavior.
3. Some parameter specifications necessitate nesting (it is meaningless to set voice volume if there is no oral component to the display), and hence some parameters are eliminated from consideration at certain times.

The steps that the modification scheme goes through are presented in Table 2. It is hoped that these steps listed in the order of operation will help the reader to conceptualize the somewhat complex, but intuitive, model presented here.

Quantitatively, this modification scheme is designed to: (1) handle the potentially large number of parameters that it must; (2) make observable changes as opposed to miniscule changes by changing one parameter at a time; (3) optimize instruction*; (4) attenuate the abruptness of changes as the system and the learner accommodate to each other; (5) adapt to changes (learning or maturation) in the learner over time. This last property can be augmented by systematically letting θ become larger, then reduce again by resetting saliency values over time.

Needed Research

Before this modification scheme can be incorporated into an instructional system and implemented for use, certain basic questions must be pursued. First, the relevant parameters must be identified and scaled. This problem is not insurmountable because only manageable parameters need to be used. Additional parameters can

Table 1

Operators for Changing Parameter Values

P = Value of a parameter of an instructional paradigm.
Pi,n = Value of parameter "i" before learner response number "n."

Operator:
A $P_{i,n+1} = (1 - \theta) P_{i,n} + \theta$
B $P_{i,n+1} = (1 - \theta) P_{i,n}$

---

*The operators function so as to maximize improvements while minimizing setbacks.

Table 2

Outline of Operation of Modification Scheme

1. The system provides a set of parameters whose values differ among individuals.
2. The instructional paradigm for each kind of instructional outcome has a subset of parameters associated with it.
3. Take the subset for the paradigm associated with the objective to be taught.
4. Establish which parameters are irrelevant to determining the display because of being nested below a parameter which has a present value that makes them superfluous.
5. Exclude the currently irrelevant parameters from the subset and draw a set of n (where "n" is small, say 3-5) parameters. Selection should consider the relative saliency of each parameter within the large subset.
6. Operate* on each parameter in the set of five.
7. Present the learning trial.
8. Look at response correctness.
   a. If correct, return the five parameter values and select a new set of five.
   b. If incorrect, reoperate on each parameter (change direction) value in the set of n and go to next trial.

Since the set of "n" is only returned after a correct response, the operator will be selected so as to move the value in the same direction as on the trial when that value was last manipulated.

be added to the system as we discover them and learn how to work with them.

Experiments must be run to validate the modification scheme. Computer-generated data could help demonstrate that this scheme leads to optimization of performance. However, subjects must also be taught in such a system. Different students should end up with different p values. If John is given Sally's p values, he should perform less well than with his own. If John is given Sally's p values, the values should change to resemble John's original set after some time on the system. These inferences suggest several experiments which are to be carried out.

Evaluation of the entire cybernetic instructional system is being considered. This evaluation will probably result in changes being made in the system, rather than in an over-all approval or disapproval of the system. Such data collection is currently only in the planning stages. Some of it must be gathered before any comments about the effectiveness of this modification scheme and of this approach to designing instructional situations can properly be made. □

References

Cronbach, L.J. How Can Instruction Be Adapted to Individual Differences? In R.M. Gagne (Ed.) *Learning and Individual Differences.* Columbus, Ohio: Merrill, 1967.

Merrill, M.D. Components of a Cybernetic Instructional System. *Educational Technology,* April 15, 1968, pp. 5-10.

Merrill, M.D. Necessary Psychological Conditions for Defining Instructional Outcome. *Educational Technology,* August, 1971.

The Human as an Information Processor: A Guide for Instructional Design

J.D. Raulerson, Jr.

Anyone confronted with the design of effective and efficient conditions for human learning finds himself in need of some theoretical framework to use as a guide. In many ways a poor but comprehensive theory is a better working tool than no theory at all. Psychological learning theories do not meet the need because they are fragmentary. Each explains only a segment of the human learning capability. A composite of these theories becomes incomprehensible to most instructors because it crosses the semantic boundaries of several schools of psychology. Even if understood, the composite is of limited value in specifying the concrete conditions required to accomplish the more complex forms of human learning.

Until the development of the modern electronic computer, man had no adequate model which would enable him to visualize the complexity of the human as a processor of information. Today many people are familiar with the concepts and terms of information processing. With the growth of educational technology, even more will be prepared to think in these terms. At the same time, developments have occurred in a number of different fields of science which make it possible to understand enough of how the human mind works to devise an information flow chart of its gross operation. This model is sufficiently detailed to be useful in deriving methods of instruction more compatible with the input characteristics of the human. In effect, an understanding of the human as an information processor can now be structured into a theory which is useful as a tool in the design of instruction. In addition, it can be an impetus for future research to refine and develop the model into a reliable predictive device. This advance will allow the designer of instruction to specify conditions and procedures which will accomplish desired educational objectives with a high probability that they will be effective and efficient.

The Human as an Information Processor

Using Figure 1 we can follow the flow of information as it is processed by the human brain. In order to simplify the explanation we will consider only the visual mode. Of course, parallel processes occur in other modes, such as audition. At the same time, interaction takes place between modes.

J.D. Raulerson, Jr. is a professional engineer and a graduate student in education at the University of South Florida.

Figure 1

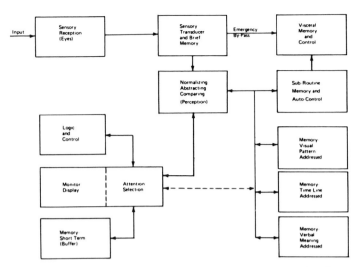

Starting with an input of information in the form of patterns of radiant energy focused on the retina of the eye, we find this energy converted to a pulse-frequency modulated code for transmission to the visual areas in the back of the cortex. At the same time, diffuse signals are sent to other areas to alert and prepare the brain for activity. Processing of the raw data begins in the visual cortex. First, a stable simplified pattern is extracted from the information. This pattern is then compared with previously stored memory patterns to interpret or "make sense" of the situation. This extraction of meaning is a highly dynamic process and is commonly called perception. We are only beginning to understand the nature of perception. We do know that it involves the immediately prior sensations and the expectations derived from the trend of events. In addition, it is influenced by the past history of the organism, along with its needs, desires and "set." From this superficial description it is obvious that seeing itself is a learned process and is in fact also a learning process. As new information flows in, it can become a part of the memory store and influence future interpretation of sensory data. Already it is obvious that the human organism is not an inert device but a highly dynamic, open system in constant intercourse with its environment. In fact, experiments with sensory deprivation show that the mind must have information to process or it becomes confused.

Normally, perception is not in awareness. However, if an exceptional situation arises and information cannot be made to relate to previous patterns, an emergency sequence is activated. The central processor is alerted and its monitor display is switched to the unusual pattern for interpretation and decision as to appropriate action. The processor is commonly known as the conscious mind, the center of awareness. The central processor can only attend to one function at a time. Attention can be switched to various modes for observation, processing or memory search activity. The monitor display within the processor can be used to view incoming visual sensory information on a direct line. In this function it is capable of an extremely high

definition color display. Only a small fraction of information in the visual display can be processed or stored.

The short term memory has a very limited capacity of about seven "words" or "chunks" of information and has destructive read-in. This means that old information is erased as new information comes in. The monitor, short term memory and logic circuits are closely connected within the central processor, and information can be processed within this group as a unit. Attention seems to be a must for transfer of information from the short term memory to long term memory. Unless information comes into attention, it is rapidly erased. There is an important exception to this effect in the case of visceral memory, but this will not be considered since it has no application in normal classroom learning.

All information that is attended is deposited in some form of long term memory. The fact that it has been stored does not mean that all of this information is available for retrieval. The key to retrieval is the way the information was organized when it was filed. If not organized so as to be associated with the address which will be formed from information available at the time it is required, then the information may be unavailable. The human long term memory has an almost unlimited capacity. Addressing a memory of this magnitude is an extremely demanding task. We are attempting to select a particular unit of information from millions of others. The search pattern must have reasonably close correspondence to the memory pattern to make the probability of success assume any reasonable value.

Moving on for a more detailed look at the long term memories, we find that the greatest barrier to our understanding of their operation is that the method of addressing is unfamiliar. The long term memory is directly content-addressed instead of the usual computer cell or location address. The basic memory units probably correspond to the short term memory capacity. There is also some evidence that no information in long term memory is destroyed. It can be lost in the sense that we are unable to retrieve it, but under special conditions it may still be available.

Several different long term memories have been identified and physically located in the brain. The most convenient classification of these memories is the means of addressing. As shown in Figure 1, one of these memories is time addressed. It is a chronological record of all that a person attends—a kind of log or diary that can be addressed in relative time. Much of this information seems lost, but under certain conditions very vivid replay can be instigated.

Another memory is addressed by a visual pattern—not a detailed photograph but a highly simplified representation of what was perceived and perhaps modified by subsequent experience, used in visual perception. As a pattern is retrieved, it can be "filled out" in a process called recall. The reconstruction is a more complete picture, which may become detailed. This process is almost a reverse of perception, where a complex stimulus is reduced to a simple pattern.

A third memory is verbal; not in the sense of the motor control for speech but for memory of the symbol or word itself. This is the only memory we have mentioned that is not duplicated in the hemispheres of the brain. We can speculate that this is an indication that speech is a relatively recent addition. The verbal memory is addressed by "meaning" which may be the same or in addition to the patterns in visual pattern memory. Probably both of these memories are actively involved in verbal communication. This brings us to the fact that although we have separated the elements for explanation, a great amount of dynamic interaction occurs.

One other activity that involves memory should be mentioned. In order to be able to do more than one thing at a time, the human can establish sub-routines which can function outside of awareness. We have already encountered this in perception. Verbal memory may be a complex sub-routine occupying a specific block or blocks of memory closely associated with audition, vision and speech motor activity. Driving an automobile is a common example of a complex process that has become so automatic that we can converse with another person while we drive. As in perception, if some unusual pattern occurs, the sub-routine demands attention on a priority basis and we stop talking to attend to the novel situation. Memory search sub-routines can also be set up. The incubation period in creative problem solving may be closely related to this activity.

As an aid to understanding, we have been looking at the similarities between human and computer information processing. However, in several important ways they are different.

The human mind is not a fast or accurate arithmetic calculator. It has a cycle time of about 100 milliseconds, which by electronic computer standards is elephantine. The human mind has the advantage of extreme flexibility and the ability to handle a problem in a dynamic approach which makes use of information and cues found in widely diverse areas.

The human is a self-programming device capable of setting up pervasive plans to accomplish long-term objectives. These plans are flexible and can be quickly modified to accomplish the objective in spite of changed conditions or unexpected effects. Much of this ability is derived from the ambulatory and manipulative capabilities and specialized sensory mechanisms capable of giving immediate, highly detailed feedback.

We have already seen that human memory is content-addressed. Content addressing with internal search pattern generation is a highly effective method for expediting the recall of random data, and contributes to the high degree of versatility and flexibility of the human organism.

These differences between man and an electronic computer may seem relatively unimportant, but this is misleading. The principal differences between a simple electronic desk calculator and a large computer are the internally stored program and the size and access time of the memory. Self-programming, immediate feedback and direct content addressing are differences of the same or greater magnitude. The interaction of these elements can produce changes all out of proportion to those predicted from summing the results of the

individual elements. Man becomes in fact a highly complex, effective, goal seeking organism, aware of time and self.

The Implications of the Theory for Human Learning

The next consideration is: What are the implications for human learning and instructional design? What information valuable to an understanding of learning can be derived from viewing the human as an information processor? The following is a list of some of these implications:

1. Attention is necessary for learning to occur. The learning path is reception, perception, short term memory, attention and long term memory.

2. The mind must have an input of information to process or it will seek other information to process, lose alertness or, if deprived long enough, become confused.

3. Visual stimuli may be monitored with a very high information content. The brain can process and retain in memory only units of limited content.

4. The short term memory capacity is about seven items of information. These items can be in the form of numbers, words or a simple pattern.

5. The most basic long term memory is the visual pattern. This pattern probably has the same information content as the short term memory capacity, about seven items. More complex patterns can be stored by organizing the information within the framework of another simple pattern.

6. Addressing of verbal memory and pattern memory is not organized identically. The conditions for learning verbal material will be different from those for learning patterns.

7. To be useful, items in memory must be retrieved. The only way this can be accomplished is by developing an address from the situation at the time of need. The address at time of learning must correspond to the address that can be developed from information available at time of need or retrieval cannot occur.

8. Memory search patterns are generated in the central processor. These patterns may be related to present or recent stimuli or may be constructed from need specifications through use of the logic capability of the processor.

The Theory and Instructional Design

A considerable amount of information useful for instructional design can be derived from these implications.

Attention is imperative for learning to occur. Attention is easy to get. The unusual, the new, the novel and the incongruent always demand attention. Maintaining attention is much more difficult. Since we see how easily attention can be lost or diverted, enough redundancy must be provided to compensate for lack of attention even in those highly motivated to learn.

The level of information input has an optimum value which will maintain a reasonable level of alertness and sustain attention. If this information flow is not adequate, attention to the material to be learned will be lost and processing of other internal material may begin, or attention may be diverted to other stimuli in the visual field. If the level of input is too great, time will not be available for proper internal processing and confusion will result.

The initial input stimuli should present the desired information in a form which can be perceived in a meaningful way within a pattern having no more than five items of information. At first this simple pattern should be presented in a form which can be easily separated from the background. In general, the stimulus should move from the simple toward the complex and from the concrete toward the abstract.

If complex material is to be taught, it must be organized into related chunks, each of which has no more than the seven items. Five is a good working number. The overall pattern relating the chunks has to be a simple pattern, also conforming to the capacity of the short term memory. As a result, our knowledge will assume a tree-like structure, with about five units at each level. Three levels will allow 25 units to be related. In order for material to be associated in learning, the prerequisite material must be readily available to short term memory. This availability can be assured by review in retrieval immediately prior to making the new association. A number of pattern schemes can be devised; concepts, spatial division, mnemonics and others. Another means of relating the chunks is chaining. Chaining can utilize some association already known or easily related. Also, the central processor can address the next unit by logical chaining. Logical chaining is particularly valuable with relational concepts and principles which have an inherent if-then quality that lends itself to logical association.

Proper organization of the material for retrieval must be accomplished at the time of learning. It is important that the overall pattern of relationships be presented first so that, as learning of the chunks occurs, they are being associated correctly within the relationship. This structure must reflect the fact that at the time of retrieval a search pattern can only be derived from sensory information available at that time. This generated search pattern must resemble the address pattern at the time of learning if the learned material is to be useful. The human is ingenious in deriving and searching, but there is no magic in the process.

Since retention in short term memory is so limited, evaluation only a few minutes after the initial instruction gives a good indication of how much has been transferred to long term memory in a form that can be addressed. At the same time, retrieval of the information by the learner is a most effective means of extending association learning. The proper procedure is not review where the original stimulus is presented again, but *rehearsal in retrieval.*

Variety has a number of potential benefits that indicate its use. In the normal functioning of the mind, attention is directed to the exceptions imbedded with the expected flow of information. This function causes attention to be diverted from the learning process as other stimuli intrude. This same effect can be used to maintain and redirect attention to the material to be learned. Variety acts to interrupt the flow of information and to change its form. Through its use, attention is directed toward the altered learning stimulus.

Since the learning stimulus never receives 100 percent attention, even among highly motivated students who want to learn, redundancy must be provided. Variety can provide redundancy without loss of attention. Even those who attended the original material can benefit from a second presentation if it is in a different form. The new stimuli can help the learner form additional associations. Also, learners have different abilities and preferences in stimuli. The new mode may fit a learner's "style" better, so learning may occur where it did not with the original material.

While it cannot be derived from the visual model, it is logical that multi-sensory stimuli will build more associations and may be more easily retrieved than single-sensory materials.

Pattern memory is more basic than verbal memory. It may be more easily learned, and more easily associated with other patterns. This should make pattern memory more easily addressed. The memory for a word seems to be more "either-or" with fewer avenues of addressing through association. As we find how to use pattern memory more extensively, the efficiency of learning may increase dramatically.

Each of the long term memories requires different conditions for learning and addressing. This provides a useful basis for classifying learning. The concept can also provide direction for applied research in creating the most effective means and conditions for learning within these classes.

Short term memory is so brief and the structuring of the material for insertion into long term memory so critical, that the length of the usual classroom teaching cycle should be questioned. Fifty minutes of presentation today, homework tonight or tomorrow, and testing next week is probably much too extended in time for efficient learning. A much shorter cycle can be arranged: A well-organized, quick review of prerequisites, and a rapid presentation of the learning stimulus, immediately followed by a period designed to actively engage the learner with the material, and concluded with evaluation and feedback. Instructional designs by the author allocate about five minutes for this cycle. There is no evidence to indicate that this is the optimum cycle time, but it is probably a good deal closer than one measured in days. These cycles can be repeated as necessary to accomplish the level of learning required. Repeating is not repetition—but includes new examples presented with enough variety to maintain attention.

Summary

Educational technologists need a concise, logical and theoretical framework which can be used as a guide to the design of instruction and developmental experiments. Our knowledge of the human mind is now sufficient to develop a workable theory based on the human as an information processor.

Instruction designed in accordance with information theory results in conditions for learning different from general practice. These differences are the result of increased emphasis on a number of points.

1. The necessity for attention if learning is to occur.

2. The efficiency of pattern memory.
3. The limited information capacity of short term memory.
4. The importance of availability of prerequisite information from long term memory.
5. The crucial part played by need-generated addresses in useful retrieval of learned information.

An information processing theory can enable the educational technologist to predict the conditions which will result in effective and efficient learning. The theory is, of course, too pragmatic to satisfy the psychologist-scientist, and too mechanical to satisfy the teacher-artist. For the educational technologist, caught in between, it has the potential of becoming a powerful tool for the improvement of education ☐

References

Atkinson, R.C. & Shiffrin, R.M. Human Memory, A Proposed System. In K.W. & J.T. Spence (Eds.) *The Psychology of Learning and Motivation. Vol. 2*, New York: Academic Press, 1968.

Bruner, Jerome S. *Toward a Theory of Instruction.* Cambridge, Mass.: Harvard Univ. Press, 1966.

DeCecco, John P. *The Psychology of Learning and Instruction.* Englewood Cliffs, N.J.: Prentice-Hall, Inc., 1968.

Gagne, Robert M. *The Conditions of Learning.* New York: Holt, Rinehart and Winston, 1970 (2nd edition).

Haber, Ralph Norman. How We Remember What We See. *Scientific American, 222* (5), May, 1970.

Hunt, Earl B. *Concept Learning: An Information Processing Problem.* New York: John Wiley & Sons, Inc., 1962.

Norman, Donald A., *Memory and Attention.* New York: John Wiley & Sons, Inc., 1969.

Penfield, W. & Roberts, L. *Speech and Brain Mechanisms.* Princeton: Princeton Univ. Press, 1959.

Woodson, W. & Conover, D. *Human Engineering Guide for Equipment Designers.* Berkeley: University of California Press, 1964.

Knowledge of Results and Other Possible Reinforcers in Self-Instructional Systems

George L. Geis and Reuben Chapman

An important contribution to the technology of education has been reinforcement theory, or popularly, "Skinnerian Psychology." Therefore, discovering, making explicit and developing reinforcers in learning situations might well be a major area of concern to the technologist.

Though this article concentrates, in a sense, on the search for reinforcers, it is recognized that unsystematic contingency setting can, even with the most powerful reinforcers in hand, result in poor learning. B.F. Skinner (1968) points out that "... it is not the reinforcers which count, so much as their relation to behavior. In improving teaching it is less important to find new reinforcers than to design better contingencies using those already available." Nevertheless, the explication of available reinforcers seems a necessary step in developing more effective contingency management in learning.

Special attention should be paid to reinforcement by those engaged in examining and designing self-instructional systems. Traditional reinforcers in education are often intimately tied up with the teacher/classroom system. The teacher is more than an exposer of material; sometimes he mediates reinforcers (e.g., reports activities to the principal, seats groups of students in certain places). At other times he directly administers the reinforcers (e.g., praises one student and applies the ruler to the hand of another). The designer who eliminates the teacher from his system is removing a reinforcing agent who has at least the potential for setting up subtle contingencies and for varying reinforcers with the moment and the student.

This article briefly discusses some potential reinforcers for self-instructional systems and then provides a detailed review of the literature relevant to one of them: knowledge of results.

Some Possible Reinforcers

Glaser (1965, p. 797) suggests an empirical approach for determining reinforcers: "Reinforcing events must be determined on the basis of detailed analysis of appropriate subject matter and component repertoire relationships." He proposes some "illustrative leads,"

George L. Geis is associate professor of psychology, McGill University, Montreal, Quebec, Canada. **Reuben Chapman** is research consultant, Ann Arbor Public Schools, Ann Arbor, Michigan. Preparation of this article was supported in part by the Center for Research on Language and Language Behavior under U.S.O.E. Contract No. OEC-0-9-097740-3743(014).

starting with an application of the *Premack principle* (Premack, 1959) which suggests that high probability behaviors can be used to reinforce behaviors which have a lower probability of occurrence. As one example, Glaser cites a learning situation in which "backward chaining" would allow the student to be reinforced with the high probability, i.e., first and better learned, behavior when he emits a previous step in the chain. Thus teaching the student Step C allows Step C to be a reinforcing event for emissions of Step B when it is being learned. A variety of other educational applications of the Premack principle have been demonstrated (see, for example, Osborne, 1969).

Manipulation or demonstrations of *mastery* or *competence* have often been cited as reinforcers or, in other terminology, as strong motives (see, for example, White, 1959). And Glaser suggests "overt control over the environment" as a second possible reinforcing event. Skinner (1968, p. 20) has suggested that a similar class of consequences be considered reinforcing: "Children play for hours with mechanical toys, paints, scissors and paper, noise-makers, puzzles—in short, with almost anything which feeds back significant changes in the environment and is reasonably free of aversive properties. The sheer control of nature is itself reinforcing."

Many self-sustaining tasks, such as science learning kits or educational construction toys, seem to have this feature. Self-instructional materials might provide the chance to manipulate materials either *during* learning or as a consequence of successfully completing a learning assignment. Moore & Anderson (1969), Gotkin (1966) and others have leaned heavily upon the reinforcing effect of manipulation to sustain the learner's behavior in their "responsive environments."

Discovery, curiosity and *exploration*, which have often been pointed to as reinforcers or motives, seem to be similar to the events just discussed. For instance, one of the supposed benefits of the "discovery learning method" is the sustained interest and motivation generated by the activity of discovering. (In all cases being cited here, specific and detailed evidence is lacking to support the contention that a certain class of events *is* reinforcing. No attempt is being made here to validate claims; this is merely a catalogue of proposed and potential reinforcers for self-instructional systems.)

Self-instruction may be narrowly interpreted to mean "teacherless." In that case, *social reinforcers* other than those mediated by a teacher might be considered. For example, the Human Development Institute (1966) has produced dyadic programs (involving two learners). A self-instruction problem-solving course for teachers (Geis *et al.*, 1969) includes exercises which utilize two teachers interviewing each other, guided by checklists in the text. The "probes" which are an important part of a recent textbook (Ferster & Perrott, 1968) require two students to cooperate on the exercises. In such cases as these it is certainly possible that the generalized reinforcers provided by another person may sustain student participation in the learning tasks. Furthermore, specific reinforcers supplied by the partner (e.g., "Now you're doing it correctly") may more precisely control learning.[1]

Extrinsic reinforcers ranging from the omnipotent "M & M" candy to points, tokens and toys have been used as reinforcers in many behavior modification studies and recently have been used in connection with self-instructional materials (see, for example, Berman, 1967; Smith *et al.*, 1969; or Sullivan *et al.*, 1967). Systems for reinforcer delivery, more elaborate than those generally present in a text or kit, are usually required when such reinforcers are used. Either a human banker or some thief-proof equipment may be called for.

Progress itself has been proposed as reinforcing; evidence of moving toward a goal may be sufficient to sustain the learner. Progress is defined a bit more specifically by Taber *et al.* (1965, p. 10). "Knowledge alone of the fact that he is performing correctly may be a less effective reinforcer for the student than being permitted to engage in further and more complex activity . . . Being able to move on, to get into and discover the fine details of the subject matter without being incorrect, frustrated or punished for being wrong may be the most potent reinforcing consequence in a programmed instructional sequence." Record keeping and progress plotting is common among behavior modifiers and has been incorporated into a number of self-instructional systems.

Aversive stimulation has not been extensively explored either in the basic research literature of psychology nor in the technology of education. Yet the continuing evidence of everyday living suggests it is a frequent and powerful controller of human behavior. Some branching programs incorporate verbal punishers in the text. Students who choose incorrectly on a multiple choice frame may be directed to a page which contains a verbal rebuke. It has been pointed out elsewhere that " . . . finding a short cut or an easier way to emit a certain response is also reinforcing for most learners" (Taber *et al.*, 1965, p. 27). Some experimental evidence supporting this modern restatement of the Law of Least Effort is available. The results of one small study (Geis & Knapp, 1963) indicate that avoidance of additional work in a program, i.e., reduction of the number of frames the student is required to do, can serve as a reinforcer.

Aversive stimulation may possibly be involved in the concept of *reduction of tension* or of uncertainty. Many people (see, for example, Berlyne, 1960) have suggested this as a major variable in the control of human behavior, especially human learning. A learning situation, it is contended, should produce a slight rise in tension followed by tension reduction after the response is emitted.[2] The authors of a large reading program for children (Smith, 1964) have informally commented on the importance of this wave-like tension profile in self-instruction. Presumably they have tried to design their programmed materials accordingly. Controlling student uncertainty less precisely, but probably based upon the same assumption, are those programs which the authors claim have error production purposely built into them in order to "maintain student interest."

The most frequently cited reinforcer in the literature on self-instructional systems, especially programmed instruction, is *knowledge of results* (KOR). Almost all published programs, as well as innumerable articles and texts, cite as one of the rules of programming: "include the correct answer in the program in order to reinforce the learner."

The remainder of this article will be devoted to a discussion and review of the literature on this, the most popular, candidate for the role of reinforcer in self-instruction.

The phrase "knowledge of results" at first glance seems self-explanatory and specific. However, it refers to a great variety of environmental changes or stimulus presentations, ranging from indicating to the learner that he is correct to providing elaborate, informative, corrective materials when he has made a mistake. "Non-verbal" feedback consequences are as varied. A student might discover how well he has assembled a piece of apparatus by plugging it in and trying it out; he might test a formula he has invented by going into the lab and blending the ingredients; he might observe a computer simulation of his patient's vital signs before, during and after the treatment he has proposed; he might watch a model of the bridge he has designed displayed on a cathode ray tube and undergoing stress from traffic and winds. (Some feedback consequences are non-verbal but do not occur "naturally" as a consequence of the student's previous performance. These have already been mentioned under the heading of *extrinsic reinforcers*.)

In fact, any consequence discriminable to the learner and regularly related to his previous performance can be designated as KOR. A child working on a teaching machine which produces a green light each time he makes a correct response is getting feedback. The child who is told that he may go to the playground when he finishes his assignment is also in a feedback situation. So is the student who, after he gives his answer in class, hears the teacher say, "Well, yes—but does anyone else have a *different* answer to suggest?" And so is the child who hears increasing giggling from his peers as he works the problem on the blackboard.

But KOR usually means something more specific than that. Some performance consequences are reinforcing in and of themselves. Suppose that a child is permitted to play with a toy when he has finished spelling five words correctly. Playing with the toy is a reinforcing activity. It can be used to strengthen a variety of behaviors; it is not uniquely tied to the task at hand. Contrast it with a procedure in which, after spelling each word, the student is shown the correct spelling of that word. Permission to play serves the same informative function as the correctly spelled words, but it is also reinforcing "in its own right."

A further distinction has to do with the specificity of contingencies. Usually KOR refers to consequences which occur immediately after each response. It is often contingent upon approximations to a more complex final performance. Other "reinforcers" are usually contingent upon completion of a large task (e.g., an assignment rather than a frame in a program).

KOR is often a mediating system, i.e., a means to an end. The child who is promised permission to play

when he has finished the assignment may also have been told he was correct (KOR) after each word or problem. It is sometimes said that being correct or "knowing you are right" is reinforcing in itself and need not be linked to other reinforcers. This claim for an autonomous status of KOR is particularly common among educators who are concerned that the use of other reinforcers either instead of or in addition to KOR not only weakens the effect of "the joy of learning for its own sake" but also smacks of immorality and bribery. We will not pursue questions concerning what particular type of reinforcer KOR may be, but will confine ourselves to discovering any evidence that it is a reinforcer at all.

We will limit the use of KOR to those cases in which the major consequence of the response is information about the learner's own performance. We are excluding all of the potential reinforcers dealt with earlier in the article which have demonstrable reinforcing effects outside of the task situation.

So far we have run the risk of appearing anti-semantic by using a variety of terms interchangeably: feedback, confirmation, reinforcement and knowledge of results.

Each of these terms has its drawbacks. *Feedback*, for example, suggests continuous guidance and an adjustment to the response producing the feedback; the speedometer on an automobile illustrates feedback better than a bit of program test. Michael & Maccoby (1961, p. 282, footnote) have noted that "the term 'feedback' and other related expressions . . . are, in a sense, misnomers, as applied to the procedures of the kind used here (providing answers in a programmed situation) in that the information is the same, from a stimulus point of view, regardless of what responses the subject has made during practice. In the knowledge-of-results procedure, as traditionally applied to practice of skills, by contrast, . . . feedback depends upon the extent and kinds of errors just made in practice. In both instances, however, . . . 'feedback' does provide a basis either for recognizing successful (correct) performance or for recognizing and correcting errors made in practice." In the context of self-instructional systems, the word "feedback" might more appropriately be used to refer to response consequences in computer-based branching programs. In such programs the information received by the student is varied depending upon his responses.

"Confirmation," on the other hand, suggests that a correct response preceded answer-observing. Though an error can, in a sense, be confirmed, general usage indicates a positive relationship between response and confirmation, making the word synonymous with "verify" and "validate."

"Reinforcement" presupposes the relationship between answer and response that is being questioned here: The purpose of this article is to explore the possibility that the presentation of an answer contingent upon a student response *is* a reinforcer.

KOR has a slight mentalistic tinge (i.e., it is subjective and non-observable); nevertheless, it seems like the least ambiguous term and will generally be used throughout this article.

Behind the proposition that KOR (e.g., the printed answer in a program) is a reinforcer lie many assumptions about the student's interaction with that answer.

Suppose that a student is working his way through a programmed text which supplies the correct answer in printed form next to each item. That printed answer cannot have an effect on the student unless he comes in contact with it. (Programmers have been accused alternately of being too artistic or too scientific, but no one has yet charged them with being metaphysical.) Observations of students working through programmed materials, to be discussed at length later, suggest that the learner does not always look at the printed answer. Providing printed answers, then, is not necessarily reinforcing. In order for an answer to become so, the student must look at and respond to the print.

Suppose the student does just that. Still, a variety of conditions can occur. The reinforcing effect of the printed answer is likely to depend upon the student being able to discover how closely his answer approximates the correct answer. In many programs, the student matches his answer to the one in the text. The matching is not always a trivial matter. Given a program in writing Thai symbols, or an audio-lingual Spanish program, the student may have a difficult time telling whether or not his production matches the model.[3] Indeed, paradoxically, some second language programs require the student to make such discriminations as confirmation before he is adequately taught to do so. The result may well be that the student accepts his own erroneous responses as correct.[4]

But suppose that all of these pitfalls are overcome. The student works through a printed program, looks at and matches a printed answer with his own and then finds out that his answer is incorrect. Ugelow (1962, p. 9) points out that "while working with knowledge of results may be preferable to working without such knowledge, knowing that one is consistently doing poorly cannot be said to be rewarding." (The student who, by observing answers in a program, repeatedly discovers that his own answers are erroneous and who nevertheless continues to observe the printed answer might be suspected of masochism.)

This short discussion indicates that the phrase, "the answers are reinforcing," ought to be approached with caution and accepted only tentatively, until a better definition and more evidence are provided. Such conservatism will be reinforced by an examination of the relevant research literature.

Review of the KOR Literature

Most studies (including those reviewed here) are not directly aimed at investigating whether or not answers are reinforcers. The question usually being attacked is a broader one: Does feedback in some way affect performance during and after programmed self-instruction?

Feedback may affect performance, but technically may not be a reinforcer, serving some other function in learning. Goldbeck & Briggs (1962, p. 184), for example, suggest that feedback " ... may provide information concerning the adequacy of responses made, may

serve as a reinforcement and reward for responses, may have a motivating effect on performance, may be used to direct the next step to be taken in the learning program."

Just as it may be mistakenly identified as a reinforcer when it is not, KOR can act as a reinforcer for behavior not being measured by the experimenter and, therefore, be overlooked. For example, one who looks at an answer in a programmed type of test may be reinforced by "seeing it." But if such answer-observing does not lead to better post-test performance (and post-test performance is being measured in the study), one might erroneously conclude that KOR does not function as a reinforcer at all.

In this article, feedback studies will be reviewed with an eye to the more specific problem: Is KOR a reinforcer in self-instruction? The review is restricted almost entirely to self-instructional situations. It has already been pointed out that there is a large literature on KOR which represents research using other than programmed instructional materials.[5] While such research seems occasionally to throw light on KOR as a variable in learning, often the situation differs so much from self-instruction that extrapolation is unjustified.

1. Feedback vs. No-feedback[6]

There is ample evidence that under some circumstances feedback affects performance. However, the results with regard to programmed instruction are ambiguous.

Feedback enhances learning. In an investigation of the relationship between test anxiety and feedback in programmed instruction, Campeau (1968) found that feedback was a significant variable in the performance of grade-school girls. Post-instructional test scores were higher for those high-anxiety girls who had feedback during learning. Low-anxiety female students who had no feedback had higher post-test scores than high-anxiety females who had no feedback. (No significant differences were found between low- and high-anxiety students under feedback conditions.) Male students showed no similar regularity.

In two studies by Anderson *et al.* (in press), large groups of subjects learned a lesson on diagnosis of myocardial infarction, using a computer-based system. *Ss* receiving KOR showed clear superiority on the criterion tests and made fewer errors within the program itself.

Using materials that might be considered "programmed," Wittrock & Twelker (1964) found an interesting relationship between KOR and rules. While rules alone proved most effective in teaching subjects to decode ciphered sentences, KOR was especially useful when rules were not supplied. It did not add to teaching effectiveness when supplied in conjunction with rules, supporting the authors' contention that KCR[7] enhances learning retention, and transfer, when the information it contains is not greatly redundant.

A number of studies regularly cited on the issue of feedback vs. no-feedback (e.g., Alter & Silverman, 1962) seem to us only tangentially relevant. They all involve contrasting a program which has both response blanks to be filled in by the student and printed answers available, with the same program in which the response words are already printed in the text (and, of course, no "answers" are available). Under the latter condition, since no particular response is specifically called for, it is logically difficult to conclude that the reinforcer (i.e., feedback) for it is being withheld. This view does not imply that straight text reading goes unreinforced; some amount of self-reinforcement indeed may take place, a viewpoint held, for example, by Krumboltz & Kiesler (1965). However, a better test of the question involves calling for a response and then confirming or not confirming the emitted response.

Feedback does not enhance learning. The studies cited above constitute the major evidence demonstrating the importance of feedback in programmed instruction; the evidence is sparse. Studies *questioning* its efficacy are more numerous.

Ripple (1963) compared teaching material in a variety of forms including a standard programmed text with and without "reinforcing feedback." The author concluded (from a comparison of criterion test scores of the feedback and no-feedback groups) that there was no differential learning or retention.

An oft-cited study by Feldhusen & Birt (1962) used a short program presented to college students. The authors concluded that the non-confirmation groups did not significantly differ from the confirmation group.

Moore & Smith (1964) also reported no differences on post-test scores between KOR and non-KOR groups of college students who used a version of the Holland-Skinner psychology program (*The Analysis of Behavior.* New York: McGraw-Hill, 1961). The experimenters tried a variety of feedback conditions (KOR alone, KOR plus pennies, KOR plus light), none of which seemed to affect learning significantly. However, errors within the program were fewer for the KOR groups.

In an earlier study by the same authors (Moore & Smith, 1961), a spelling program for fifth and sixth grade children was presented with and without confirmation. Again, there seemed to be no difference between the two treatment groups in terms of achievement test results.

Hough & Revsin (1963, p. 290) also reported no effect of KOR when it was used in a 555-frame college level program. Echoing a common theme found in this literature, they state: "The program used in this study has a low error rate. When students 'know' that their response is right, and thus presumably reinforce themselves, it would seem reasonable that further confirmation in the form of a reinforcement frame would be redundant."

Becker (1964) used a 180-frame program on time-credit loans with a small group of adult learners. Though both KOR and non-KOR groups showed dramatic gain scores, the differences between groups did not prove to be significant.

While findings which indicate no effect of feedback are disconcerting, even more damaging would be evidence that feedback actually hindered performance. Swets *et al.* (1962) report such data. Subjects were taught to identify multidimensional, non-verbal sounds utilizing a computer-based teaching system. Detrimental effects of extensive feedback were demonstrated when the performances of feedback and no-feedback groups were compared.

Jacobs & Kulkarni (1966) had groups of high school students work with a program on gas laws and groups of junior high students work with a program on solving equations. The three experimental conditions were: regular program, a program with KOR omitted, and regular program with the order of some sections inverted. For the junior high students, although the non-confirmation group averaged more than twice the number of errors in the program (a finding consistent with that of Krumboltz & Weisman, 1962, see below), their post-test scores were not significantly different from those of the other two groups. In the high school groups, errors in the program were again high for one high school non-confirmation group with little evidence of a related effect of these high errors on post-test scores. This trend in error data did not hold for the other high school group, although it also showed high post-test scores. In contrast to the results obtained with junior high *Ss,* in both high schools the post-test differences among groups were significant, with the regular program group learning *the least.* It may also be noted that the non-confirmation group generally showed a more positive attitude toward the program materials.

The results in the literature, then, are conflicting and puzzling. A number of design and interpretation problems may lie behind some of the ambiguity. One suggestion of particular relevance stems from a study by MacPherson, Dees & Grindley (1948-1949). In presenting the results of the study of skill learning, they suggest an interpretation which has implications both for those theorizing about the effects of feedback and those reviewing or designing research in the area. The authors propose that the important function of KOR varies with the stage of learning. In the initial stages of learning, they contend, the directive or informational effect of KOR is important; after performance has stabilized, the "incentive" function of KOR assumes greater importance; finally, when proficiency has reached a high level, overt, formal KOR seems to be of little value. This does not seem to be incompatible with the view presented earlier by Wittrock & Twelker and others, namely, that the effect of KOR varies with its redundancy.

A second suggestion relates item difficulty and the reinforcing effect of confirmation. Holland (1965, p. 91), after a review of the literature, points out that no difference between confirmation and non-confirmation is found when programs with low error rates are used. On the other hand, studies which utilized high error rate materials tended to show an advantage in the confirmation group. In such programs, students' confidence in their own answers would not be great. "The relation between item difficulty and relative effectiveness of confirmation may be indicative of the nature of the reinforcer in the program. The reinforcer may be an answer known by the subject to be correct either because he is told it is correct or because he was already confident of his answer."

2. Schedules of Reinforcement

One test of whether a particular consequence is a reinforcer is to present it under various scheduling conditions and observe whether or not predicted changes in behavior occur. A large literature on the effects of various schedules, on human and infra-human subjects, strongly suggests regular effects, and a comparison can easily be made between the results of a new study and that literature. If a consequence thought to be a reinforcer fails to produce the expected results, its status as a reinforcer is suspect.

A technical difficulty which can assume critical proportions is present in many of the confirmation studies in the programming literature. Data (to be presented later) suggest that learners rarely look at all available answers. This presents somewhat of a problem when comparing no-feedback with feedback conditions. However, when schedule of reinforcement is the independent variable, one might well question whether, for example, "50 percent of answers available" is equivalent to "50 percent of answers observed." In short: Is the schedule of reinforcement to be defined formally, in terms of the number of answers available to the subject, or functionally, in terms of the actual number of answers observed?

A second problem concerns the usage of the term "reinforcement." Traditionally, a schedule of reinforcement refers to a contingency involving a single operant class (roughly: "one kind of response"). However, the studies to be cited here involve "reinforcement" of classes of different responses. Thus, a 50 percent partial schedule does not mean that one half of the emissions of responses in a certain response class are reinforced. Rather, it means that half of the answers were present and available in the program. In point of fact, if the answers are indeed reinforcers, each one usually is reinforcing a different response.

By way of preview it might be pointed out that the literature on schedules of reinforcement in programs resembles, in one respect, that reviewed in the previous topic: the findings of different investigators are in disagreement.

Studies showing schedule effects. Lublin (1965, p. 299) studied a large group of college students in a programmed psychology course. Students were on schedules of reinforcement including no confirmation, 100 percent confirmation, fixed ratio 50 percent confirmation, and variable ratio 50 percent confirmation. She found that the variable ratio 50 percent and the No Confirmation group scored higher on the criterion test than did those students under the continuous confirmation treatment; and she suggests that "omission of the answers may have caused the subjects to look for confirmation of their responses in succeeding frames." Presumably, this is tied somehow to better attending and, consequently, improved learning. Conversely, the continuous confirmation group may not have engaged in these beneficial searching behaviors and may have learned little from the frames. In addition, Lublin suggests that the post-test more closely resembles the no-answer program, so that the students whose program responses were continuously confirmed may have been handicapped when faced with the post-test.

Krumboltz & Keisler (1965) propose that, in a low error rate program, response requests without answers provide the occasion for self-reinforcement. Using a 177-frame program on educational test interpretation, they found that the 100 percent, 20 percent and 10 percent confirmation groups did show a difference in behavior. The partial confirmation (i.e., less than 100 percent) groups clearly made more errors in the program and on the immediate post-test. Post-test scores *decreased* as the number of confirmations and number of response requests decreased, a finding contradicting Lublin's. The 100 percent response requests and confirmation condition had the least frame errors, data similar to that obtained in the earlier study by Krumboltz & Weisman (1962). Time to complete the program decreased as response requests and confirmations were removed. The authors suggest that the findings of the study support their hypothesis, though perhaps the measures of "self-reinforcement" are too few to be persuasive.

In a study by Moss & Neidt (1969) the problem was looked at in the context of information theory: both KOR and amount of certainty were varied. University and high school students served as subjects, and a short (42-frame) program in insecticides was used. Decrements in learning were found both when items of information were omitted, (i.e., lower percentage of KOR) and when uncertainty was reduced. The authors conclude that the effectiveness of KOR is intimately related to the degree of uncertainty: KOR is useful and important when uncertainty is high.

Studies showing no schedule effect. Glaser & Taber (1961) investigated the effects of partial "reinforcement" using a symbolic logic program for high school students. None of the four experimental groups (100 percent confirmation, 50 percent fixed ratio, 50 percent variable ratio, and 25 percent variable ratio) differed significantly from each other on the criterion test. The authors suggest that the reinforcing effectiveness of feedback may depend upon the age of the student, specific subject matter, IQ and probability of correct response.

Scharf (1961) used a symbolic logic program with high school juniors and with 50 percent and 25 percent variable schedules and 100 percent and 50 percent fixed schedules of confirmation. No significant relationship was found between confirmation schedules and post-test errors, program errors, or post-test time to completion. The only important difference among groups seemed to be that the 50 percent variable schedule group took the longest time to complete the program.

Krumboltz & Weisman (1962) also found no difference in criterion tests scores for variable vs. fixed ratio schedules, nor for 0 percent, 33 percent, 67 percent and 100 percent schedules. There also was no interaction effect. However, students made fewer frame errors in programs with more confirmation.

Driskill (1964) used a 52-frame program on powers and roots of numbers with Air Force men. He provided 40 percent or 100 percent feedback. No significant difference was found between the gain scores for the two groups.

Rosenstock *et al.* (1965) used four different schedules of feedback with a mathematics program: 100 percent, 20 percent fixed, 20 percent variable, and 0 percent. Partial knowledge of results did not seem to enhance learning, but again, fewer program errors occurred under conditions of increased KOR.

Blank & Pysh (1967) investigated schedules of reinforcement with a short program on the English money system using sixth-grade students. The program was chosen for its difficulty, having a predicted high error rate. The study, therefore, attempted to answer criticism of previous studies to the effect that the failure to find differences due to various schedules of confirmation was a result of using low error programs.[8] In this study no significant differences were found among post-test, gain, or error scores for the various groups (100 percent, 67 percent variable ratio, 33 percent variable ratio, 0 percent, and "logical confirmation," the latter group having answers supplied on the terminal frame for each concept). The only significant difference was found in a sub-group taught by teaching machine. For that group, the difference in gain scores between the 100 percent and the 67 percent treatments was statistically significant.

The authors (Blank & Pysh, 1967, p. 13), in their introduction, state: "By and large the conclusion suggested by (studies on confirmation) is that either (a) it is incorrect to regard confirmation in programmed instruction as equivalent to reinforcement as used in the sub-human context, or (b) these studies have failed to meet the necessary conditions that there be little chance for inter-frame cueing. If the latter conclusion is true, then varying schedules of confirmation in the form of knowledge of results should manifest their differential effects where the probability of error response is high.

"A further possibility . . . is that the conceptual material found in most programs does not lend itself to random partial reinforcement."

On the basis of their analysis of the literature and the findings of their own studies, the authors severely question the traditional observation that confirmation is a reinforcer. The results of a later, more elaborate, study (Pysh *et al.*, 1969, p. 62) again question the role of confirmation as a reinforcer. In that study the authors conclude: "In summary, it would appear that the pivotal assumption, that programmed instruction's effectiveness derives from the explicit provision of KR in the form of a confirmation frame with which the learner compares his antedating response, requires a reappraisal."

3. Delay of Confirmation
Another probe to discover the reinforcing effects of any consequence involves delaying the proposed reinforcer for a time after a correct response is emitted. A large literature exists which, though not entirely consistent, strongly suggests that delaying the presentation of the reinforcing consequence reduces its effect on the behavior upon which it has been made contingent. This literature has, for the most part, involved infra-human subjects (although a fairly large sub-set concerns the behavior of retarded children). Evidence for delay

noticeably affecting the performance of humans is less solid than evidence of such effects with lower organisms (see, for example, Renner, 1964).

Much of the research that seems to be at all relevant to the issue raised in this article involves feedback in test situations or in situations involving memorization of discrete associations. These results are not consistent and are not always clear. Sometimes immediate feedback seems to be more effective than does delayed feedback (see, for example, Sassenrath *et al.*, 1968); sometimes delayed feedback seems more effective, especially when long-term retention is being measured (see, for example, Sassenrath & Yonge, 1969; Sturges, 1969; Brackbill, 1964).

Delay produces effects. A few studies are directed specifically at the programmed instruction situation. Evans, Glaser & Homme (1962) investigated delay using a program in symbolic logic. Delays in confirmation seemed to have only a little effect on criterion performance. The authors suggest that when the correct response is highly probable, the effect of confirmation may be minimal, a theme we noted occurring elsewhere in the confirmation literature.

A study by Meyer (1960) involved presenting a 19-lesson program on Latin prefixes in English to eighth-grade students. One group had immediate feedback (answers were available in the text), and another group had delayed feedback (no answers were available in the text). For both groups, the answers were "corrected" by the experimenter and returned to the students the next day. Students in the delayed feedback group committed more errors in the program. The author suggests a lack of potential for self-correction in the form of the program used by this group. Repetition of previous errors by these students, therefore, probably accounted for their poorer performance. Comparison of post-test scores for these two groups revealed a difference just short of significance (p = .06), with the difference in the predicted direction: the immediate feedback group showed higher scores.

Meyer (1960, p. 69) concludes: "It was hypothesized that immediate confirmation of correct responses and disconfirmation of incorrect responses would lead to superior acquisition. The hypothesis was supported by the data."

Delay produces no effect. Boersma (1966) used a modification of the symbolic logic program used by Evans with college students. He found a significant interaction effect of delay of feedback (i.e., time from response to feedback exposure), and post-feedback delay (i.e., time between end of feedback exposure and presentation of next frame) on program errors, but not on criterion scores. There were more program errors in the *feedback-delay, no post-feedback delay* condition and in the *no feedback delay, post-feedback delay* condition. However, more importantly, delay of feedback did not produce a significant main effect on the program or on criterion error scores. (Delay in this study was short: eight seconds in length.)

4. Other Kinds of Evidence
A general observation can be made at this

point: the evidence is weak that confirmation is a reinforcer. The results reviewed are inconsistent; if there is a trend, it is toward showing no real reinforcing effect of feedback.

Some "secondary" generalizations do emerge from the literature. For example, students with less, or no, opportunity to view answers commit more errors in the program. This finding seems explainable in terms of those in confirmation groups being able to peek at answers and to correct their errors. When the opportunity to peek is controlled for, usually there is an increase in errors noted in the confirmation group. That error or peeking has any effect on learning (in terms of criterion test scores) is not at all clear.

It could be argued that the reinforcing effect of confirmation is subtle and that the experiments cited have not been sensitive enough, in terms of design or the measures of the dependent variables, to pick up an existing effect. Some suggestions have already been made about confounding or masking variables that ought to be considered. (For example, the argument has been repeatedly raised that the probability of correct response interacts with the effect of confirmation, an hypothesis to be returned to later.)

Organism variables. Permanent or momentary organism-centered variables (e.g., anxiety, IQ, sex, age, achievement motive) might confound experiments in which other variables are being manipulated. Assuming that the literature search made in the preparation of this paper was fairly comprehensive, one would conclude that the only extensive research on such variables has been conducted by Campeau (1968), whose work was reviewed earlier. A major variable in her research has been anxiety, specifically test anxiety as measured by the Test Anxiety Scale for Children. Accentuating the test-like features of the situation by omitting answers in the program should, the author contends, adversely affect high-anxiety *Ss.* Furthermore, a comparison of high- and low-anxiety *Ss* under feedback conditions should reveal higher achievement scores for the high-anxiety group (implying, in the context of this paper, that feedback may be reinforcing, or at least more reinforcing, to anxious students). The differences Campeau found in her studies were not significant for the male *Ss.* High-anxiety girls did somewhat better, but not significantly better, on immediate post-tests than did low-anxiety girls when both groups had received feedback in the program. High-anxiety girls in the feedback group showed dramatically better gain scores than those in the no-feedback group. The evidence is not very clear, however, that feedback is more reinforcing to high- than to low-anxiety students.

Though a number of writers (e.g., see Taber *et al.*, 1965, p. 170) suggest that factors such as age, motivation and IQ may well interact with feedback, little research has been directly aimed at investigating such relationships.[9]

Task variables. A second set of variables which might affect the status of feedback involves the task itself: the *kind* of task (e.g., motor skill learning as contrasted with verbal discrimination), the degree of interaction of the parts of the task (e.g., learning rote material in which the components have little interaction with each other *vs.* learning concepts which are related) or task complexity. For example, some pilot work by the authors (Geis & Chapman, 1970) utilizing a program teaching Russian script (i.e., the Cyrillic alphabet) suggests that students are more likely to request feedback when the task requires production, in this case writing a letter, than when a discrimination alone is called for, as when the student is asked to choose the better of two letters. More generally stated: feedback might be more reinforcing when one is executing a complex motor coordination than when he is merely recognizing a correct item in a choice situation. This may be related to the idea that the probability of error interacts with the reinforcing effect of feedback, since the chance of making some error is usually increased when a chain of responses is called for, as in the case of production.

Kinds of feedback. A third area might be called "kinds of feedback." Certain types of feedback may, in an absolute sense, be more reinforcing than others, or may be more reinforcing under certain conditions. For example, given a two-choice discrimination task in a program frame, the student might be reinforced by an indication of "correct response" in the form of a light going on after he emits the right answer. Failure to produce the "correct" signal is logically equivalent to producing an "incorrect" signal, in the two-choice situation.[10]

At the other extreme might be a complex motor task. When learning to pronounce a French word or to write a Thai symbol, binary feedback limited to "correct "-"not correct" may prove unreinforcing. On the other hand, a more elaborate feedback system (e.g., pointing to particular dimensions of the student's response which fail to meet criteria and providing a correct comparison model for him at the time) might be highly reinforcing.

"Kind of feedback" might also refer to varying conditions for the same feedback, i.e., the same information. (Thus, in a study by Anderson to be discussed later [Anderson *et al.*, in press], one group received answers only after they had made an incorrect response while other students received feedback only after they had made correct responses.)

Branching programs often provide elaborate and varied response consequences. In examining possible evidence for the reinforcing effects of various kinds of KOR it might be appropriate to include the branching literature. Unfortunately, there seems to be no research specifically directed to explorations of kinds of branches, number of alternatives in a branching system, etc. (This seems a fallow area for research.) The assumption is commonly made that a branching program, especially a computer assisted one, is bound to be superior to a more pedestrian linear program. Holland (1965), summarizing his review of the area, noted no significant advantages had been demonstrated for branching programs. Two years later, Anderson (1967) came to the same conclusion, despite additional research that had been conducted in the intervening time. There may be advantages to branching; certain kinds of branching consequences may be reinforcing. But at present there is little evidence to that effect.

The research literature on kinds of feedback in programmed instruction is small but interesting.

Kind of feedback affects learning. Krumboltz & Bonawitz (1962), using their educational test construction program, varied the form of confirmation. The "isolation" approach involved presenting as feedback the word or phrase that was desired as a response. The "context" approach presented the confirming response by repeating the relevant part of the stimulus frame. The experimenters found no differences on a sub-test of knowledge of technical terms, but a significant advantage was found for "context" confirmation on a sub-test of applications of test construction knowledge. The authors caution that the findings are for a small group of subjects. Nevertheless, there is a suggestion that kind of feedback may interact with the development of certain kinds of terminal behaviors and not others.

Gilman (1968, p. 2) has investigated the effect of various kinds of feedback in a computer assisted instruction (CAI) system. He points out that "if there were no purpose to feedback other than to provide the student with reinforcement, statements such as 'you are correct' should prove equally effective as confirmation of a correct answer." University upperclassmen were taught 30 general science concepts by means of a CAI self-instructional system, using a multiple choice format. Various modes of feedback were used: no feedback, "correct" or "wrong," feedback of correct response, feedback appropriate to the student's response, and a combination of the three latter modes. Students repeated items which were missed until a perfect run-through was obtained. The no-feedback group and the "correct" or "wrong" group performed less well on the program, making a significantly greater number of responses and requiring a greater number of iterations of the program in order to reach criterion. On the post-test, the combined feedback group scored significantly higher than did the others.

These two studies seem to suggest that more elaborate feedback may be reinforcing, or at least more effective in some way, in changing student behavior. However, other studies do not support this hypothesis.

Kind of feedback does not affect learning. McDonald & Allen (1962) varied the kind of confirmation in a program which taught a game similar to chess or checkers. The variations in confirmation included: no response request and no confirmation; response request with correct response as confirmation; response request, correct response and an explanation of correctness or incorrectness as confirmation. The experimenters found no differences among groups on immediate and delayed criterion tests.

Bivens (1964) used a short program in elementary set theory with 89 eighth-grade students. Confirmation was offered in *simple* and *complex* forms. The simple form was a presentation of the explicit desired response. The complex form was an example of a different but similar problem already solved. All students had the complex form of confirmation available. Those in the "simple" group were told to check the answers against the simple answers and merely read the other solved problems. Those in the "complex" group were instructed to search through the solved problems to determine if their own answers were correct. There were no differences found between the groups on the criterion test after learning.

Anderson *et al.* (in press) used several feedback arrangements involving a computer and a program on diagnosing myocardial infarction. In one experiment, using several groups, they presented the correct response (1) only after a correct response had been emitted, or (2) only after a wrong response had been emitted, or (3) always (100 percent), or (4) never (0 percent), or (5) after a correct response, but the subject had to "loop" back to the same frame after the wrong response. Criterion test scores were higher for the 100 percent feedback and the "looped" groups. The only group with significantly lower test scores was the no-feedback group (0 percent). Of interest here is the fact that no significant difference was found between the 100 percent and the "looped " group, although the latter students underwent much more elaborate feedback procedures. Furthermore, there was no evidence in these studies that KOR functioned as corrective feedback. The group receiving KOR only when errors were made did not perform significantly better on the criterion test than the other KOR groups. Again, whatever reinforcing function KOR might serve was not established. The KOR-only-when-correct group performed at the same level as the other groups.

In a second experiment by the same authors, the 0 and 100 percent groups were again used. Various groups of subjects *(Ss)* who always received KOR were exposed to one of the following variations: S was forced to repeat wrong frames until he made the correct response; or, after each of four sections (about 25 frames) in the program, S repeated any wrong frames in the preceding section until he made a correct response; or, when he made an error S saw the frame and KOR for 15 seconds; or, S was presented with frame and answer but was instructed to respond before looking at KOR. (This last group was similar to groups of students using programs used outside of experimental settings and without mechanical presentation devices in that "peeking" was possible.) Again, the 100 percent group proved to have undergone the most effective procedure both in terms of reduced number of frame errors and increased criterion scores. And again, no difference in favor of the more elaborate feedback procedures was found in this study.

Melaragno (1960) investigated *negative* feedback using a set of 50 multiple choice items for teaching the names, uses and meanings of five logic symbols. The material resembled programs of the day, having easy small steps. A small group of junior college students acted as subjects. Five ambiguous items with no correct answers were inserted to determine the effect of negative reinforcement on post-test scores. Members of all groups were shown a green light after each response to an item in the program except for the five ambiguous ones. The green light indicated that the previous response had been correct. (S received the green light, or "correct" signal, even if he had made an error on the frame.) Following responses to the ambiguous items: *Group I* saw the green light after each response to the ambiguous items, which indicated they were correct. For this group the ambiguous items were spaced throughout the sequence. *Group II* saw a red light indicating responses to the ambiguous items were wrong. Again, the five items were interspersed throughout the program. *Group III* also saw "incorrect" feedback lights on the five items which were in this case massed at the middle of the total set.

All groups were given a 45-question criterion test upon completion of the learning sequence. *Group III* had lower post-test scores than the other two groups. The author concluded that some spaced negative reinforcement does not impair learning, but that massed negative reinforcement seems to do so.

5. Prompting and Cueing

In pursuit of the specific conditions under which confirmation might be reinforcing, the literature on prompting was examined. The conjecture was one already repeatedly discussed in this paper: namely, that the reinforcing function of KOR may depend in good part upon the probability that S emits a correct answer. Frames with a high degree of prompting reduce the chances that an erroneous response will occur and, therefore, confirmation following such frames should be minimally reinforcing.

There is a large literature on prompting versus confirmation, much of it involving non-programmed materials (e.g., Cook & Spitzer, 1960). A comprehensive review by Aiken & Lau (1967) examined three types of learning: verbal learning, perceptual learning and signal monitoring. The authors conclude that response prompting is as effective as, or is more effective than, response confirmation. (A possible exception, the authors note, is discrimination learning.) While cautious in their conclusions and extrapolations, the authors stress that one should neither ignore the potential importance of antecedent stimuli in controlling behavior and effecting learning, nor subsume all consequent, response-contingent events under the rubric "reinforcer."

From the literature, two opposing suggestions emerge concerning prompting in programs. The first is derived from paired-associate learning studies in which the superiority of prompting over confirmation seems to have been established. Extrapolating to programmed materials from such data, one would recommend heavily-cued frames. The second view (e.g., Margulies & Speeth, 1968) suggests that over-prompting in a program, especially one involving non-rote materials, may reduce the effectiveness of learning, since it eliminates searching, problem solving and some of the other (probably covert and assumed) behaviors in which the programmer intended his student to engage.

There are about half a dozen studies on the issue of prompting which do utilize programmed materials.

No effect. Silberman *et al.* (1961) used 61 teaching items on topics in logic with 44 junior college students. A version of the program providing confirmation after each item was contrasted with one which presented the same items of information in statement form, one at a time, and with one which presented the same information in paragraph form allowing review. Though the two "prompted" versions took less time to complete than the confirmation versions, there were no differences among groups on post-test scores.

Hershberger & Terry (1965) used lessons resembling programs and studied the effect of typographical cueing on learning. The essential material, tested by the criterion test, was prompted by underlining, size of type and color. This type of prompting failed to increase learning, though in a related study (Hershberger, 1963) it had been found that a simpler form of typographical cueing, using only color, helped students learn more of the core content.

Some effect. Wittrock & Twelker (1964) used program-like materials with 184 college students to teach ten ways to decipher coded statements. In this study, cited at length earlier in this article, prompting consisted of seeing the decoding rule with each problem. Confirmation involved S seeing the decoded sentence after attempting to decode the problem sentence. Scores on post-tests, retention tests and transfer tests were highest when prompts were given, about the same when prompts and KOR were given, lower when KOR alone was given and lowest when neither KOR nor prompts were provided. The authors conclude that KOR is effective, but only when it is not redundant (i.e., KOR plus prompts was no more effective than prompts alone).

Anderson *et al.* (1968) modified the Holland-Skinner psychology program for use with 108 high school teachers in an educational psychology course. The first 1,052 frames were used, with one additional prompt added to about 90 percent of the frames of the "prompted" version. Time to complete the program and post-test scores were compared for the prompted and a non-prompted version. Ss in all groups could look at the confirmation on the page containing the next frame. Ss in the prompted version took significantly less time and produced lower test scores. The authors suggest that there is a limit to the efficacy of prompting, that limit having been reached with this kind of program.

The authors related their findings to two other bodies of research on prompting: Cook's work referred to earlier and Holland's research on "blackout ratios" (see Holland, 1965). They propose that their findings complement Holland's contention that the response in a program must be contingent upon attention to critical material in the frame. Anderson *et al.* (1968, p. 93) state that "learning is reduced when the prompts are of such a nature that it is possible for the student to respond correctly without attending to the cues."

Although a study by LeFurgy & Sisseron (1968) does not utilize programmed material, it seems highly relevant here. The authors utilized concept cards with geometric figures to teach 30 young girls the concept that "the one with the most sides is the correct one." One group received confirmation of correct choices on acquisition trials. Another group saw a light go on in front of the correct figure on the card ("prompting"), then made a choice. A third group could decide which procedure, prompting or confirmation, they would like to follow on each trial. No differences (trials to criterion, errors, time, etc.) were found among the groups during acquisition. However, the free-choice group was superior on the generalization post-test and in its ability to verbalize the concept. The confirmation group did *least* well on both tasks. It is also interesting to note that (1) on the average, Ss in the free-choice group chose the prompting procedure on about 50 percent of the acquisition trials and (2) that they requested prompts with decreasing frequency as acquisition proceeded, providing a self-controlled vanishing procedure. This latter finding recalls the repeated suggestion that KOR may play different roles as acquisition proceeds.

Lumsdaine (1961, p. 490) investigated and discussed a variety of issues in the prompting and confirmation controversy. He strongly argues that the importance of feedback clearly depends upon the adequacy of prior prompting: "With a well-prompted program of the Skinner type, students may frequently pay little attention to the confirmation/correction panel since the program is sufficiently well-cued so that they are generally certain of the correctness of the response they have made." He further suggests (Lumsdaine, 1961, p. 482), specifically, that "at any point during acquisition, the strength of unconditional cues or prompts provided the learner should satisfy the dual conditions of being: (1) just sufficient to elicit the correct response, but (2) no stronger than is required for this purpose."

The point which emerged early in the paper seems to be strengthened and clarified with each additional section: if KOR can function as a reinforcer at all, it is likely to do so under special conditions which involve low probability of correct response (or, conversely, high probability of error). Lumsdaine seems to be suggesting that the programmer produce materials which are delicately designed to "keep the student on the edge," i.e., barely cueing the correct answer.

6. Student Use of Feedback

One of the most obvious ways to discover the actual reinforcing effect of KOR would be to make it available to the learner and notice whether or not he takes advantage of its availability. If a reinforcer is defined as strengthening the response which precedes it, and if KOR is indeed a reinforcer, then the response of producing KOR should be at high strength. Or, as Anderson (1967, p. 149) puts it: "If an explicit 'observing response' were required of students in order for them to receive KOR, then the rate at which this observing response occurred would be by definition the measure of strength of KOR as a reinforcer."

Melching (1966) used a 364-frame linear program on magnetism with 17 enlisted Army personnel. All answers had been deleted from the program, which was then administered individually to each student. The experimenter, sitting opposite S, provided feedback (the printed answer) after each response upon request from S. The learner requested feedback on about one-quarter of the frames. Percent requests by subjects ranged from 57 percent to 6 percent. The first conclusion, then, is that Ss tended to request feedback much more often when they were wrong than when they had correctly responded. Low ability students (as defined by scores on a measure of "general intellectual ability") requested feedback about three times as often as high ability students. They also made about three times as many errors in the program.

A series of studies by Geis et al. (1970) strongly supports Melching's findings. Several different programs were used with college students as subjects. The answer to each frame was either on the back of a card containing the frame, or, in some instances, was exposed when S removed a piece of masking tape. It was consistently found that: (1) on the average, students checked far less than 100 percent of the answers; (2) students varied among themselves in regard to the percent of answers they checked (data indicate that each S was consistent in his checking rate over a variety of programs); (3) clear, significant and positive correlations were obtained between erroneous responding and checking. Thus, though the checking rates differed widely from student to student, with only a few exceptions, the probability of checking, regardless of base rate, is higher after a student has emitted an erroneous response than when he has been correct.

Anderson's (1967, p. 149) comment on Melching's data holds for these findings as well: ". . . the only decent thing to do in the face of these data is to question the assumption that KOR is a reinforcer." Nevertheless, that broad statement seems to require an amendment. Under certain circumstances, namely after an error has been committed, the probability of observing behavior is raised and, by Anderson's definition, the printed answer may be said to be reinforcing.[11]

Summary and Conclusions

Knowledge of results is most frequently cited as the reinforcer in self-instructional systems. The printed answer in a programmed text, for example, is supposed to reinforce the response the student emits previous to observing that answer. Some other possible reinforcers were briefly discussed in this article before the literature on KOR in self-instruction was selectively reviewed. The review was organized as a search for evidence that KOR might appropriately be called a reinforcer. Studies comparing programs with and without feedback were examined; the weight of evidence from these global studies was that feedback did not enhance learning, as measured by immediate post-test scores or by retention tests. In at least one case there seemed to be a decrement in performance traceable to the presentation of feedback. One recent and sophisticated study (i.e., Anderson et al., in press) did show clear advantages for feedback and thereby implied that KOR may be a reinforcer.

Studies in which "schedules of reinforcement" were varied failed to show effects that would be expected if KOR were acting as a reinforcer. (However, high error scores within the program are consistently noted when percent of KOR is reduced.)

One major study involving delay of KOR (i.e., Meyer, 1960) did report the effect expected when delivery of a reinforcer is delayed. Other studies on delay do not replicate this finding.

Finer-grained analyses of student behavior and KOR begin to reveal specific conditions under which KOR seems to be acting as reinforcer. A few studies scattered throughout the literature report on manipulation of subject and task variables and of kinds of feedback. The results of these and the results of studies in prompting *vs.* confirmation and student-controlled feedback suggest, each in a different way, that KOR may well be a reinforcer when uncertainty or probability of emitting an incorrect response is high, or where confidence is low.

It is clear that the printed answer (or its analog in other media) is not globally and automatically a reinforcer. The review provides the springboard from which one might jump into broader questions such as how, when and why information on one's own performance in a learning situation becomes reinforcing and contributes to more effective learning. □

Notes

1. In descriptions of his partially self-instructional system, Keller has stressed the reinforcing effects of peers who act as student "proctors." See, for example, Keller, 1967, especially pp. 17-19.
2. Seemingly related is the concept of *closure* or *completion* advanced by Gestalt psychologists.
3. In non-language learning programs a similar problem occurs when the author slyly adds the phrase, ". . . or synonymous answer," to his answers.
4. For further explication of this point see Gagne (1965 pp. 26-27).
5. For a broader survey, the reader should consult a recent comprehensive book (Annett, 1969) which deals with a great variety of tasks involving feedback.
6. As Annett (1969) points out, *intrinsic* feedback is unavoidable; it occurs as part of the performance itself, e.g., hearing your own overt verbalizing. "No-feedback" means no experimenter-supplied feedback.
7. The abbreviations KOR, KCR and KR are equivalent.
8. As noted earlier (Taber *et al.*, 1965, p. 92), again and again suggestions are made in the literature that "confirmation at the frame level may have little effect on student motivation except in situations when the student has real doubts about his answer, as in unusually difficult frames."
9. Though there is a small literature on student characteristics and programmed instruction. See, for example, Woodruff *et al.*, 1966.
10. There is some indication that feedback for right and no-feedback for wrong answers is not completely equivalent to identifying the answer as right-wrong. However, generally speaking, the feedback for correct responding in a two-choice situation seems to exhaust all of the possibilities.
11. Little attempt has been made in this article to answer the question: What is being reinforced by feedback? While the ill-defined term "learning" intuitively seems like the proper and relevant answer, "the response just previous to feedback" is less assailable. It is assumed that the observing response is somehow related to learning and to continued participation in the program, but the relationship is not clear.

References

Aiken, E.G. & Lau, A.W. Response Prompting and Response Confirmation: A Review of Recent Literature. *Psychological Bulletin*, 1967, *58*(5), pp. 330-341.

Alter, M. & Silverman, R. The Response in Programed Instruction, *The Journal of Programed Instruction*, 1962, *1*(1), pp. 55-78.

Anderson, R.C. Educational Psychology. *Annual Review of Psychology*, 1967, *18*, pp. 129-164.

Anderson, R.C., Faust, G.W. & Roderick, M.C. Overprompting in Programmed Instruction. *Journal of Educational Psychology*, 1968, *59*(2), pp. 88-93.

Anderson, R.C., Kulhavy, R.W. & Andre, T. Feedback Procedures in Programmed Instruction. *Journal of Educational Psychology*, (in press).

Annett, J. *Feedback and Human Behavior.* Baltimore: Penguin Books, 1969.

Becker, J.L. The Effect of Withholding Reinforcement in Auto-instructional Programs. In G.D. Ofiesh & W.C. Meierhenry (Eds.) *Trends in Programmed Instruction.* Washington, D.C.: DAVI, National Education Association and National Society for Programmed Instruction, 1964.

Berlyne, D.E. *Conflict, Arousal and Curiosity.* New York: McGraw-Hill, 1960.

Berman, M.L. The Experimental Analysis of Performance on Programmed Instruction. *NSPI Journal*, 1967, *6*(10), pp. 10-13.

Bivens, L.W. Feedback Complexity and Self-Direction in Programmed Instruction. *Psychological Reports*, 1964, *14*, pp. 155-160.

Blank, S.S. & Pysh, F. The Effects of Varying Confirmation Schedules in a High Error Rate Program. *Canadian Psychologist*, 1967, *8a*(1), pp. 12-18.

Boersma, F.J. Effects of Delay of Information Feedback and Length of Postfeedback Interval on Linear Programmed Learning. *Journal of Educational Psychology*, 1966, *57*(3), pp. 140-145.

Brackbill, Y., Wagner, J.E. & Wilson, D. Feedback Delay and the Teaching Machine. *Psychology in the Schools*, 1964, *1*(2), pp. 148-156.

Campeau, P.L. Test Anxiety and Feedback in Programmed Instruction. *Journal of Experimental Psychology*, 1968, *59*(3), pp. 159-163.

Cook, J.O. & Spitzer, M.E. Supplementary Report: Prompting versus Confirmation in Paired-Associate Learning. *Journal of Experimental Psychology*, 1960, *59*(4), pp. 275-276.

Driskill, W.E. Partial and Continuous Feedback in a Linear Programmed Instruction Package. In G.D. Ofiesh & W.C. Meierhenry (Eds.) *Trends in Programmed Instruction.* Washington, D.C.: DAVI, National Education Association and National Society for Programmed Instruction, 1964.

Evans, J.L., Glaser, R. & Homme, L.E. An Investigation of "Teaching Machine" Variables Using Learning Programs in Symbolic Logic. *Journal of Educational Research*, 1962, *55*(9), pp. 433-452.

Feldhusen, J. & Birt, A. A Study of Nine Methods of Presentation of Programmed Learning Material. *Journal of Educational Research*, 1962, *55*(9), pp. 461-466.

Ferster, C.B. & Perrott, M.C. *Behavior Principles.* New York: Appleton-Century-Crofts, 1968.

Gagne, R.M. The Analysis of Instructional Objectives for the Design of Instruction. In R. Glaser (Ed.) *Teaching Machines* and *Programmed Learning, II: Data and Directions.* Washington, D.C.: DAVI, National Education Association, 1965.

Geis, G.L., Chapman, R., Smith, C.W. & Moore, C.J. *Improving Instructional Systems.* Mimeo. Foreign Language Innovative Curricula Studies, Ann Arbor, Michigan: U.S.O.E. Grant No. 3-7-704431-4389, 1969.

Geis, G.L. & Chapman, R. Feedback in Programmed Instruction. Progress Report. Center for Research on Language and Language Behavior, U.S.O.E. Contract OEC-0-9-097740-3743(014), January 1970.

Geis, G.L., Jacobs, W., Spencer, D. & Nielsen, S. The Role of the Printed Answer in Programmed Instruction. *NSPI Journal,* 1970, *9*(6), pp. 8-11.

Geis, G.L. & Knapp, S. A Note on Nonfunctional Branching in a Linear Program. *Journal of Programmed Instruction,* 1963, *2*(1), pp. 15-17.

Gilman, S.A. A Comparison of Several Feedback Methods for Correcting Errors by Computer-Assisted Instruction. Paper presented to the American Psychological Association, 1968. Also: ERIC document: ED 024 287.

Glaser, R. Toward a Behavioral Science Base for Instructional Design. In R. Glaser (Ed.) *Teaching Machines and Programmed Learning II: Data and Directions.* Washington, D.C.: DAVI, National Education Association, 1965.

Glaser, R. & Taber, J.I. *Investigations of the Characteristics of Programmed Learning Sequences.* University of Pittsburgh, Programmed Learning Lab, Coop. Research Project 691, Chapter 4, 1961.

Goldbeck, R.A. & Briggs, L.J. An Analysis of Response Mode and Feedback in Automated Instruction. In W.I. Smith & J.W. Moore (Eds.) *Programmed Learning.* Princeton: D. Van Nostrand Co., Inc., 1962.

Gotkin, L.G. The Machine and the Child. *AV Communication Review,* 1966, *14*(2), pp. 221-241.

Hershberger, W. Learning *via* Programmed Reading. Palo Alto, California: American Institutes for Research, Contract No. Nonr-3077(00), Office of Naval Research, Technical Report AIR-C28-7/63-TR No. 5, July 1963.

Hershberger, W. & Terry, D.F. Typographical Cuing in Conventional and Programmed Texts. *Journal of Applied Psychology,* 1965, *49*(1), pp. 55-60.

Holland, J. Research on Programming Variables. In R. Glaser (Ed.) *Teaching Machines and Programmed Learning, II: Data and Directions.* Washington, D.C.: DAVI, National Education Association, 1965.

Hough, J.B. & Revsin, B. Programmed Instruction at the College Level: A Study of Several Factors Influencing Learning. *Phi Delta Kappan,* 1963, *44*(6), pp. 286-291.

Human Development Institute. (J. Berline & J.B. Wyckoff) *General Relationship Improvement Program.* Human Development Institute, 1966.

Jacobs, P.I. & Kulkarni, S. A Test of Some Assumptions Underlying Programmed Instruction. *Psychological Reports,* 1966, *18*, pp. 103-110.

Keller, F.S. Neglected Rewards in the Educational Process. In *Proceedings of the American Conference of Academic Deans.* Los Angeles, 1967, pp. 9-22.

Krumboltz, J.D. & Bonawitz, B. The Effect of Receiving the Confirming Response in Context in Programmed Material. *Journal of Educational Research,* 1962, *55*(9), pp. 472-475.

Krumboltz, J.D. & Keisler, C.A. The Partial Reinforcement Paradigm and Programmed Instruction. *Journal of Programed Instruction,* 1965, *3*(2), pp. 9-14.

Krumboltz, J.D. & Weisman, R.G. The Effect of Intermittent Confirmation in Programmed Instruction. *Journal of Educational Psychology,* 1962, *53*(6), pp. 250-253.

LeFurgy, W.G. & Sisseron, J.A. Effect of Prompting, Confirmation and Free Choice upon Children's Acquisition, Verbalization and Generalization of a Concept. *Psychonomic Science,* 1968, *12*(6), pp. 277-278.

Lublin, S.C. Reinforcement, Schedules, Scholastic Aptitude, Autonomy Need, and Achievement in a Programmed Course. *Journal of Educational Psychology,* 1965, *56*(6), pp. 295-302.

Lumsdaine, A. Some Conclusions Concerning Student Response and a Science of Instruction. In A. Lumsdaine (Ed.) *Student Response in Programmed Instruction.* Washington D.C.: National Academy of Science and National Research Council, Publication No. 943, 1961.

MacPherson, S.J., Dees, V. & Grindley, C.G. The Effect of KR on Learning and Performance II. Some Characteristics of Very Simple Skills. *Quarterly Journal of Experimental Psychology,* 1948-49, *1* pp. 68-78.

Margulies, S. & Speeth, K. What Determines What the Student Learns? *Programmed Learning & Educational Technology,* 1968, *5* (4), pp. 255-270.

McDonald, F.J. & Allen, D.W. An Investigation of Presentation, Response, and Correctional Factors in Programmed Instruction. *Journal of Educational Research,* 1962, *55*(9), pp. 502-507.

Melaragno, R.J. Effect of Negative Reinforcement in an Automated Teaching Setting. *Psychological Reports,* 1960, *7*, pp. 381-384. Also in J.P. DeCecco (Ed.) *Educational Technology: Readings in Programmed Instruction.* New York: Holt, Rinehart & Winston, 1964.

Melching, W.H. PI Under a Feedback Schedule. *NSPI Journal,* 1966, *5*(2), pp. 14-15.

Meyer, S.R. A Test of the Principles of "Activity," "Immediate Reinforcement," and "Guidance": as Instrumented by Skinner's Teaching Machine. *Dissertation Abstracts,* 1960, *20*, pp. 4729-4730.

Michael, D.M. & Maccoby, N. Factors Influencing the Effects of Students' Participation on Verbal Learning from Films: Motivating vs. Practice Effects, "Feedback," and Overt vs. Covert Responding. In A. Lumsdaine (Ed.) *Student Response in Programmed Instruction.* Washington, D.C.: National Academy of Science and National Research Council, Publication No. 943, 1961.

Moore, J. & Smith, W.L. Knowledge of Results in Self-Teaching Spelling. *Psychological Reports,* 1961, *9*, pp. 717-726.

_____ Role of Knowledge of Results in Programmed Instruction. *Psychological Reports,* 1964, *14*, pp. 407-423.

Moore O.K. & Anderson, A.R. Some Principles for the Design of Clarifying Educational Environments. In D.A. Goslin (Ed.) *Handbook of Socialization and Research.* Chicago: Rand-McNally, 1969.

Moss, D.E. & Neidt, C.O. Applicability of Information Theory to Learning. *Psychological Reports,* 1969, *24*, pp. 471-478.

Osborne, J.G. Free-Time as a Reinforcer in the Management of Classroom Behavior. *Journal of Applied Behavior Analysis,* 1969, *2*(2), pp. 113-118.

Premack, D. Toward Empirical Behavior Laws: I. Positive Reinforcement. *Psychological Review,* 1959, *66*, pp. 219-233.

Pysh, F., Blank, S.S. & Lambert, R.A. The Effects of Step Size, Response Mode and KOR upon Achievement in Programmed Instruction. *Canadian Psychologist*, 1969, *10*(1), pp. 49-64.

Renner, K.E. Delay of Reinforcement: A Historical Review. *Psychological Bulletin*, 1964, *61*(5), pp. 341-361.

Ripple, R.E. Comparison of the Effectiveness of a Programed Text with Three Other Modes of Presentation. *Psychological Reports*, 1963, *12*, pp. 227-237.

Rosenstock, E.J., Moore, J.W. & Smith, W.I. Effects of Several Schedules of Knowledge of Results on Mathematics Achievements. *Psychological Reports*, 1965, *17*, pp. 535-541.

Sassenrath, J.M. *et al.* Immediate and Delayed Feedback on Examination and Immediate and Delayed Retention. *California Journal of Educational Research*, 1968, *19*(5), pp. 226-231.

Sassenrath, J.M. & Yonge, G.D. Effects of Delayed Information Feedback and Feedback Cues in Learning on Delayed Retention. *Journal of Educational Psychology*, 1969, *61* (3), pp. 174-177.

Scharf, E.S. A Study of Partial Reinforcement on Behavior in a Programmed Learning Situation. In R. Glaser (Project Director) *Investigations of the Characteristics of Programmed Learning Sequences*. University of Pittsburgh, Programmed Learning Lab, 1961.

Silberman, H.F., Melaragno, R.J. & Coulson, J.E. Confirmation and Prompting with Connected Discourse Material. *Psychological Reports*, 1961, *9*, pp. 235-238.

Skinner, B.F. *The Technology of Teaching*. New York: Appleton-Century-Crofts, 1968.

Smith, D.E.P., Brethower, D. & Cabot, R. Increasing Task Behavior in a Language Arts Program by Providing Reinforcement. *Journal of Experimental Child Psychology*, 1969, *8*, pp. 45-62.

Smith, D.E.P. (Ed.) *Successive Language Discrimination Program*. Ann Arbor: Ann Arbor Publishers, 1964 on.

Sturges, P.T. Verbal Retention as a Function of the Informativeness and Delay of Informative Feedback. *Journal of Educational Psychology*, 1969, *60*(1), pp. 11-14.

Sullivan, H.J., Baker, R.L. & Schutz, R.E. Effects of Intrinsic and Extrinsic Reinforcement Contingencies on Learner Performance. *Journal of Experimental Psychology*, 1967, *58*(3), pp. 165-169.

Swets, J.W., Millman, S.H., Fletcher, W.E. & Green, D.M. Learning to Identify Nonverbal Sounds: An Application of a Computer as a Teaching Machine. *Journal of the Acoustical Society of America*, 1962, *34*(7), pp. 928, 935.

Taber, J.I., Glaser, R. & Schaefer, H.H. *Learning and Programmed Instruction*. Reading, Mass.: Addison-Wesley Publishing Co., Inc., 1965.

Ugelow, A. Motivation and the Automation of Training, a Literature Review. Final Report. Behavioral Sciences Laboratory, 6570th Aerospace Medical Research Laboratory, Aerospace Medical Division, Air Force Systems Command, Wright-Patterson Air Force Base, Ohio, Technical Documentary Report No. MRL-TDR-62-15, March 1962.

White, R.W. Motivation Reconsidered: The Concept of Competence. *Psychological Review*, 1959, *66*(5), pp. 297-333.

Wittrock, M.C. & Twelker, P.A. Prompting and Feedback in the Learning, Retention and Transfer of Concepts. *British Journal of Educational Psychology*, 1964, *34*(1), pp. 10-18.

Woodruff, A.B., Faltz, C. & Wagner, D. Effects of Learner Characteristics on Programed Learning Performance. *Psychology in the Schools*, 1966, *3*(1), pp. 72-77.

Comprehensive Instructional Mission-Systems for Universities

Lawrence E. Fraley

Instructional system technology in the academic arena has as its prime function a total system approach to instructional development. Currently this endeavor is typically manifested in projects associated with establishing new instructional facilities and methods, often in a direct attack on stagnated classroom lecture approaches. Instructional technology organizations are being created which are intended to do either all or some combination of the following things: design instructional systems for courses or blocks of courses, design the associated learning activities, design the materials for those activities, produce the materials, interface the system with its target population, manage the on-going instruction, evaluate the results and recycle the instruction.

The actual production of operational instructional systems for courses of instruction depends on a fully functional, total system approach to instructional development. The total system approach demands that all necessary resources be applied to the overall system, that these resources (men, money, materials, machines, facilities, ideas, etc.) all become intrinsic elements of the system. The total resources required are marshalled and integrated into the system.

The era of technology has proven the validity of the system concept in organizing projects to solve problems. It should no longer be a seriously questioned notion that the total system approach yields significant increases in time efficiency, cost efficiency and product quality. If one professes a sincere desire for these characteristics in new instructional developments, then there needs to be a willingness to reorganize resources around the mission-oriented system concept.

Instructional system creation and operation is one long, continuous process. And it is a "system" which best accommodates a "process."

At the present time the resources for instructional system development at most universities are quite scattered. Instead of being grouped around the institution's prime objectives (missions), the resources have instead been doled out to various relatively independent and autonomous protectorates within the university.

Responsibility for instruction has been slipped under the closed doors of faculty offices and classrooms, wherein there is frequently a pitiful dearth of qualifications which have anything to do with instruction.

Lawrence E. Fraley is an instructional technologist, College of Human Resources and Education, West Virginia University, Morgantown.

The philosophy behind the parcelling out of these resources was, of course, related to the desire for efficiency. The various resources simply went to those elements which, by tradition or solid qualifications, were deemed most able to guard, preserve and use them. But it must be noted that this unsystematic dispersion of resources occurred because, at the time, there was no mission-oriented, total system approach to instructional development with which to integrate resources or around which to reorganize them.

It is now time for the universities to delineate their missions (instruction in this case being a prime one) and create major systems directed along the thrusts of those primary missions. The available assorted resources of the universities could then be fed directly into those systems and integrated in a way that would insure their efficient application toward the attainment of system goals. Modern instructional needs cannot feasibly be fulfilled by ad hoc committee actions or by the loose consortiums so frequently used in academia to protect the interest of assorted autonomies. The problems now demand the technological approach of total mission-oriented systems.

A university is typically not a very system-conscious organization. Although a university has many goals and has many functions to perform, there tends to be a lack of specifically organized missions involving specifically designed systems into which all necessary resources are directed to facilitate specific processes in order to overcome specific problems. The system approach to problem solving is often passed over in the university in favor of the pretechnological approaches of consortiums, ad-hocracies and politically competitive foraging for resources. In an earlier unpublished paper, I wrote the following lament of a frustrated system technologist trying to work in a university setting:

> First, one of its primary functions is defined to be instruction. However, no comprehensive system is developed to accommodate the process of instruction. No mission is organized to accomplish instruction. Instead, the responsibility for instruction is endlessly fragmented and scattered among all of the content specialists. These are the people who know about rocks, music, grammar, law, math, and things like that, but not necessarily about instruction.
>
> Next, many of the key resources for instruction are divided up and doled out to various autonomous little units for preservation and safekeeping. This is because there is no comprehensive mission or instructional system to which they can be applied. Television is put at one place, document production at another, facilities design and maintenance at another, budget control elsewhere, data processing someplace else, equipment maintenance and repair at still another place, and other media wherever you can find them. Those charged with instruction are then told that this resource is here, that resource is there, the other resource is someplace else, etc. And lots of luck!

The frustrations expressed by this statement often are not understood within the university because, ironically, many of the nonsystem dispersions of system-needed resources were actually intended by the university to be useful centralization moves—moves in pursuit of the same efficiencies that are benefits of the very system approaches which they prevent.

Within universities, the centralizations of resources are often around (1) pools of content, (2) geographic locations or (3) existing missions other than those for which the resources should be allocated. Technologically speaking, resources are most efficiently used when centralized around *processes;* that is, applied to the systems designed to facilitate specific processes such as the process of instruction.

An example of resources needed in one mission-system being allocated to a different mission-system would be the shift of instructional materials production capabilities to such service units as the university publication facility. These units have the primary mission of producing high-volume university publications; they do not ordinarily recruit instructional specialists, or others specialized in the design and production of instructional systems or materials. Yet because there has traditionally been no comprehensive system organized to facilitate the instructional process, many instructional resources have had to be appended to such scattered service units for want of a more appropriate place to put them.

An example of geographic centralizations would be the simple pools such as motor pools or the old audiovisual equipment pools. These usually represent a lack of any specific organized mission-oriented system into which these resources could efficiently be incorporated. Pools are certainly not always undesirable, but they are frequently symptoms of nonmission-system approaches rather than parts of any such systems.

An example of the centralization of system-needed resources around pools of content is the allocation of instructional development resources to traditional academic departments. These departments are frequently not able to efficiently incorporate instructional development resources because they have no instructional system into which they can feed such resources. Most academic departments have little or no expertise in either instructional system design or instructional materials design; they have almost no instructional materials production capability; they have little, if any, structure for instructional management beyond teachers with some graduate student aides; they have little or no systematic data collection and performance analysis of their instruction; they have no repair and maintenance capability; and, finally, most academic departments have instructional facilities suited for little more than assembling groups of students to hear professors or other students talk. The accumulative experience of most university faculty members has been within departmental settings such as this.

About all that the academic departments have is an assortment of content specialists and the responsibility for instruction. What they lack is an adequate capability for determining, accommodating and facilitating the instructional process.

In the long run, academic departments will contribute their content expertise as a resource into major instructional mission-systems. In the immediate future, while instructional responsibilities remain dispersed among multitudes of academic departments, there must be instructional development mission-systems capable of assisting those departments in making a quantum jump transition from wherever they are now to the more significant, efficient and successful approaches of the technological present.

A number of universities around the nation are now turning out well-trained and highly competent instructional system technologists who can be assembled to work in this field. They are not really dangerous radicals; they are simply trying to bring the effectiveness of technology to an arena which has long tended to shun it and which is deteriorating for lack of it. They are accused by some of trying to give process more significance than content, but process already *has* more significance than content. Content has transient relevance to situations along the evolving continuum, but it is process by which values are actualized, and that *is* more significant. Technologists are alert to this distinction.

Below are three currently advocated schemes for establishing the locus of responsibility for instruction (within universities). Instructional *system* development is accommodated successfully only by the third plan, because the first two lack the efficiency to keep the required system elements above their operational critical minimums.

1. The responsibility for instructional development could be pushed downward into the various academic departments to be presided over by the pools of content-knowledgeable academicians that reside there.

2. Instructional development responsibilities could be placed in some separate organizational entity or office, but without any integral operational capability. This approach would have production, operational and evaluation functions fragmented and scattered among many different university service units, all of whom have primary missions other than the specifics of instructional development.

3. Instructional system technology could be an integral university-wide, mission-oriented system, operating as a division under the direction of the university president, and providing the locus of application for instructional improvement resources. This system would be integral and capable of producing, managing and researching prototype instructional systems.

Alternative I: Instructional Responsibility in Academic Departments

The first alternative, which leaves instructional development responsibilities in the hands of the academic departments, has the basic flaw of leaving the decision making in the hands of persons not qualified in most of the areas of expertise required. Academicians have been notorious for failing to realize the scope and characteristics of the mission required to accomplish substantial instructional development projects at a level commensurate with the current state of the art. Thus we find individual colleges and departments plunging naively into the technological system approach.

Often this is done by simply adding a staff person who has some competence in a related area such as educational psychology, media, system theory, instructional materials design, etc. The error here is that one man finds himself expected to substitute for an entire mission-system. The task is typically something like this: Design and develop a suitable learning environment, design instructional systems for courses, design the associated learning activities, design the materials for those activities, produce the materials, interface the system with its target population, manage the on-going instruction, evaluate the results and recycle the instruction. Of course, nothing much is going to happen, and in some cases it may be years later before it comes to be understood *why* so little has been accomplished.

Academic subdivisions, many of which were not even successful in fully exploiting the old audiovisual aids concepts, do not have the expertise and resources to independently operate in the sophisticated and complex world of instructional system technology.

Some universities respond to this problem by providing big instructional development service units to which the faculty members can resort for the vast assistance which they need. The process of instructional system development, however, is so big and complex that the faculty member may find himself unprepared to play the role of leader of a large, professional mission team. The efficiency of such a sophisticated team may be significantly reduced both by lack of adequate leadership from the faculty member and by having to protect itself from his poor judgments. Most college faculty members are qualified to join the instructional development mission team as content experts, but are not adequately prepared to assume responsibilities in the equally important areas of learning theory, system analysis, media, communications, materials production, etc.

The problem here is a simple one. Instructional system development is a technological team effort, and the academic content specialist has a place on the team. But according to the traditional academic approach, such persons are supposed to enjoy some automatic favored position of control and leadership because of their professorial status, whether qualified for it or not. Just as no Black man was once deemed fit to sit forward on a bus, no instructional technologist has been deemed fit to take control of the instructional process from the traditional content area academician. Thus there are many excellent, professional instructional design teams whose potential is partially wasted because control resides in the hands of persons who are not adequately qualified to exploit the organization's potential. It is analogous to placing an ordinary Sunday afternoon private pilot in the cockpit of a Boeing 707.

Instruction belongs in the hands of instructional system technologists. Good instruction is not an art; it is a science; its disciplinarians are instructional technology theorists and instructional engineers. Content specialists in other academic fields enjoy no valid *a priori* qualification on the basis of their content area specialty to have anything to do with the instructional process beyond contributing that content to an instructional mission-system at the appropriate time and place.

Alternative II: Instructional Responsibility in a Separate Nonoperational Unit

This second alternative for locating the responsibility for instruction within a university is a nonsystem solution to a system problem, an approach which universities and governments sometimes seem determined to perpetuate *ad infinitum;* that solution violates the basic principle that responsibility and capability should not be separated. The break-up of intimately cooperative and symbiotic working relationships in a mission-oriented team, which would be a consequence of this second alternative, is simply a system-destructive scheme. What is proposed here can only be likened to the suggestion that it would be just as possible for an administrator to operate if his secretary's office were located in another part of the city.

If one is a system-senstive and system-conscious person, then it is easily realized that organizational structure and administrative prerogative are also critical, internal system resources and that their divorce from the system is indeed system-destructive. But even if these resources are included in the system, the loss of operational capability through the dispersion of other system functions renders the mission impotent.

One further point must be made emphatically clear here:

Instructional system development is a creative team process and its products do *not* form by the accretion of externally acquired services or elements. They are synthesized through the mutual, often simultaneous, system-sensitive inputs of all team members functioning as a dynamic whole. The products emerge qualitatively greater than any one of the members could conceptualize.

Workable organizational structures should evolve around the functional milestones in the instructional development process: design, production, operation and evaluation. In this way the organizational structure reflects the conceptual framework underlying the instructional development mission which it facilitates. To disorganize or scatter such a unit's structure can be construed as a repudiation of the concepts of comprehensive instructional system technology which such an organization's structure must be custom designed to support.

One of the most notable characteristics of instructional development efforts in general is the great difficulty which all of them seem to experience in gaining an initial foothold in a new university. The encroachment of technology as a philosophy into the traditionally nontechnological academic arena is frequently met with fear, distrust and entrenched resistance at all levels. This is especially true when the encroachment is into areas that for hundreds of years have been jealously guarded as the private domain of the academic content specialists.

However, this resistance will give way to change. That is not now a serious issue. But neither is *how* this will happen, and herein lies a truly significant issue. The die is cast; the whole evolutionary course of our culture brings us to this: Instruction as a process *will* be approached as a technological problem; there *will* be a technological quest for cost efficiency, time efficiency and product quality in instruction; the necessary resources of all kinds *will* be marshalled in mission-oriented systems to do a better job with the instructional process. These are fundamental and obvious generalities.

The more relevant questions are simply *who* will be doing these things, where will be the loci of leadership, and from which institutions will the long-awaited answers be emanating. It is already much too late to be first, but not too late to join the first wave. Those who counsel delay are typically characterized by having vested interests in the status quo, or else they are too imperceptive to appreciate a valuable opportunity when the time is right to move ahead.

Alternative III: Instructional Responsibility in an Institution-Wide Instructional Mission-System

This brings us finally to the last option, the establishment of the instructional development mission under the direct guidance and control of the university president. The power and the significance inherent in the potential of this mission-system is too great for it to be any place else. That simply is where it belongs—all of it, the entire mission-system, integral, with its operational capabilities intact. Instructional system technology is clearly a university-level and university-wide function. All moves to bury it elsewhere are to be perceived as moves to stifle the concept, or at least stifle its effects.

The set of concepts and supporting organizational structures of instructional system technology represent a substantial quantum jump from the old approaches to the problems which they attack. This gives the technological approach so much more potential for successes than the traditional approaches enjoy that defensive resistance arises from many sources. Stated simply, because of the way that an instructional mission-system continuously evaluates and recycles its product instructional systems, its on-going operations acquire a self-validating character. Flaws in its products tend to be automatically exposed and system-corrected as a normal internal system function. This is instruction as a science.

A perceptive person can see that such an approach to instruction as is being described here also tends to reveal and expose not only the flaws in its own products, but also many of the flaws inherent in what others have done using other approaches to instruction. Instructional system technology must be constituted to reveal instructional inadequacies, and the concomitant spill-over in such revelations to other instructional endeavors is in many instances viewed as threatening. In a mission-system that is cranked up for the rapid operational testing and modification of theories of instruction, validity and accountability need not remain the elusive and latent Holy Grail to be endlessly (and

ineffectively) pursued by academicians as a career-long game.

Implications for Academic Departments

Obviously, the purposes and responsibilities of traditionally organized academic departments must change. They were organized around content, and the technological approaches that are now required are organized around processes. The typical academic department is not capable of accommodating the instructional process; yet, in most universities, that is where many of the instructional resources and responsibilities continue to be deposited. Not only are the academic departments dysfunctional in the instructional process, but their divisive compartmentalizing of the content inhibits the easy scholarly pursuit of knowledge that cuts across the content area border lines.

Research, another of the traditional responsibilities of academic departments, has been operated more as a license than a responsibility. Academic departments, operating more as scholarly gentlemen's prestige clubs than as research mission teams, have tended to subsidize assorted semi-private, personal research often on a release-time, scholarly hobby basis. Although the research has generally, if not always, had some relevancy to the legitimate concerns of the department or to its field of discipline, it has remained true that most academic departments have been no more systematic about their research endeavors than they have been about their instruction.

There is a need to reorganize resources around research missions. The instructional mission-systems previously discussed in this article incorporate their own system-related research and evaluation functions as on-going internal system elements. This continuous system-intrinsic applied research provides the continuous feedback for the recycling of the instructional process. It is very questionable whether the remaining responsibilities for a university's applied and basic research endeavors should remain dispersed among assorted academic departments. It is time to consider the establishment of major university-wide research mission-systems to accommodate, facilitate and integrate the research process. The content area of particular research projects is not significant enough to justify its being the locus for the allocation and concentration of all research resources.

Universities simply need to reorganize around systems to accomplish their missions, instead of around loose aggregates of enclaves more suited to the protection and preservation of outmoded, professional academic life styles. □

Psychological Background and Rationale for Instructional Design

John F. Feldhusen and Donald J. Treffinger

In all instructional situations, certain important common problems confront the instructor or designer of educational materials. These problems include: clarification, for oneself and for the students, of the objectives of the instruction (i.e., deciding what should be learned); selection and administration of instructional activities which will help students attain the objectives; assessment of the outcomes of instruction to determine if the students have attained the objectives; and production of learning at a level or depth which will enable the students to retain and to use what has been learned in other settings and on subsequent occasions. These general problems may be summarized under the headings: *Analysis of Concepts and Principles, Objectives* and *Instruction.*

In approaching these three major problems, the following questions arise:

(1) *Analysis of Concepts and Principles*

How does the instructor analyze the concepts and principles to be taught so that essential attributes and interrelationships among them are specified and so that suitable examples and nonexamples are identified?

(2) *Objectives*

How does the instructor then formulate objectives, use them in developing instruction, and communicate them to students in order to evoke maximum student motivation and guidance in attaining the objectives?

(3) *Instruction*

What instructional techniques can we use to assure thorough learning, long-range retention and maximum transfer effects or usefulness?

The first problem encountered in designing instruction is that of analyzing the concepts and principles to be taught. Analysis of concepts and principles really implies identification of all the ideational content, the

John F. Feldhusen is professor of education and psychology at Purdue University, chairman of the Educational Psychology Section, and director of the Graduate Educational Research Training Program. Donald J. Treffinger is assistant professor of educational psychology at Purdue University.

knowledge, or the information which must be taught. Thus, it is closely related to the statement of objectives at the first level of the *Taxonomy of Educational Objectives, Cognitive Domain* (Bloom, *et al.*, 1956), the knowledge level. However, since level two, comprehension, also involves use of knowledge or information in higher level cognitive operations, the analysis of the ideational content of instruction is also really relevant to that level of the *Taxonomy,* too.

Within this first problem we can identify four steps which will facilitate instructional design. *The first step involves identification of the major information, ideas, concepts and principles to be taught.* This and the subsequent steps to be described next should precede the writing of objectives. In a sense this first step is developing a list of topics to be taught. Enthusiasts of behavioral objectives often advocate that the first step in instructional design is to write objectives. We argue that it is better to start by analyzing the ideational content of instruction. If we wish to teach a unit on cybernetics we might be identifying the topics or concepts which we believe are essential for the level of instruction and the readiness level of the students. Careful delineation of the topics might result in the following list:

> input
> output
> servomechanism
> throughput
> types of machines
> man-computer analogies
> a definition and illustration of cybernetics

The second step involves *identification of the essential attributes of each topic or concept.* As illustrations, we will begin with the concept of servomechanisms. Markle and Tiemann (1970) argue that identification of essential attributes of concepts is as crucial as and parallel to task analysis in analysis of performance prior to instruction. They have also developed a training program (Markle and Tiemann, 1969) for development of skill in conceptual analysis in instructional designers. Attribute analysis requires clear discrimination of essential and nonessential attributes and appropriate exemplars of the concept and attributes. For the concept of servomechanism, an essential attribute or characteristic, denoted by function, is goal seeking. A second attribute is control of a power source or function. That is, a servomechanism serves as a control agent. Thirdly, it has the attribute of facilitating the process of corrective feedback which keeps a mechanism directed to the goal.

In teaching the subconcept of servomechanism with the three attributes identified we are next faced with the task (third step) of selecting appropriate exemplars. A torpedo with a built-in target-seeking device which helps to continually correct its course in pursuit of a moving target is one good exemplar. The first attribute of goal seeking is clearly present. The goal is the target. The second attribute, control of a power source or function, is also present in that the servomechanism in the torpedo does control the functions of the torpedo. Thirdly, the servomechanism enables the torpedo to correct its path from time to time in pursuit of a target.

A comparable exemplar in human behavior could be found in the complex behavior of reaching for and picking up a coin. Here the servomechanism, based in neural structure, guides the hand to the goal, the coin; it controls the energy or power source which moves the hand; and through eye-hand coordination provides constant corrective feedback when the hand strays from the path to the coin.

The fourth and final step in analyzing the concepts and principles to be taught is to *organize them into an appropriate hierarchical arrangement.* Gagne's conception (1970) of learning hierarchies provides clear guidelines for this stage of the analysis. Essentially, the task here is to decide which subordinate skills or abilities (Gagne refers to them as sets) are prerequisite to the learning of any higher order skill or ability.

In our illustration of instruction on cybernetics the hierarchy may emerge as follows (one moves from bottom to top):

Define
cybernetics.

Define
servomechanism.

| Describe the input function in man and machine. | Describe the throughput function in machine. | Describe the output function in man and machine. |

With the hierarchy established on at least a temporary basis, we are ready to proceed to the second problem, specifying objectives.

Objectives

Conceptualizing or formulating objectives is certainly a crucial problem in designing instruction. Gagne (1965) suggested three reasons for the importance of specifying objectives. First, knowledge of the end-product performances which students must learn provides a guide for the instructor in planning instructional activities, particularly the exercise or practice activities. Second, concern for testing or measurement absolutely demands that the instructor know the objectives of instruction. Third, ensuring that the objectives are known and clear to the students may heighten student motivation and encourage students to join actively in pursuit of the objectives. If the students do not know the objectives, they must remain passive receivers of instruction or "wander about" aimlessly in the learning environment.

The first problem under the heading of objectives is that of deciding on the cognitive and/or affective levels of the knowledge which must be taught. The *Taxonomy of Educational Objectives: Cognitive Domain* by Bloom *et al.* (1956) describes cognitive learning outcomes which the authors assumed would be common

ends of instruction in many educational settings. At the base of the *Taxonomy* is a level called "knowledge." The higher levels of the *Taxonomy,* in ascending order, are "comprehension," "application," "analysis," "synthesis" and "evaluation." These five higher levels of learning outcomes are described as "intellectual abilities and skills." It seems likely that some kinds of ideas, information or knowledge will often underlie our teaching of higher order cognitive skills and abilities. The ideas, information, or knowledge will probably be the cognitive or mental guides which students should learn to use in directing their own performance of higher order skills. *The Taxonomy of Educational Objectives, Affective Domain* by Krathwohl *et al.* (1964) describes five levels of affective functioning, which can be used as guides in formulating objectives related to interest, attitudes, values and philosophy. The five levels are receiving, responding, valuing, organization and characterization by a value or value complex.

The second problem under the heading of objectives is that of *writing* or *specifying objectives.* Mager (1962) defined three essential ingredients of a well-stated objective. First, it denotes or describes an action representing what a student will be able to do when he has completed instruction. Second, it describes the conditions, settings or circumstances under which the student will perform whatever he is supposed to learn. And third, it suggests a criterion level of performance which will be acceptable. The following is an example of a well-stated objective:

The student will be able to identify at least 90 percent of the punctuation errors in a sample of descriptive prose.

The action denoted is "identifying," the criterion is "identifying 90 percent of the errors," and the conditions of performance are specified to be "in a sample of descriptive prose." Kibler, Barker and Miles (1970) have also proposed a useful distinction, between *planning objectives,* which contain all the elements just described, and *informational objectives,* which are briefer, and emphasize only the desired terminal behavior. The former are used in instructional design; the latter are used by the teacher or instructional designer to communicate the goal to the learner.

One useful procedure in writing objectives is to be guided by an adaptation of the test maker's specification chart. The test specification chart typically has two axes or dimensions: (1) the content or subject matter topics, concepts, principles, etc., and (2) the levels of objectives. For the latter, the six levels of the *Taxonomy of Educational Objectives, Cognitive Domain* might be used.* Figure 1 is an illustration using as subject matter our topic of cybernetics. The writer of objectives begins with a blank chart but with topics listed on the

---

*Of course, the five levels of the affective taxonomy might be used in the same way, or even the five cognitive operations defined in Guilford's (1967) structure of intellect model (cognition, memory, convergent production, divergent production and evaluation). The critical point here is really that the teacher or designer is considering psychological processes as well as the logical structure of the material to be taught.

Figure 1

Topic	Knowledge	Comprehension	Application	Analysis	Synthesis	Evaluation
Input	Define input	Describe the input function in man and machine				
Throughput	Define throughput	Describe the throughput function in man and machine				
Output	Define output	Describe the output function in man and machine				
Feedback	Define feedback	Describe the feedback function in man and machine				
Servomechanism		Describe the interrelationship among parts of a servomechanism		Given a description of a servomechanism, identify the parts and interrelationship among them	Design a servomechanism to guide or control teacher behavior	Evaluate several models as true or inadequate servomechanisms
Cybernetics			Describe the man-machine analogies in pairs of given mechanisms			

vertical axis and the six levels of the *Cognitive Taxonomy* on the horizontal axis. He begins by asking himself, for the first topic, input, "Do I wish to formulate an objective at the knowledge level?" If he decides in the affirmative, he writes it. Then he proceeds horizontally to each higher level, and decides whether he wishes to formulate an objective at that level. The blanks in the chart simply indicate that there was no interest in an objective at that level for the given topic.†

This specification chart for objectives serves the heuristic function of systematically reminding the objectives writer of all his topics for which objectives must be formulated and of all the cognitive levels at which he might consider writing them. Of course, it should be noted that, in developing the learning hierarchy as proposed by Gagne, the objectives are virtually completely written or formulated in the process of formulating the hierarchy.

The third problem under the heading of objectives is *how to communicate the objectives to students to elicit motivation to learn or to attain the objectives.* Carpenter and Haddan (1964) suggested that the objectives of a unit or course of instruction should be presented or listed for the students in clear, understandable language. Instructors should note the value of things to be learned in future instruction and/or out-of-class experience. It also seems likely that some discussion or exchange between the students and the instructor would often be needed to clarify objectives and the value of attaining them and to help students formulate additional objectives more closely related to their own unique needs and interests. When objectives are finally well articulated, student achievement, or learning, will be significantly greater than it is in instructional situations in which the objectives remain ambiguous or unknown (Mager, 1962; Mager and Clark, 1963; Miles, Kibler and Pettigrew, 1967).

Instructional designers and teachers continue to argue the merits of explicit statements of objectives. Kibler, Barker and Miles (1970) have reviewed the pros and cons of explicitly stated objectives and conclude that explicit statements lead to increased instructional effectiveness.

However, it seems likely that in some instructional situations, particularly in mathematics and science, the performances to be learned are so well understood by instructional designers and students that explicit statements of planning or informational objectives may not be necessary. In teaching conversion of temperatures for centigrade to Fahrenheit in science or solving pairs of equations in algebra, the skill or performance is so well identified that an explicit statement may be redundant. However, the English teacher who comes to Chaucer or the social studies teacher who must teach protective tariffs may have no such certainty about what students should learn or how they would have to demonstrate their learning. Thus, careful attention to the formulation of planning and informational objectives would be especially necessary in these cases.*

---

†This raises, of course, the interesting question of whether or not there can be any "gaps" in any row of the chart. Since the cognitive taxonomy purports to be hierarchically arranged, inclusion of intent to write an objective at one level would imply the necessity of objectives at each level. However, research which has been conducted to examine this problem indicates that performance at higher levels may often not be dependent on lower level achievements (Smith, 1965; Smith, 1968).

*In this article we have assumed that the instructional designer, teacher, or programmer is someone other than the student himself. Many recent analyses of American education (e.g., Kohl, 1969; Holt, 1969; Rogers, 1969) have taken a different and critical view. In general they stress the need for self-determination and self-direction on the part of the student. While the implications of their views for our approach and extensive analysis of possible applications of our approach within their framework are of considerable interest, they are beyond the scope of the present article.

Instruction

If we agree that there may be some need to teach information or knowledge, how best can this be done? This is the third general problem with which this article is concerned. Ausubel (1963) argued that "reception learning" is most efficient in transmitting knowledge, even though it has been popular to ridicule it as rote and passive learning in the last two decades. In meaningful reception learning the instructor selects and organizes the knowledge to be taught and presents it to the student in some appropriate verbal or symbolic form. Ausubel contended that the learner's retention and future use of the knowledge can be greatly increased if "advance organizers" or "subsuming concepts" are first taught to the student as a kind of scaffolding for the main ideas to be taught later. The "advance organizer" is a general concept which is taught at the outset of instruction and which serves as a system into which the ideas which are to be taught later can be fitted meaningfully. Thus, if one wishes to teach something about motivation, learning would be improved if the instructor first taught a general framework of ideas. An example in teaching about motivation might be to teach first a general framework, such as Maslow's (1943) hierarchy of needs, which the students could use as a conceptual framework to take in and understand the later ideas about motivation which will be presented to them.

From a position which is almost diametrically opposite to the one set forth by Ausubel, Bruner (1966) argued that learning of knowledge and skills will be most effective only if the student is *actively engaged* in discovering ideas or generalizations which the instructor wants him to learn. Bruner acknowledged that not all knowledge needs to be discovered (1966, p. 96) but yet contended that there is little value in giving or presenting information to students (1966, p. 94). The most important ends of learning, in his view, are intellectual skills, and these are acquired only through active pursuit of understanding in problem situations. To be sure, the student may have to learn how to acquire, process and use information (1966, p. 28), but above all he needs to become autonomous in using his own intellectual resources in solving problems. He should not be or remain dependent upon the instructor.

"Reception" and "discovery" are concepts which provide useful guides for planning instruction in short-term settings. The instructor who plans to design courses using these concepts will have to study thoroughly the literature of this now well-developed field. (Several suggested works are Cronbach, 1966; Gagne, 1966; Shulman & Keislar, 1966; and Wittrock, 1966.) The payoff in improved instruction, increased student achievement, and better application outside or beyond the classroom will more than justify his efforts.

Summary

In this article we have suggested the instructional designer should begin by doing a thorough analysis of the concepts and principles to be taught prior to formulating objectives. Secondly, he should formulate the objectives following guidelines suggested by Mager, Bloom, Krathwohl and others and employ an objectives specification chart as a heuristic device to assure adequate coverage of content and all levels of the taxonomies. Thirdly, he must decide on a method of instruction. Discovery learning techniques, as well as traditional didactic methods, should be employed. ☐

References

Ausubel, D.P. *The Psychology of Meaningful Verbal Learning.* New York: Grune and Stratton, 1963.

Bloom, B.S. *et al. Taxonomy of Educational Objectives, Cognitive Domain.* New York: David McKay, 1956.

Bruner, J.S. *Toward a Theory of Instruction.* Cambridge, Massachusetts: Harvard University Press, 1966.

Carpenter, F. & Haddan, E.E. *Systematic Application of Psychology to Education.* New York: Macmillan, 1964.

Cronbach, L.J. The Logic of Experiments on Discovery. In L.S. Shulman & E.R. Keislar (Eds.) *Learning by Discovery: A Critical Appraisal.* Chicago: Rand-McNally, 1966, 77-92.

Gagne, R.M. The Analysis of Instructional Objectives for the Design of Instruction. In R. Glaser (Ed.) *Teaching Machines and Programed Learning, II: Data and Directions.* Washington, D.C.: National Education Association, 1965, 21-65.

Gagne, R.M. *Varieties of Learning and the Concept of Discovery.* In L.S. Shulman & E.R. Keislar (Eds.) *Learning by Discovery: A Critical Appraisal.* Chicago: Rand-McNally, 1966, 135-150.

Gagne, R.M. *The Conditions of Learning,* New York: Holt, Rinehart and Winston, 1970 (second edition).

Guilford, J.P. *The Nature of Human Intelligence.* New York: McGraw-Hill, 1967.

Holt, J. *The Underachieving School.* New York: Dell, 1969.

Kibler, R.J., Barker, L. & Miles, D.R. *Behavioral Objectives and Instruction.* Boston: Allyn and Bacon, 1970.

Kohl, H.R. *The Open Classroom.* New York: Vintage, 1969.

Krathwohl, D.R. *et al. Taxonomy of Educational Objectives, Affective Domain.* New York: David McKay, 1964.

Mager, R.F. *Preparing Instructional Objectives.* San Francisco: Fearon, 1962.

Mager, R.F. & Clark, C. Explorations in Student-Controlled Instruction. *Psychological Reports,* 1963, *13,* 7-16.

Markle, S.M. & Tiemann, P.W. Conceptual Learning and Instructional Design. *British Journal of Educational Technology,* 1970, *1,* 1-12.

Markle, S.M. & Tiemann, P.W. *Scripts for Really Understanding Concepts.* Chicago: Tiemann Associates, 1969.

Maslow, A.H. A Theory of Human Motivation. *Psychological Review,* 1943, *50,* 370-396.

Miles, D.T., Kibler, R.J. & Pettigrew, L.E. The Effects of Study Questions on College Students' Test Performances. *Psychology in the Schools,* 1967, *4,* 25-26.

Rogers, C.R. *Freedom to Learn.* Columbus, Ohio: Charles E. Merrill, 1969.

Shulman, L.S. & Keislar, E.R. (Eds.) *Learning by Discovery: A Critical Appraisal.* Chicago: Rand-McNally, 1966.

Smith, R.B. An Analysis of the Scalability of the Knowledge and Comprehension Levels of the *Taxonomy of Educational Objectives: Cognitive Domain.* Paper presented at the annual meeting of the National Council on Measurement in Education, Chicago, 1965.

Smith, R.B. A Discussion on an Attempt at Constructing Reproducible Item Sets. *Journal of Educational Measurement,* 1968, *5,* 55-60.

Wittrock, M.C. The Learning by Discovery Hypothesis. In L.S. Shulman & E.R. Keislar (Eds.) *Learning by Discovery: A Critical Appraisal.* Rand-McNally, 1966, 33-75.

A Basic Difference Between Educational and Training Systems

Robert Fromer

The world of education and training is currently undergoing a strong revolutionary movement. This movement is not characterized by innovations in the application of special hardware, nor by novel architectural designs of educational institutions or training centers; rather, its **most significant** aspect is the current attention being directed toward the "systems approach" to designing and developing education and training. This is supported by the many recent articles in educational journals on systematic procedures for developing such programs (Harmon, 1968; Gagné, 1968; McIntosh, 1968; Merrill, 1968) and by numerous recent books and manuals covering such topics as "instructional systems," "instructional objectives," "instructional technology," etc.

Most of the procedures described and discussed in the current literature are based upon a general systems development model. They all include elements such as problem definition; statement of objectives; selection of methods and techniques for achieving the stated objectives; identification of appropriate content; design and development of a system of personnel, hardware and software to implement the methods, techniques and content designed to achieve the selected objectives; design and development of measurement instruments to evaluate and diagnose the system's effectiveness, and a feedback control system to optimize system effectiveness.

Most of the above elements are the same for either the design of educational systems or training systems. There is one group of elements, however, where a clear distinction between training and educational system design should be made. The purpose of this article is to clarify this distinction.

The distinction has to do with statement of objectives. It is an area that has recently received a great amount of attention, but one that this author believes is accompanied by a great amount of confusion. One problem, perhaps, is that different

Robert Fromer is senior scientist, Education Systems, Computer Sciences Institute of Computer Sciences Corporation, El Segundo, California.

authors have used a variety of terms to represent the same concept (more or less), and some have used similar or identical terms to represent different concepts. It is not my intention here to suggest a standardization of terms. Rather, I would like to point to the distinction between two general classes of objectives and their relationships to educational and training systems.

As a prelude to discussing these two classes of objectives, I would like to indicate that their distinction is not based upon factors such as cognitive vs. sensory-motor or covert vs. overt behavior. Their distinction will be based upon their task specificity vs. task generality and whether they represent descriptions of tasks or of the knowledges and skills necessary to perform tasks. To avoid confusion, I will refer to the two classes of objectives as Class I and Class II.

Class I objectives are task-specific. They are behavioral descriptions of tasks that are performed in meeting the requirements of a specific job. Indeed, these objectives are so specific that they differ for different examples within a single job classification. For example, "Computer Programmer" is a single job classification; however, the specific tasks performed by an IBM computer programmer are different from those performed by a Univac computer programmer. Variations in software and hardware result in different sets of Class I objectives. The extreme task-specificity involved in generating Class I objectives represents its major distinction from Class II objectives.

Class II objectives are behavioral descriptions of the knowledges and skills required to perform the tasks included in Class I objectives. In other words, Class II objectives represent the knowledge and skill prerequisites for the task performance represented by Class I objectives. For example, developing computer programs in Fortran might be a task required of a specific computer programmer's job. This task can be analyzed into a number of knowledge and skill components, such as, knowledge of Fortran statements, their functions and the rules of syntax; flowchart interpretation; translation of flowchart symbols to Fortran statements, and selection of appropriate statements, program execution, program editing and program debugging. Some of the knowledges and skills are fairly specific to the task from which they are derived; others, however, are quite general, and would be useful for the performance of a large variety of tasks.

Much confusion concerning the distinction between the two classes of objectives is related to the fact they both must be stated in behavioral terms (action verbs, object nouns and qualifiers); because of this, they are often confused with one another. The purpose of behavioral descriptions is to enable an unbiased observer to determine objectively whether or not an objective has been achieved. Despite their similar appearance, however, there is an important difference between Class I and Class II objectives — the former describes job-related tasks, the latter, knowledges and skills necessary for task performance.

A specific knowledge or skill represented by a Class II objective may be related to more than one task represented by a Class I objective. Indeed, a single Class II objective could be related to a very large number of Class I objectives. For example, a skill such as adding digits is related to many tasks performed within a single job, or even across job classifications. Indeed, it is difficult to think of a cognitive, perceptual, or motor skill that is not related to many tasks. Also, the performance of a specific task represented by a Class I objective may require the acquisition of a variety of skills and knowledges.

The final point of this paper is to describe the relationship of the two classes of objectives to educational systems and training systems. Stated directly and simply, Class I objectives are much more meaningful for designing and developing a training system than for an educational system. This is so, because the purpose of a training system is to produce individuals capable of performing the tasks required to accomplish a specific job or set of jobs, whereas one of the main purposes of an educational system is to prepare individuals for a large variety of possible jobs, some of which may not yet exist.

In order for a training system to achieve its goals, both classes of objectives must be identified and defined. First, the Class I objectives are identified through an appropriate job analysis; then, the Class II objectives are identified through an analysis of the Class I objectives. There are a variety of analytical procedures that can be used for this purpose (see Cotterman, 1959; Folley, 1964; Miller, 1963; Paulson, 1967); it is not within the scope of this paper to present them here. After both classes of objectives have been identified, instructional methods and techniques are then developed to achieve these objectives.

The problem of achieving the goals of an educational system is much more difficult. There are no specific job-related tasks that can be identified

for an educational system. The problem, then, is to identify an optimum set of knowledges and skills that will best prepare students for a very large variety of job possibilities. The problem is compounded by the fact that it is not an easy task to derive Class II objectives even when Class I objectives are available; it is much more difficult (perhaps impossible) to derive them in the absence of Class I objectives.

One possible approach to this problem would be to attempt to define those knowledges and skills that undergird the performance of the largest numbers of Class I objectives. Unfortunately, there is no body of data or system of principles that make it easy to do this. In the past, educators have made intuitive guesses in this regard; hence, the three R's. Some intuitive guesses might result in reasonably good choices, but others might be very poor, and thus very costly to society at large.

The main point to be made here is that the identification of Class I objectives is not appropriate to the development of educational systems, and a great deal of time, effort and money may be saved with this realization. The same rigor and care must be applied to preparing behavioral descriptions of Class II objectives as for Class I objectives, but the behavioral descriptions of Class II objectives are used only to permit objective assessment of knowledge and skill acquisition; they are not the end products of the educational system for which they are designed. □

References

Cotterman, T. E. **Task Classification: An Approach to Partially Ordering Information on Human Learning.** Wright-Patterson Air Force Base, Ohio: Wright Air Development Center, WADC TN 58-374, 1959 (AD 210 716).

Folley, J. D. Guidelines for Task Analysis. **USNTDC T.R. NAVTRADEVCEN.** 1218-2. June, 1964.

Gagné, Robert M. Educational Technology as Technique. **Educational Technology,** November 15, 1968, 5-13.

Harmon, Paul Developing Performance Objectives In Job Training Programs. **Educational Technology,** November 30, 1968, 11-16.

McIntosh, John H. Army Training Reexamined. **Educational Technology,** August 30, 1968, 18-19.

Merrill, M. David Components of a Cybernetic Instructional System, **Educational Technology,** April 15, 1968, 5-10.

Miller, E. E. A Classication of Learning Tasks in Conventional Language. **USAF MRL TDR.** July, 1963.

Paulson, C. F. Specifying Behavioral Objectives. **National Research Training Institute Manual.** Teaching Research, Monmouth, Oregon, 1967.

Getting with Instructional Systems and Getting Instructional Systems with It

Noel F. McInnis

There are today at least two general trends in American education which claim to be innovative.

One trend may be seen as an effort to more efficiently transmit an ever-increasing body of data to an ever-increasing number of students.

Although this trend legitimately claims the title of being innovative, it is nevertheless little more than an attempt to more effectively rationalize the traditional form of education, whose primary concern is the mastery of a body of content. The dominant elements of the educational process, including faculty, students, information and examinations, are carefully programmed to achieve maximum student attainment of predetermined, mostly symbol-manipulative, objectives.

The other innovative trend in American education is much more radical in that it attempts to devise an entirely **new form** for the educational process.

Whereas traditional education in America has emphasized the **transmission and storage** of information, the other form emphasizes the **acquisition and assimilation** of information. The differences between the transmission model of education and the acquisition model of education lie in three areas:

1) in their location of the source of initiative in the educational process
2) in their assumptions about the primary criterion for the organization of data
3) in their predominant behavioral outcomes.

In the transmission model, the initiative lies with the teacher (person, book, machine, or some combination) who presents pre-packaged information in a form which the student is expected to replicate.

In this model, the learner is viewed essentially as a recipient of education. His principal obligation is to preserve the pre-packaged information relatively intact, so it can be reproduced in its original form in response to the appropriate cue. The emphasis on maintaining the information pattern as transmitted derives from the assumption that the primary criterion of relevance for a given bit of information is its relationship to other bits of information. The dominant behavior conditioned by this model of education is manipulative — manipulative not only of information but, by extension, of everything in the environment to which information refers, including people.

In the acquisition model of education, to which more technologists should address themselves, the initiative lies primarily with the learner, who seeks information which will help him to make more sense out of himself and his various situations. In this model, the learner is viewed essentially as the **incipient** of his education. His strategy is to discover and utilize that information which can be most meaningfully related to his own particular needs to know, to do and to be. This strategy assumes that the primary criterion for the organization of data is the accumulated experience and present understanding of the learner at the moment of encounter with the information. The dominant behavior conditioned by this model of education is associative, and again is generalized beyond data and information to the human and material environment codified thereby.

I think that the wave of the future lies neither with the institution which innovates along the lines of making the transmission model of education more efficient, nor does it lie with those institutions which specialize in developing the acquisition model (or the "dialogue" model, "process" model, "learner-centered" model, whatever you want to call it). It lies, rather, with those institutions which do **both** of these things.

Noel F. McInnis is director of Educational Advancement at Kendall College, Evanston, Illinois.

89

Technology is providing the machinery for more effective transmission of data; or, if we decide to move in another direction, a technique for developing the acquisition model of learning. This is the technique of the instructional system, which can be used for either model of learning — but which has tended to be used primarily for data transmission.

Instructional systems became inevitable when we set about programming instruction, because in order to program it we had to become extremely specific. We had to be very precise in our knowledge of the capabilities of the students coming into our course, so we would know where to begin the program. We had to be very precise in defining the abilities that we wanted the student to have at the end of the course, so we would know what to put in the program to get him there. And we had to be very precise about sequencing the information in the program, in order to get the student from where he was to where we wanted him to be.

In other words, when we began to program instruction we had to face up to the old truth that "you can't get there from here."

Everybody knows that you can't get there from here. Wouldn't it be nice if everybody taught that way? Most of us teach on the basis of unfounded assumptions about the preparation and abilities of our students to receive, digest and make meaningful the information we want to give them. At best we usually start somewhere in between their present understanding and ours — we don't start with their "here" and come to our "there," we start somewhere in between.

At worst, of course, we just begin where we are at — and never relate to the students. The first ambiguous tendency which the instructional systems approach corrects is that which leads us to pitch the ball in such a way that it ends up out in left field having never approached the batter.

A second ambiguous tendency which is corrected by the instructional systems approach is that which characterizes our course objectives. The instructional systems approach to instruction makes the teacher aware of what he is doing, primarily by focusing on the purpose and the result of his instruction: behavioral change. Educators tend to be very resistant of the charge that they are in the business of changing behavior.

Yet I have never met a teacher who would declare that he intended his students to be in no way different at the end of his instruction than they were before they began. And if, in fact, we expect that students are going to be somehow different at the conclusion of our period of instruction, then we are assuming that there is going to be a change in their behavior. Some aspect of their behavior obviously is expected to change, or there is not going to be a difference.

Instruction begins to be systematic when, upon the recognition of his attempt to change behavior, the instructor asks "what behavior do I want to change?" In the jargon of instructional systems, this question becomes "what terminal behaviors should I be able to detect in my students at the conclusion of my instruction that they do not exhibit at the beginning?" The specification of terminal student behaviors to be detected at the conclusion of a period of instruction is a dramatic antidote for fuzzy thinking.

When one applies the systems test of "how do you achieve this objective and how do you measure its attainment?" many traditional statements of purpose are shown in all their meaningless ambiguity: "I teach students to appreciate the subject matter of my course," "I am teaching my students to be better citizens," etc. Most statements which appear in the opening pages of college catalogues likewise fail to pass this test.

The clarity with which one views both his objectives and the methods for their attainment in the instructional systems approach is, I believe, a conclusive argument for getting with this type of approach. But it is also a conclusive argument for getting beyond instructional systems, as presently limited, in many instances, to the mere transmission of data. My personal teaching experience becomes relevant at this point.

I did not discover the instructional systems approach via the literature on the subject; I stumbled on it via self-examination of my own teaching experience. At the end of my first semester of teaching, I sat down to make a final examination and discovered that I couldn't do it without consulting the textbook and the lecture notes. I found myself asking, "If I can't prepare an examination without referring to the textbook and the lecture notes, how can I expect my students to take an examination without reference to the same materials?"

It was when I found myself unable to make an examination which I expected my students to take that I asked myself just what, specifically, were my objectives in the course? Just what type of behavioral change was I working for? What did I really want my students to do at the end of the course that they couldn't do at the beginning of the course? And, when I asked myself what effect I was having on student behavior, the only thing I could come up with was that I was making them more effective manipulators of the data of U.S. history. And, when I asked the next logical question, "Why am I making them more effective manipulators of the data of U.S. history?," I was aghast at what I finally had to accept as the honest answer, "So that they could pass my final examination."

Making students more effective manipulators of information to the end that they become more effective manipulators of information was never my **professed** role as an educator. But at one time this was my actual, though not admitted (because not conscious), objective. I began my teaching career primarily as a preparer of students to take my exams. This system was totally self-validating and self-justifying. But it wasn't very self-satisfying, either for the students or for myself. The only thing which appalled me more than that particular revelation was my later discovery that instructional systems often seem to have fallen into the same trap, and have made a **virtue** of this trap.

The trap is an easy one. The only aspects of human behavior we can measure with objective accuracy are those which involve the replication of a skill or the duplication of a body of information. Beyond this we are in the subjective, or what psychologists call the "affective," domain. We know how to measure quite accurately the ability to manipulate data, but we haven't even begun to know how to measure the assimilation of it, the incorporation of it into a style, way, or philosophy of life and being.

Those of us whose interest is to teach people rather than subject matter have few objective procedures for the evaluation of whether and how well we have done this. Objective measurements are mostly designed to measure only replicated subject matter. The principal reason for our almost exclusive preoccupation with the manipulation of data is our ability to measure with accuracy only the manipulation of data. The medium is the message.

The problem is that while the medium may be the message, the medium does not necessarily validate the message. Our examinations do not validate the course objectives. The fact that we can objectively measure only certain things does not validate an exclusive interest in those things which we can measure. I cannot buy the arguments of those who make a virtue of rigid adherence only to the objectively measurable.

To say that we have no business teaching self-confidence because we have no way of conclusively measuring whether and how much our students have attained it — this argument is as self-defeating as its basic assumption is self-justifying. We will never learn to do anything until we set about to do it. We will never learn to measure the attainment of self-confidence until we set out to **teach** the attainment of self-confidence.

It was only in 1967 that I took sufficient courage to deliberately adopt a set of subjective goals for my instruction. I decided that my students should develop four behaviors as a result of my course:

1) increased ability to perceive interrelationships across disciplinary boundaries

2) increased ability to establish human relationships
3) increased autonomy (self-reliance, independence, individuality, etc.)
4) increased self-affirmation (self-esteem, sense of self-worth, etc.).

Assuming that the ability to perceive relationships across boundaries would be facilitated by my refusal to establish any boundaries, and assuming that the ability to develop autonomy would be facilitated by an atmosphere of freedom, I turned my class over to my students — totally and completely.

I announced that I would assign no reading, require no papers and give no examinations. If the students wanted to read, they would choose their reading assignments. If they wanted to write, they would write as the spirit moved them. If they wanted to be examined, they would have to devise their own examinations.

Furthermore, they would decide what to do with the class sessions. And at the end of the semester, they turned in their own grades. The only criterion the student would have for grading himself would be his self-evaluation of how well he utilized this opportunity to learn free, somehow converting his conclusions into an "A," "B," "C," "D," or "F."

The most significant pedagogical insight derived from this experiment was my totally new perspective on the evaluation process. I overcame the objectivity bind, which might be defined as the compulsion to attempt greater and greater degrees of objectivity as one becomes more and more aware of the subjectivity inherent in any objective system of measurement. I overcame this bind merely by the discovery of a means of assessing subjective behavior. This discovery was the result of my doing two things that most teachers probably would never think of doing: I prepared a purely subjective examination, and then I took my students' answers at their word.

The examination consisted of 14 questions:
1) What has this experience done for me?
2) What have I done for this experience?
3) How am I different as a result of this experience? Why?
4) What have I learned from this experience? Both generally and specifically? What contributed to this learning?
5) What questions have I become aware of as a result of this experience? Why?
6) What conclusions have I drawn as a result of this experience? Why?
7) Have I developed new interests as a result of this experience? How? Why?

8) Have attitudes toward others and myself been affected by this experience? How? Why?

9) To the best of my knowledge, have the interests and attitudes of others in the group been affected by this experience? How? Why? Please use specific examples.

10) Has this experience affected my other coursework? How? Why?

11) Has this experience affected my relations with others outside the group? How? Why?

12) Has this experience affected my manner of living? How? Why?

13) What has prevented this experience from being more effective for myself and for others?

14) How would I improve this experience?

The purpose of asking so many similar questions was to elicit a greater depth of response from the students.

The two major criteria which determine the accuracy of a reactive behavioral measurement (one in which we are getting a response from the person being measured) are the honesty of the person being measured and the validity of the examination itself (does it measure what it sets out to measure?).

Since the only "right" answers on a truly subjective examination are the honest answers of the person who is taking it, it is quite unlikely that one can cheat on such an examination without being detected by someone who already knows him. Honesty of response on my exam was therefore essentially assured.

The examination validated itself, not because of any quantitative assessment, but by virtue of a pattern of behavior reported in most of the responses. The students consistently reported certain types of reaction to the course, which indicated that to some degree (and the degree, of course, is unmeasurable) they had attained some or all of the objectives of the course. As it turned out, I even had a control group in this experiment. The only

examinations on which the prevailing patterns failed to show up at all were those of students who had already demonstrated a pattern of self-deception. Students who told me what they thought I wanted to hear produced the traditional "snow job." They did not, in fact, tell me what I was looking for. Those who weren't trying to **did.** I took this to be additional confirmation of the validity of a test designed to assess the attainment of integral behaviors. It was the student without integrity who failed.

Of course, it can be argued that qualitative measurements can never approach the accuracy of quantitative measurements. For instance, I am unable (probably forever) to assess the percentage of increase in self-esteem and autonomy on the part of either a total group of students or on the part of individual members of the group severally. But I think it is rather meaningless to try to reduce qualities to quantities. Those who can trust only quantitative instruments can stick to teaching only the ability to manipulate data.

I prefer to enable my students to develop not only the ability to manipulate data, but the ability to self-actualize, to realize their human potential. I think that more instructional systems designers, as more teachers generally, should be concerned more often with this latter ability.

Objectivists who are concerned with what they can quantitatively measure can count numbers. I will try to devise techniques for perceiving patterns. Objectivists may continue to specialize in rendering unto objectivity that which is objectivity's. Others, I hope, will begin or continue to generalize, and render unto both objectivity and subjectivity that which is respectively appropriate. If they do so, I am convinced we can devise academically legitimate instruments for self-evaluation.

I shall perhaps be accused of unsubstantiated faith; and, if so accused, I will plead guilty to the charge. My faith is as unsubstantiated as the faith of one who makes the subjective decision that item "four" on his final examination is worth as many points as items "one" through "three." □

Teacher Education:
Rube Goldberg or Systems Management?

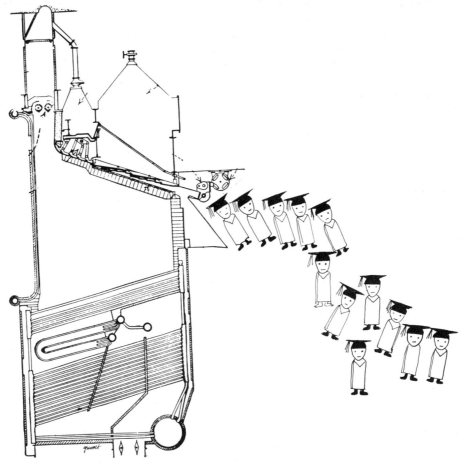

Albert H. Yee

Almost everyone agrees that a school is not much better than the quality of its teachers. Most people agree that pedagogical skills and competencies can be learned and that teacher education should provide the professional preparation and enhancement of teachers. If teacher preparation is an important factor determining the nature of schooling in modern American society, this question must be raised: How systematic and effective is teacher education in the United States? Answers, now familiar to everyone, from Conant (1963), Mayer (1961), Sarason **et al.** (1962), Stinnett (1962) and others indicate teacher education resembles many of the characteristics of a Rube Goldberg cartoon rather than a meaningful process of professional preparation.

Albert H. Yee is graduate program chairman, Department of Curriculum and Instruction, University of Wisconsin School of Education, Madison.

This paper pursues answers to the same question of teacher education's efficacy. It attempts to provide constructive criticisms of teacher preparation today and suggest necessary changes. To do so, we will examine teacher education from the systems management point of view. The systems approach frame of reference has proven highly effective in analyzing and perfecting organizational and machine systems in many areas of modern business, governmental and scientific-technological endeavors, and should be applied more often to educational settings (Gagné, 1965; Lehmann, 1968).

Teacher education systems, as all social organizations, contain the potential for four basic elements of cybernetic systems (Smith & Smith, 1966; Wiener, 1956 & 1961): (1) an **input component** providing selection and entrance of necessary raw materials; (2) an **operations component** providing development of a product by manipulation of the input according to a purposive design; (3) an **output component** providing release and distribution of the system's products for use by others; (4) a **feedback component** supplying control and guidance to the other components. In a teacher education system, (1) would deal with the screening, selection and orientation of students; (2) would concern teaching-learning operations, mainly on campuses; (3) would provide extensive clinical experiences in schools and close relationship between student, school personnel and teacher educators; (4) would be continuous evaluation of system processes and student progress.

Input component

There is no question that perfunctory admissions policies characterize teacher education centers. Entrance into elementary school programs is usually screened only on the basis of an individual's grade-point average — usually a "C" average is all that is required for admission. Due in part to such admissions policies, the education major usually stands at the bottom of the intellectual totem pole on campuses. It is common for students failing in other areas to turn to teaching for a career. Surely selection procedures can be developed to provide much more information than is now obtained; few would seriously argue that everyone with a "C" grade-point average can be properly prepared to teach youngsters.

Not only do the screening procedures select candidates, but also they influence who shall be recruited. Teacher education does not appeal to many of our brightest college and university undergraduates. However, many of these bright young people, upon graduation, without any background in education, will join the Peace Corps to teach foreign children for two or more years in the most underdeveloped corners of the world. But, ironically, most will never teach children in their own country upon their return. Better quality applicants would be attracted to enter teacher education if the entrance requirements represented an intellectual challenge. Present admissions policies have helped to create an unflattering stereotype of typical education students. With present policies, the Teaching-Learning and Output components must be assumed to provide great effects in developing the professional characteristics and behaviors of competent teachers. This assumption of effects, of course, cannot be made.

Feedback information within and from the system to the field has not been systematized for continual evaluative purposes. With such meager information on the input characteristics of teacher candidates, little diagnosis of individual needs can

be provided to maximize the effects of teaching-learning operations through individualization of instruction and evaluation of learning behavior. Also, lack of information on the nature of inputs drastically weakens the opportunity to continually improve the system through predictive procedures.

With adequate information concerning the student's characteristics, behavior and background experiences, the Input component should perform the following functions:

(1) A **screening function** to answer the question: **Who is admitted and who is not admitted into the system?** The Input component can be developed into a filtering process which provides some guarantee of success through the system to the individual student and the teacher educators. If meaningful screening continues to be neglected in teacher education, then the Teaching-Learning and Output components must perform the major screening function necessary to establish and maintain quality control in output. In typical programs today, only the obviously poor candidates seem in jeopardy, and most of them unfortunately become identified late in their preparation, usually in student teaching. Because of the efficiency desired in the system and consideration due the student's well-being and efforts, it would be practical to make the screening function a critical aspect of the teacher education system.

(2) A **diagnosing function** to answer the question: **What are the needs and interests of the student?** The system should counsel and guide accepted candidates and provide a beginning study program appropriate to the objectives of the program and the individual needs of students. Above the lower bounds of entrance criteria, the characteristics of students accepted into the system will vary in their intellectual and experiential readiness for professional training. Some may require further studies in language, mathematics, or the social sciences; perhaps some will require more familiarity of real community and world affairs; while some may show considerable strength in preliminary professional studies and readiness to begin more challenging work, especially in special areas of interest. If the preparation system is designed for individualization of instruction, then diagnosis of the student's needs, his strengths, shortcomings and wants at the input level must be considered essential.

(3) A **predictive function** to answer the questions: **What estimate can be given at this point for a student's probable success as a teacher? How much confidence can be placed upon the estimate?** The development of this function may be thought of as the long-range extension of the screening and diagnosing function. To some extent, the first two functions may operate on logical groups in the absence of scientific knowledge concerning relevant predictors. However, reliance on logical procedures

alone would phase out as empirical studies and technical facilities provide the necessary scientific procedures.

For this third function, the proper coordination of evaluation within and between all system components and adequate technical storage-analyses of data should provide probability estimates that can be given with greater confidence the longer students become involved in the system's operations. In other words, teacher education systems should be able to perfect the intra- and intersystem feedback functions to the point sometime in the future that the progress of individual students can be assessed at major stages in terms of probability statements. By the time students enter their clinical exprience, teacher educators should have high confidence that the student will complete the program, and proceed with the task of rounding out the professional development of the intern.

The predictive function, at least at the input level, is hardly new to major institutions in business and government. In ancient China, those performing highest in scholarly examinations were appointed to civil service positions. It is interesting that the U. S. Army provides more screening, diagnosis and prediction of effectiveness for their buck privates than teacher education typically provides students. Private corporations utilize scientific predictive procedures for many job classifications, such as secretaries and engineers; and the U. S. Government requires competitive examinations for most civil service positions.

The well-known problems confronted with the "criterion-of-effectiveness" paradigm (Gage, 1963) in the past need not deter teacher educators from research on multiple criteria and their joint contributions to prediction. The fact that teacher educators, after so many years of "research and development," cannot declare for sure what teaching effectiveness is indicates a lack of systematic analysis and an over-load of entropy in teacher education. Perhaps the greatest single problem of teacher education is its lack of clear, behavioral objectives which direct the training operations. Viewing the system as a whole, we can see that all of the functions in the Input component may be considered a subset of the total evaluation process handled by the Feedback component.

The operations or teaching-learning component

This component fulfills the pre-clinical operation designed to prepare candidates to work with pupils. It answers the question: **What studies, experiences and sequential teaching-learning patterns does the system provide to develop students' professional teaching behavior?**

In the main, the operations here have been independent lecture courses in a number of content and methods areas, such as art, reading, social studies and science education. The courses have been largely uncoordinated in regard to the characteristics and needs of individual students and the behavioral changes desired. To further each student's progress, professors and students have relied upon within-course feedback for evaluation; and, to a much lesser degree, the joint development or programming of the course. Thus, a teacher education program providing several sections of a required social studies methods course will probably find that the course will vary more by professors than for and by students. Also, although professors may occasionally consult each other concerning the progress of a student, continuous, systematic feedback for all students throughout this component has not been possible in traditional programs. Certainly letter grades for courses provide trifling feedback information to the student and scant evaluative value to teacher educators and potential employers.

Millions of dollars and years of human endeavor have been expended in the operation of teacher education programs that have vague designs based heavily on administrative rather than teaching-learning planning. Intelligent planning by professors for effective teaching and learning in education courses is not rare. But the planning we find lacking is in the overall structure of each course, its meaningful relationship to other courses, and the design of the whole program to achieve clear and certain objectives.

Thus, the planning needed to develop and continually improve an educational program depends on the program's objectives. Because the objectives of teacher preparation have been equivocal and often unrelated to teaching youngsters, the programs have lagged and meandered. Stating objectives for an institution only in global, philosophical terms creates uncertainty, for the vagueness of such objectives can only lead to uncertain planning and designs.

Objectives should be clear and definite enough to allow development of specific procedures to attain the objectives. Stating what is to be taught and learned with a minimum of ambiguity and equivocality becomes the first major step toward intelligent planning of an educational program. It may be possible, however, that specification of all objectives cannot be completed when planning is started, especially in developing innovative programs. In such cases, the delineation of objectives may need to be held in abeyance until objectives may be specified in the future. A developing educational design may resemble a skyscraper in construction. Thus, completion of a design, as it is for a building, properly occurs after the objectives or purposes have been formulated and specified. In specifying objectives and planning accordingly, B. F. Skinner (1968) has observed:

> . . . when we know what we are doing, we are training; when we do not know what we are doing, we are teaching. Once we have taken the important first step and specified what we want the student to do as the result of having been taught, we can begin to teach in ways with respect to which this outworn distinction is meaningless. In doing so we need not abandon any of our goals. We must simply define them.

If individualization of instruction is a teaching-learning strategy that should be utilized by classroom teachers because it is most efficient in effecting human learning, then one might hypothesize that it is only appropriate that teachers also learn through individualization. The greater implementation of multi-media, computerized instructional facilities could be significant in developing the many channels or routes through the Teaching-Learning component for individual students; also, in providing greater direct experiences with classroom and teacher-pupil situations through simulation and multi-media facilities.

The application of available and specially-designed technical aids in this component can help overcome the inflexible scheduling of professor-class relations in present teacher training programs. Programming immediate feedback and branching teaching-learning sequences to students through greater use of technology can help provide individualization of instruction worthy of the term.

Another important advantage a wide use of instructional modes provides over present programs would be the opportunity to systematize many aspects of professional concern, such as classroom discipline and handling standardized tests, in a manner that allows students many examples and replications of realistic teaching-learning experiences. For instance, it may be possible to provide self-controlled dial access systems so that students at their convenience could go to a computerized teaching-learning station and request what is desired from program storage. Simulation of classroom situations could also be made available, with the interactive responses of the student determining outcomes. As with many aspects of the system discussed in this paper, the actual accomplishment of the operations will require greater systems management of teacher education.

The output component

Several functions are fulfilled in this component. The first answers the question: **What realistic experiences does the system provide so that the student practices more fully the behaviors, responsibilities and routines of teaching?**

Andrews (1964) has characterized this general area of professional training as follows:

> Nowhere are the vast extremes between excellence and inadequacy in student teaching more striking and more shocking than in the dimension of quality. Some student teachers have skillfully guided growth experience which leads them to an artistic and professionally effective performance in directing learning, while others have a continuously frustrating, emotionally disturbing experience during which they receive little positive direction or assistance, and may in fact learn unwise and professionally unsound procedures.

Postulating the student-teaching triad (three-person group concerned with practice teaching — the student, college supervisor and cooperating teacher) as a socio-psychological model, Yee (1967 a,b; 1968) studied the group dynamics operating in practice teaching. It was found that the triad seldom approaches levels of social interaction and professional activities worthy of the purposes for practice teaching. The opportunity to develop intersystem feedback between the professional school and the public schools for the benefit of the whole process of teacher education as well as for the three individuals involved has been ignored in teacher education programs.

The chief causes for such superficiality in interpersonal relations may be attributed to the inadequate resources to handle the large number of candidates and the administration of practice teaching which force many students to work under unqualified and ill-prepared cooperating teachers and supervisors. Quantitative concerns to help overcome the teacher shortage have been one major hindrance to progress in student teaching and teacher education in general. Systematic improvements in student teaching and indeed in all aspects of teacher education would be easier to develop if such quantitative concerns were deemphasized and the qualitative preparation of students were made primary.

For the first function, therefore, the Output component should provide extended clinical experiences in actual classrooms where the student carries much responsibility for actual teaching-learning operations and receives professional supervision and critique. It goes beyond previous exposure to classroom situations and settings through simulated conditions, multi-media experiences and short-term classroom experiences in the laboratory experiences of the Teaching-Learning component. Now the student becomes involved with learners as a responsible teacher, one who must become familiarized with each pupil as an individual learner, plans teaching strategies, develops learning and evaluative materials, works cooperatively with colleagues, etc.

Another function of the Output component concerns close relationships between professionals working in the teacher education program and those in the schools. It answers the question: **How can greater communication and cooperation be developed between teacher educators, school administrators and teachers, and those in state departments of education?** In present teacher education programs, nothing approximates this function. There is little meaningful structure for it and a gross lack of necessary coordination. Close working relations have to be developed between university, school, and state personnel in the greater development of teacher education.

Since school systems provide the realistic classroom situations for the practice of student teachers, teachers and principals should be more involved in this component than in the past from several points of view. As consumers of output from teacher education systems and with the responsibility to protect their pupils from possible unprofessional practices of student teachers, the public schools can only gain by being more closely involved in operations of the Output component. From an in-service point of view, the public schools could also gain much from more meaningful participation in this component.

Through purposeful involvement in the total teacher education system, the state, school and university can share responsibility for the determination of: (1) appropriate professional education for the needs of the student and the society; (2) laboratory and clinical experiences rewarding to all persons involved; (3) professional criteria for certification; and (4) improved curriculum development in the schools.

The feedback component

Viewing social organizations as systems of communication, we can analyze and evaluate their feedback processes for self-improvement and self-regulation through systematic information exchange. The primary function of such information processes deals with the quality control of whatever the organization produces — how well it is achieving its objectives or mission. An organization's viability and capacity to be productive and efficient are determined by the nature of its information network composed of channels of communications between antecedent and subsequent events. A vital, progressive institution operates with an efficient feedback

system of process self-regulation and product evaluation, while a lack of adequate feedback processes — entropy — characterizes a chaotic, unorganized institution.

Teacher education programs typically function without systematic feedback components. They tend to have inefficient methods of providing feedback to students, no self-regulation procedures for learning sequences, nor methods of assessing the effectiveness of the program or the graduate. Also, they maintain minimal communication with schools and American society in general. As discussed earlier, the student-teaching situation provides great opportunity for feedback between schools and teacher education, but it is the least developed area of professional preparation. To be relevant for the realities and needs of American classrooms and in order to evaluate its training processes, teacher evaluation must establish feedback processes with schools. Through the view of systems management, a meaningful relationship between schools and teacher education seems so obvious; that such feedback agreements have not been developed characterizes the deplorable lack of system in this society's preparation of teachers.

Conclusions

Critical to the maintenance and progress of American society are the great educational functions intended to promote the growth and development of its people. Believing that, Americans provide multiple opportunities for all youngsters in a program of universal schooling. Since American teachers bear major responsibility for school achievement, they must be better screened and prepared than they have been to match such expectations.

Utilizing a management systems viewpoint to evaluate teacher education, this paper analyzed the major problems of teacher education programs today and proposed ways of improving them. An ideal teacher preparation system was outlined and compared to today's teacher education programs, which bear strong resemblance to Rube Goldbergian rattle-traps. Identification and analysis of the essential component tasks of teacher education help to identify key problems and areas for improvement. Greater systematic programming and coordination of the various components and application of modern instructional techniques would seem to be essential developments necessary for effective teacher preparation today and in the future.

America's increasing urbanization requires educational systems which are relevant to a great range of diverse social needs and capable of progressive improvement. One of the most important steps to improve education in American society will be to replace today's quasi-professional programs with truly professionalizing processes in teacher education and certification.

Almost 80 years ago, J. M. Rice, the writer credited as first to recognize the Progressive Movement in American schools, asked whether it was more talent or training that was needed to improve the illogical and harsh teaching that he often observed across the United States. His research and reflection told him more training was needed and that schools should be developed with "scientific management." He wrote: ". . . the school is as the teacher, and consequently the advancement of the schools of any particular locality means practically the elevation of the standards of its teachers (1893, p. 159)." Such a statement would be a truism, but for a continuing lack of implementation.   □

Stinnett, T. C.   Teacher Certification. **Review of Educational Research,** 1967, 248-259.

Wiener, N.   **Cybernetics.** New York: Wiley, 1961.

   The Human Use of Human Beings. New York: Doubleday, 1956.

Yee, A. H.   Interpersonal Relationships in the Student-Teaching Triad. **Journal of Teacher Education,** 1968, 95-112.

   Student Teaching: A Problem in Group Dynamics. **California Journal for Instructional Improvement,** 1967, 188-201(a).

   The Student-Teaching Triad: The Relationship of Attitudes Among Student Teachers, College Supervisors and Cooperating Teachers. U.S. Department of Health, Education, and Welfare, Office of Education. Cooperative Research Project No. 5-8354. Austin: The University of Texas, 1967(b).

A Cybernetic Instructional System

Frank F. Gorow

A teacher has a subject to be taught and students who are to learn. What the teacher does, and how he does it, is the result of his own learning about teaching, his conceptions and misconceptions, and the inputs which he receives in his first years of experience. There is little agreement among teachers as to the "best" teaching procedure and little empirical evidence to support any particular procedure. What is needed is a cybernetic, or self-correcting, instructional system which will enable teachers to continually improve their teaching to the point of optimum results.

"The name of the game is learning—and we play to win." This implies that teaching is a means to an end; the end is learning; the function of the teacher is to assure that every pupil will learn as much as he can learn. When pupils fail to learn as much as they can learn, the fault lies in the "system," and modification is indicated.

The paradigm for a cybernetic instructional system, shown diagrammatically below, was developed for use in a course titled "Instruction and Evaluation in Secondary Schools." The aim of the course is to help each prospective teacher build his or her own instructional system by successive approximation of the ideal—instead of dispensing prescriptions for planning lessons, maintaining discipline, and the like. The paradigm is simple but the demands made upon students are rigorous; they receive little help from traditional textbooks.

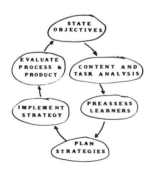

State Objectives. The student's first task is to examine courses of study and other curriculum publications to determine the overall objectives of a course which he (or she) proposes to teach. Guiding questions are: What is worth learning? What will pupils be able to do at the end of the course which they could not do before? What changes in pupil behavior can the course bring about? Each student produces a short list of the most important, overall objectives of a course (subject to later revision) and "validates" his list by consultation with a teacher of the subject and a subject matter expert.

Content and Task Analysis. Time limitations preclude the analysis of content and learning tasks of an entire course. One

Frank F. Gorow *is professor of secondary education at California State College, Long Beach.*

segment (or unit or topic) is analyzed in two ways: the kinds of content (complex ideas, concepts and specifics of knowledge); and the kinds of learning tasks (memory, understanding, verbal chaining, multiple discrimination, classifying, rule using and problem solving—as described by Gagne, 1965). A task analysis of one typical learning task is also made.

At this point, objectives are re-examined. Attention has shifted from the course-as-a-whole with its overall objectives to one segment. Content and task analyses enable the student to select and state explicit objectives for that segment. Objectives in performance terms are then written to provide the bases for planning instruction and for evaluation.

Preassess Learners. Lacking pupils to preassess, we are limited to hypothetical questions, such as: What kinds of information about the pupils in a class are needed to plan effective instruction? What formal and informal techniques of preassessment might be used? How might you modify objectives as a result of various possible findings?

Plan Strategies. Instead of teaching "about" various methods of instruction, we begin with the instructional objectives which were previously written for one segment of a course. The first problem is to search the methods literature and identify many approaches and techniques which could be used to enable pupils to achieve the kinds of objectives in the various lists. The next concern is with the varieties of pupils: the more and the less able, the self-starters and the reluctant ones, those with limited reading abilities and with other "different" characteristics. (Without attempting to construct "taxonomies" of techniques or of pupils or to suggest a close match between the two, we attempt to promote variety and flexibility.)

The actual planning of strategies for helping pupils to achieve specified objectives is at two levels: the single-class-period lesson plan (based on McDonald's 1965 model) and the longer unit plan based upon specified objectives and including a variety of learning activities and teaching techniques, the application of five learning principles (suggested by Popham, 1965) and evaluation of achievement. The products are model lesson and unit plans.

Implement Strategy. Because student teaching *follows* the course, we are limited to hypothetical problems, such as: developing rapport with pupils, teacher behavior which leads to undesirable and desirable discipline conditions, classroom management and student demonstration of teaching techniques.

Evaluate Process and Product. (Construction of "professional education" courses in California credential programs forced us to include measurement and evaluation in the general methods course.) Students learn to write test items to measure various levels of learning and to compute simple statistical measures "on their own time" using books written for this purpose (Gorow, 1962, 1966). Groups of students with a common subject interest produce samples or descriptions of evaluation procedures for a variety of kinds of objectives. Having experienced "criterion-referenced" tests in the course, these are compared with "norm-referenced" tests as to design, construction, use and interpretation. Practice is given in interpreting a set of test scores, including transformation to standard score and absolute or percentage scales. Attention to the problems of "A, B, C" grading is given and each student produces a statement of grading procedures for his course.

Process evaluation is the critical element in a "cybernetic" instructional system. Throughout the course, every product and conclusion has been considered to be "tentative" and subject to the test of application in a real teaching situation; thus the groundwork has been laid for modification. Focus is on the kinds of questions to ask in appraising the quality of learning experiences as well as quantitative achievement, ways to find answers, and the system elements most likely to require improvement.

Summary

This brief description of a course in "instruction and evaluation" is intended to illustrate one attempt to improve a traditional secondary education course. We have sought to enable our students to achieve specific, definable competencies and simultaneously to become adaptable and to work systematically toward excellence in teaching. We have assumed that "learning how to teach" is *their* problem, and that our function is to help them. We have developed an instructional model which appears to be useful. Correspondence, criticism and suggestions are invited.

□

References

Gagne, Robert M. *The Conditions of Learning.* New York: Holt, Rinehart & Winston, 1965. (Chapter 2, Varieties of Learning, pp. 31-61.)

Gorow, Frank F. *Better Classroom Teaching,* San Francisco: Chandler, 1966.

.... *Statistical Measures: A Programmed Text.* San Francisco: Chandler, 1962.

McDonald, Frederick J. *Educational Psychology.* Second Edition. Belmont, California: Wadsworth Publishing Company, 1965. (Chapter 3, Instructional Strategies and Learning, pp. 71-106.)

Popham, W. James. *The Teacher-Empiricist.* Los Angeles: Argus Press, 1965, pp. 15-40.

A Faculty Development Institute in Learning Systems Technology

Many institutes have been conducted to introduce teachers to the merits of educational media and to foster proper usage of these media. We decided to go one step further and hold an institute for college and university faculty of the Finger Lakes region, not simply on educational media production and utilization, but on instructional problem-solving. We were going to use the so-called systems approach to learning. Emphasis of the institute would be on the diagnosis of instructional problems by the participant professor, with the assistance of a team of specialists, which would include a learning psychologist, a tests and measurement psychologist, a specialist in communications theory and a media expert. Participants would have the opportunity to share each other's problems.

The institute was scheduled to meet on 30 consecutive Saturdays, for a minimum of five hours per session. Since this was a year-long institute, few faculty were willing to sacrifice their Saturdays during a whole academic year for this type of instructional adventure. On the other hand, those who applied to participate, in spite of this, were highly motivated. Since the participating faculty was to be recruited from the Finger Lakes region (proximity to the Ithaca area was another important factor that participants had to consider), skeptics had predicted that we would never be able to recruit 20 faculty. However, that did not prove to be a problem.

In the brochure advertising the institute and under the heading "Criteria for Eligibility," it was specified that participants must be involved in undergraduate instruction, have a minimal background in educational media and a keen interest in making their teaching effective through proper use of technology. They were expected to obtain the support of their immediate supervisor, i.e., departmental chairman or dean. But most important of all, they had to demonstrate that at least one problem existed in their own teaching situation, a problem which they were willing to let the team of specialists study and analyze. Possible solutions were then to be field-tested.

It was for this purpose that the participant was expected to secure, beforehand, his supervisor's approval and willingness to assist in implementing some of the strategies recommended by the team of specialists.

The program of the institute included instruction in three main areas of concentration:

1. *The Socio-Psychological Dimension of the New Media*
   (a) Human Communication Theory in the Classroom
   (b) Educational Procedure and Objectives
   (c) Tests and Measurements in Instructional Development
2. *Integrating the New Media into the Teaching Program*
   (a) Instructional Television

John E. Keshishoglou is associate professor of radio-television-film at Ithaca College and director of the Instructional Resources Center.

   (b) Instructional Film
   (c) Audio-Visual Aids
   (d) Integrating Programmed Learning into the College Teaching Program
   (e) Computer Assisted Instruction
   (f) Facilities for Housing Media and Cost Analysis
3. *Consultation on Specific Instructional Problems*
   Each participant met separately with the team of specialists to discuss his instructional problem.

It is interesting to note some of the "problems" which the participants brought to the institute for assistance. Fifty percent of them had to do with teaching problems in large group instruction. Their comments, submitted beforehand to the institute administration, ranged from, "I do not want to just feed them information," to requests for help on effective incorporation of multi-media presentations in a course plan. With the ever-increasing school populations and the amount of information that has to be communicated to the learner, large group instruction is not likely to be eliminated in the near future—this, in spite of the popularity of auto-tutorial stations, extensive use of dial-access systems and experimentation with computer assisted instruction.

The other 50 percent of the participants had more specific problems. A professor who is teaching an introductory course in speech, and is fortunate enough to have a wide variety of audio-visual equipment at his disposal, wished to learn about message design and evaluation through the use of technology. Two others were also concerned about making their courses more realistic, and thought that perhaps the incorporation of educational media might partially solve the problem. The problems presented by still others had to do with individual student differences in learning a given body of information, inadequate background information when enrolling in a given course which makes it difficult for the learner to follow the course, and the design and evaluation of auto-tutorial courses.

With these problems on hand, the institute team of specialists met to plan strategies for the various sessions. It was obvious from the beginning that some of the problems were too general to be tackled within the scope and time allotted to the institute. It was felt that these had to be narrowed down to just a few or even to a single concept. The team would then attempt to discuss possible ways of solving the problems, and it would be up to the individual professor to plan similar strategies for the other similar concepts of his general problem.

While the team of specialists studied the problems submitted by the individual participant and held interviews with the person involved to obtain a better perspective of the problem, the participants received instruction in both the theoretical and practical aspects of educational media. The areas discussed were instructional television and film, still photography and transparencies, programmed learning, educational measurement, learning theory, communications theory, computer assisted instruction, dial-access and telelectures. A discussion of the issues involved in instructional development was also included in the program.

Two months after the institute began, each participant met individually with the team of specialists to discuss his problem at length. It was at this time that the team and the participant attempted to narrow down the problem, if all parties felt this was necessary, and to recommend possible strategies.

Perhaps it would be appropriate to include mention of the production facilities utilized by the institute, in the design and production of the audio-visual materials. It should be emphasized again that the systems approach was also used in the design and production of A-V materials to insure that the information presented on a slide, transparency or film communicated the message and met the objectives for which it was designed. The extensive production facilities of the Instructional Resources Center were complemented by those of the Department of

Communication Arts at Cornell University, backed by an experienced staff of specialists. Classes were held both at Ithaca College multi-media lecture halls and at Cornell. Faculty and guest lecturers were recruited from Cornell University, Syracuse University and the State University of New York.

Toward the end of the institute, all participants were asked to submit two assignments using the guidelines sent to them in the form of a memo by the institute director. These guidelines were as follows:

Assignment #1

The purpose of this assignment is to assist you in the specific designation of an instructional problem which can be solved by the resources of the institute. The first round of individual conferences held in November and December attempted to uncover this problem in a general way. Now we want to isolate a more specific part of that problem, suggest solutions to it, and make plans for any production that is needed. It is our hope that the solution to the specific problem chosen will act as a model for you and your associates to use in considering further changes in your courses.

Your written paper should include:

1. *A brief statement identifying the instructional problem.* (This is the problem you agreed to attack after the first personal consultation in November or December.)
2. The *specific objectives* in terms of measurable student behavior.
3. Identify, for each objective, the *type of learning* involved, using Gagne's eight types of learning.
4. Identify the characteristics of stimuli needed to produce learning and the medium which would most effectively display the stimuli. Where stimuli could be effectively displayed through more than one medium, indicate the considerations leading to your final choice. (Aspects to be considered would include: cost, convenience of use, ease of production, etc.)
5. Propose an evaluation design to measure the amount of learning that the instructional message produces.

The institute faculty experienced difficulty in attempting to convince the participants that their teaching would benefit from the consideration of such matters as (1) listing specific learning behaviors, (2) identification of types of learning, (3) understanding media characteristics and (4) evaluation of specific objectives. Of the 20 participants, five were successful in their application of the requirements of Assignment 1. Five others had difficulty in considering learning experiences in such specific terms. The rest were successful for the most part, but some difficulties arose in the evaluation part of the assignment. Perhaps additional consultations with the tests and measurements psychologist were necessary. Perhaps too, the belief by many that a professor is a dispenser of information, not a manager of learning experiences, was another reason for this.

Assignment #2

Each participant is asked to submit a final paper. These papers will be presented to the members of the institute for discussion and criticism on April 12, 19 and 26 and May 3. As far as is possible, these papers should cover the following areas of consideration:

A. Background Information
  1. A course description.
  2. Student population characteristics.
  3. Teaching methods used in the course.
  4. Methods of evaluation of student achievement.
B. The General Problem—(Perhaps as stated in your original application to the institute.)
C. The Specific Problem—(Adapted from Assignment #1.) This is the problem that the institute tried to solve.
D. Possible Application to Other Courses.
E. Summary and Conclusions.
F. Barriers to Instituting Innovation in Your Situation.

The reader will note the final item under Assignment #2. Participants were asked to express their personal opinion as to what were the barriers to instituting innovation in their own environment. A great many of them listed *time* as the main barrier. One of them summarized the problem as follows: "The problem of time has two main parts: (1) professional activities which compete with teaching for one's time and (2) rewards—the alternative uses of time (research, articles, etc.) offer much greater rewards than do attempts to improve teaching."

Other barriers mentioned by the participants are administrations unsympathetic to instructional innovation, uncertainty among administrators as to priority for curriculum changes, inadequate funds for the production of instructional aids, lack of information on media utilization and lack of programs in instructional media.

The institute was planned on the premise that college professors should not become media specialists, but that they should be made aware of the issues involved in using media and should know where they could get skilled assistance to carry out their plans for innovation and improved teaching. The design of the institute reflects this premise. □

Instructional Products: An Engineered Course in Educational Technology

Stephen Yelon

The central purpose of a course titled Seminar in Instructional Products was to give students the opportunity to create and test instructional products. An instructional product was defined as some empirically tested object or material which, when presented under specified conditions, would result in a relatively permanent change of a particular behavior. An underlying purpose of this course was to give students a chance to apply principles derived from research on learning and instruction.

Entry Skills

To be admitted to this class, the student had to demonstrate the ability to write objectives in operational terms with unambiguous conditions and criteria. Each student had to be able to do a task description and analysis and be able to extract the concepts, principles and skills from his task description. He had to be able to analyze and prescribe instructional situations according to empirically verified principles of learning.

A second sort of entry behavior was required. The instructor wanted students who were truly interested in this course, and students who would persist in completing their instructional products. The instructor measured persistence by the amount of times the student would ask to get into the course. To be admissible, the student had to ask at least twice to join this course. Six people met this requirement. One was a nurse, one an employee in a learning systems institute at MSU, another a teacher of art and photography, one a remedial reading teacher, and two students were studying in the area of instructional media.

Course Preparation

The students were all instructed that they were free to choose before the first meeting of the class an instructional product which they would like to develop. The class met and the objectives were presented to the students. The major objective was as follows: the learner will produce an instructional product of his own choice. The product will meet the relevant specifications of a prepared checklist for planning and implementing instructional products.

Students were then given en route objectives, that is, those objectives in which they would participate which would lead to the terminal behavior described above:

Stephen Yelon is assistant professor and assistant director of the Learning Service at Michigan State University.

1. The learner will present an oral report describing the plans for his product. These will include objectives, task analysis, method of implementation, and costs and time of construction. These will all be in accord with the criteria given on a checklist. Amendments of these plans will follow the class presentation based on the criticism of the students in the class so that they may conform to the criteria.
2. The learner will present a prototype of his product in class. The product must fit the description of the plan presented and meet the checklist criteria.
3. The learner will test the completed product on at least five subjects. The evaluation procedure data will be presented in an oral presentation. The evaluation procedure must follow the checklist criteria. Hypothetical causes of error based on testing results will be presented. The revisions will be suggested in order to eliminate the possible causes. These revisions will meet the checklist criteria and will follow from the hypotheses.

The checklist referred to was an elaborate list of questions derived from many types of curricular handbooks. Some parts of the checklist were drawn from applications of well tested learning principles. For example, the first part of the checklist incorporated the methods employed in a systems approach to instructional planning: writing objectives for the product, and performing a task analysis from a task description. Other sections of the checklist were derived from learning principles, such as this question, which reflects a learning principle, "Are the prerequisite concepts, principles and skills practiced before new tasks are undertaken?" The checklist was quite rough and detailed. The students were charged by the instructor to revise and criticize the checklist during the course of instruction as well as use it for a critical analysis of their own work. In this way, the students were told, the checklist could become more refined.

The specific nature of the questions on the checklist used is relatively unimportant for those who would care to reproduce this course, although the major characteristics of the checklist are important. The checklist must be:
1. Rough—it must have overlapping categories, poorly phrased statements and plenty of jargon.
2. Lengthy and detailed—a great many criteria must be derived from a great many sources.
3. Incomplete—one section of the checklist must be omitted completely.

When these characteristics are present in the checklist, the following behaviors will most likely take place in the course as described: the students will look at these criteria as ever-changing, evolving, relative to a particular instructional product and in constant need of refinement based upon empirical evidence. The students will practice refining statements of criteria as well as generating their own statements of criteria. For example, no criteria were given for the process of remediation after initial testing. The students and the instructor had to fashion their own criteria based on the interpretations of the data presented, within the constraints of what the group knew about learning and instructional research. In this way, also, students will learn to discriminate between relevant and irrelevant criteria. Instead of working from global criteria to specific, there may be more to gain from choosing those criteria which are relevant from those which are irrelevant, as the students might do when a curriculum recommendation guide or catalogue comes across their desks.

Thus, there was another en route objective, *not* stated to the students: The learners will state suggestions in class for refining statements of criteria. They will generate statements of criteria of their own and will state in their plans which of the criteria were relevant and which were not.

Course of Instruction

During the initial meeting of the course, a great deal of time was spent discussing what each part of the checklist was for and what to look for in each of the student presentations. The students were, of course, cautioned as to the constraints of the course. There were only ten weeks of time and no money could be provided.

The instructor made a presentation just as he expected the students to do. The instructor planned a simulated instructional game and presented his plans for that game. In the first presentation, the instructor elaborated on the plans for his product. He presented his objectives, the task description and analysis, the cost and time of construction, the probable target population, and the knowledge, the skills, the concepts and the principles acquired. The plans were criticized by the students; point by point the checklist was used to evaluate the plans. For example, the objectives were too grandiose. The game that was planned was trying to do too much, and the instructions were much too complex for the target population. The students recognized this and suggested narrowing the purpose down to do one of the many objectives proposed. In this way the product was specified further and the checklist itself was clarified and revised.

While the students were preparing their plans and prototypes, the instructor presented his prototype. The prototype was to be a very cheap, pliable mock-up version of the final product. The instructor explained the use of the instructional game he developed and each student got to play the game. Then the students criticized the game in light of sections of the checklist, and in light of the plans that were presented at the previous meeting.

In addition to the actual demonstration, the instructor discussed plans, prototypes and problems that he encountered in planning other instructional products. This was done to insure the sensing of problems that might not have been encountered in the instructor's prototype. For the same reason, several guests who had developed instructional products of their own presented their products to the group, discussed these products and had them evaluated according to our criteria.

All this time the students were planning and constructing their products. The products that were presented were criticized just as the instructor's product.

The products completed were the following:

1. A programmed text on quality control for first line managers. This was a pencil and paper program which taught a first line supervisor the methods to use in filling out a standards chart for office management, and a quality control chart so that he could make decisions regarding quality control. They would learn to set standards, measure current quality, compare the quality to the standard and periodically review the standards.

2. An instructional film to teach the rules for girls' basketball. At the end of the film the learner could pick out infractions of rules for foul shooting in girls' basketball.

3. A programmed text to teach hospital nurses a new process of filing called phonetic filing. This is a new system where similar names of patients are grouped by a code reducing each name to one letter and three digits. In the programmed text, the student is taught to code and decode names using this phonetic filing method.

4. An instructional game which teaches prospective teachers in special education how to categorize and diagnose learning difficulties. It is called Di-Teg and it is a discrimination game where, when given a description of a child's learning problem, a student can state what category of learning disability the behavior fits in. By becoming more and more accurate in their identifications, they get closer and closer to a goal in competition with other players.

5. A slide and tape unit that taught the elements and principles of visual design. At the end of a series of units, such as the one built, a student would be able to, when given two very similar visual designs, pick the one that was a better design and explain why it was better in terms of the elements and principles of visual design.

6. A series of materials including tests and games to teach a child to read initial consonant blends.

Each student presented his plans and the prototypes for the projects described above in class. Four out of the six students presented data in class based on limited field tests. The total time required of the whole class was ten three-hour evening sessions.

Evaluation

The plans and prototypes were each evaluated on the checklist, as were the instructor's materials. Not all of the students accomplished the en route objectives described. Only four out of the six students were able to test their products and produce enough data to revise them. All six did their planning and produced prototypes.

All the students showed which of the criteria were relevant and which were not relevant to their particular product, and thus could demonstrate this discrimination. They did refine some of the statements when criticizing each person's products, and in presenting their own product. The group generated a whole section of criteria based upon the data brought in and the revisions made. Statements were made in the final evaluation which had to do with the refinement and generation of criteria.

The students were asked to comment on the value of this course to them personally. The course was described as challenging, fruitful, stimulating, exciting and interesting. Here are some sample comments in answer to the question of the course's value to them:

"It felt wonderful to be wrapped up in a course to the extent that time and effort spent was no object. It was all relevant to the course."

"I have learned a procedure to follow in developing an educational product. I found great satisfaction in not only making the product but also learning how to evaluate others' products."

"Enjoyed the opportunity of sharing ideas on product development with others. Interesting to see strong and weak points in instructional design and be able to discuss these with a developer."

A second question was asked, "What in the course should remain and why?" Most replied, "Developing the product," of course; but others stressed specific points. Keeping the en route objectives was desirable as they were helpful in thinking through and clarifying the product. Most wanted to keep the group interaction, commenting, discussing and evaluating the product.

When asked, "What in the course should be changed, and how?" the following comments were made. Several students suggested having more time, perhaps a greater number of meetings or a two-term course so that they could test out the products more fully. Others wanted to have a completed checklist already revised. The major comment regarding the checklist was that it was too rough, too lengthy and too detailed. Some students thought the guest speakers should not be invited because they break up the continuity of the course progress. Others thought that they would like to have invited a speaker who buys products for a company, or who produces or markets instructional products, to tell what he looks for and what he wants in an instructional product.

Suggestions for the Course Next Time

In planning for a rerun of this course the following additional plans will be put into effect:

1. Either more credit hours or a two-semester sequence.
2. A subject pool available for field testing products.

Conclusion

Many students studying in various areas such as teaching, educational psychology, educational technology, instructional development and media technology need systematic, tested courses which facilitate the synthesis of the skills and knowledge they have already learned into a meaningful experience. This course of instruction was constructed with that purpose in mind. □

Developing a Training System

Paul Harmon

This article describes the development of a complete training system for the Job Corps Men's Urban Centers. The effort described, although hardly complete, has taken over two years and has involved the personnel of two companies (Xerox Education Division and, more recently, Cybern Education, Inc.) as well as several consultants, the headquarters staff of Job Corps and numerous Job Corps Center personnel. The objective of this article is to identify some of the problems that have been encountered and overcome and to describe the system as it now stands as an **example** of training system development effort.

Background

The Office of Economic Opportunity was established in 1964, and the Job Corps program was one of OEO's first commitments. There are several different types of Job Corps centers, including men's conservation centers, women's centers and men's urban centers. The men's urban centers each contain from 1,000 to 2,000 young men between the ages of 16 and 21. These urban centers offer the

This article reports work that was done, in part, in fulfillment of Job Corps Contract OEO-4001. Miss Mary Ann Hammeral was the Job Corps Project Monitor. Dr. William Laidlaw of Cybern Education, Inc., was the senior scientist on the project.

Paul Harmon is a project designer with Praxis Corporation, New York. Formerly he was with Xerox and Cybern Education, Inc.

more sophisticated vocational training options, and were originally intended to admit only young men with grade equivalent reading scores of 6.0 years or better. Each men's urban center was contracted to a different institution to operate. Most of these institutions are currently industrial corporations. Each contractor was asked to develop and implement a curriculum.

Each center incorporated or developed different teaching approaches, different curriculum conceptions, different staff organizations and different reporting procedures. This diversity continued during the first two years of Job Corps' Men's Urban Center operations.

Before the end of these two years, it became apparent that there were certain disadvantages in each center having a separate curriculum.

For example, when a corpsman was transferred from one center to another, there was no convenient technique for evaluating what the corpsman had learned at the first center to facilitate his placement into a program at a new center.

Further, centralized evaluation and comparison of corpsman progress was impossible, since progress reports differed so much between centers that it was impossible to compare or compute reported achievements of corpsmen on a national basis.

Outside observers also noticed that the historical development of the separate men's centers (they were opened very hastily, under great pressure and often with personnel of different educational philosophies competing for predominance) had left most centers with inconsistent and often contradictory elements within their individual curricula.

These considerations plus the success of a CAS system in the Conservation Centers* led Job Corps headquarters to believe that there would be distinct advantages in consolidating the training innovations and evaluation practices of each men's urban center into a common and consistent system.

The corpsman advisory system

Initial discussions with Job Corps personnel indicated that a total systems approach would be applicable. It was the consensus that the individual corpsman would gain from his Job Corps experience if he were allowed to follow a more integrated program that was consistent with his employment goals, social and academic development, and also sensitive to his personal needs and difficulties. To achieve this, each corpsman was to be provided an advisor who would be able to meet with that corpsman to help him gain an overview of the center's activities as they affected him and his goals.

It was assumed that the corpsman would gain if his life at the center was made more rational and understandable. To achieve this, the corpsman's efforts and achievements in curricular areas needed to be directly and obviously tied to any rewards he received while at the center. In brief, his experiences were to be structured so as to convince him that a "good day's work" resulted in a "good day's pay." To be sure, each corpsman understood how the system was related to his own self-interests; the corpsman's advisor could personally explain the system to the corpsman, pointing out in a matter-of-fact way that he was achieving certain goals and that he was being rewarded for that achievement, just as he would later be rewarded for effort in the real world of employment.

The men's urban center Corpsman Advisory System is intended to interrelate four basic subsystems:

1. **A curriculum subsystem** that details the possible achievements of corpsmen in a behaviorally exact and efficiently communicable series of units (the primary unit being a behavioral objective).

2. **A data-communication subsystem** that relays corpsman achievement in the curriculum subsystem to the advisory and reinforcement subsystems and to other groups needing these outputs.

Since the Nixon Administration assumed office, two of the six men's urban centers have been closed. The information given in this article was current at press time for the four remaining centers (Gary Job Corps Center, Texas; Breckenridge JCC, Kentucky; Atterbury JCC, Indiana; Clearfield JCC, Utah). The future of the system described in this article is uncertain, given extensive personnel changes occurring at Job Corps headquarters in Washington. Without enthusiasm at the leadership level, the Corpsman Advisory System may "wither away" at the Centers. It is believed, however, that the Nixon appointees' emphasis on evaluation may mean that the system will be continued — at least the curriculum and data-communication sub-systems. It is obvious, of course, that nothing is certain about the Job Corps at this time. — Editor.

---

*The problem of inter-center inconsistency was first noticed and resolved in Job Corps Civilian Conservation Centers. This first "Corpsmen Advisory System" was designed and developed by Dr. Stuart Margulies, Dr. Kathleen Speeth and Dr. Irving Goldberg.

3. **An advisory subsystem** that provides the corpsman with personal feedback about his achievements in the curriculum subsystem and in the reinforcement subsystem.
4. **A reinforcement subsystem** where all possible reinforcing events available to a corpsman are catalogued and arranged so that they are contingent upon the corpsman's achievement in the curriculum subsystem.

The interaction of these four subsystems may be graphically represented in the following manner:

Figure 1

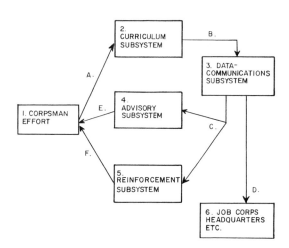

A. The corpsman makes efforts to achieve behavioral objectives in the center curriculum.
B. The corpsman's achievements in the curriculum subsystem are reported out.
C. The data-communication subsystem informs both the advisory subsystem and the reinforcement subsystem of individual corpsman achievement in the curriculum subsystem.
D. The data-communication subsystem informs other groups (e.g., Job Corps headquarters) of the accumulated achievements of all corpsmen in the curriculum subsystem.
E. The advisory subsystem informs the corpsman of his total achievements in the curriculum subsystem and what he may expect, as a consequence, from the reinforcement subsystem. The advisory subsystem mediates between the entire Corpsman Advisory System and the individual corpsman — hence the system name.
F. The reinforcement subsystem presents the corpsman with reinforcing events proportionate to his achievement in the curriculum subsystem.

The model integrates the diverse subsystems of center life, and provides the corpsman with insight into these various subsystems by means of a personal advisor (an element of the advisory subsystem).

The effort required to implement such a system is extensive. It is hardly something that can be done quickly or without extensive analysis of each particular subsystem. Such analysis must take into consideration the rational needs of the subsystem, the practical and technical limitations of each existing center and curriculum, and also the feelings and the personalities of the various centers and their personnel who were asked to implement the system. The subsystem deemed to be primary to the total analysis effort was the curriculum subsystem. This subsystem is primary because all other subsystems would function with outputs resulting from the curriculum subsystem.

Further, all Men's Urban Centers already had curricula, and the effort to build a common Corpsman Advisory System would obviously be dependent upon the ability to obtain agreement among all centers on a model of the curriculum subsystem.

The curriculum subsystem

The curriculum of a center includes all of those elements of introduction, instruction, practice, practical experience, personal interaction and evaluation concerned with finally producing behavioral changes in the individual corpsman that will enable him, upon leaving the Job Corps, to find employment, achieve economic success and to function in psychologically and socially effective ways in a community.

The curriculum subsystem of the Corpsman Advisory System (CAS) includes those elements of a center's environment that interact to result in discrete and measurable achievements (behavioral changes) for individual corpsmen.

An analysis of the commonality of existing Job Corps Men's Urban Center curricula resulted in a curriculum subsystem model (see **Figure 2**).

The elements and components of the curriculum subsystem model's flowplan are defined as follows:

1. The INPUT to the Curriculum Subsystem are efforts on the part of center corpsmen.
2. The Curriculum Subsystem is composed of three elements:

    2.1 the instructional element
    2.2 the evaluation element
    2.3 the curriculum development element.

Figure 2

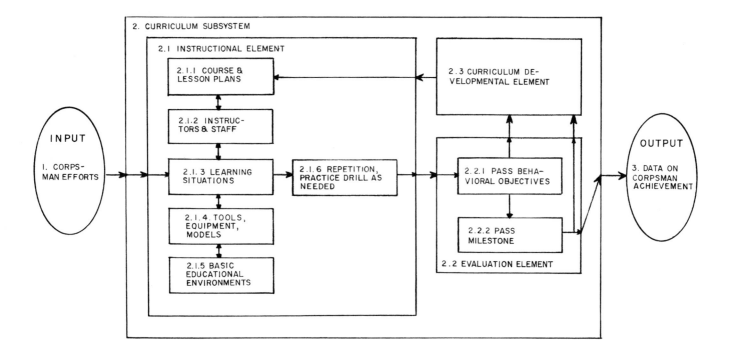

2.1 The Instructional Element includes six basic components, four of which (2.1.1, 2.1.2, 2.1.4 and 2.1.5) support or contribute to (and are constantly being integrated into) the two components that make up the "critical path" of the instructional element. The "critical path" is comprised of those components in which Corpsman effort is actually shaped or modified to effect changes which become the "outputs" of the Instructional Element. The six components are defined as follows:

2.1.1 The course and lesson plans that specify the interactions and desired results of the other components.

2.1.2 The instructors and other staff members that physically and intellectually integrate all the components to create the learning (2.1.3) and repetition (2.1.6) components.

2.1.3 The learning situations that the corpsmen are exposed to and participate in.

2.1.4 The tools, equipment, models, etc., that are used to facilitate behavioral shaping in ˙ the learning (2.1.3) and repetition (2.1.6) components.

2.1.5 The basic educational environment, including classrooms, buildings, fields, etc., within which the other instructional components physically interact.

2.1.6 The repetition, practice and drill (over-learning) that is needed following the initial learning presentation to insure sufficient retention on the part of the corpsman or to assure that the corpsman can integrate his new learnings with past learnings (chaining, generalization, or discrimination practices).

2.2 The Evaluation Element includes two basic components:

2.2.1 The behavioral objective test to determine if the corpsman has successfully added a specific new behavior to his repertoire.

2.2.2 The more formal milestone test (a milestone in the CAS system is a group of related behavioral objectives equivalent to about two weeks of classroom effort) to determine if the corpsman returns to receive more drill (2.1.6) or advances to a new area of learning. If the corpsman advances to a new area of learning his new efforts would in effect become INPUT again and he would experience new learning situations (2.1.3). When the corpsman advances to a new area of learning (that is to say when he passes the milestone test) a record of this fact becomes an OUTPUT of the Curriculum Subsystem and is sent to the Data-Communications Subsystem (3) to be distributed to other subsystems for reinforcement, counseling and general administrative purposes.

Whether or not the corpsman successfully passes the behavioral objectives (2.2.1) or the milestone test (2.2.2), information is relayed to the Curriculum Development Element (2.3).

2.3 The Curriculum Development Element of the Curriculum Subsystem was found to be the least systematic and is therefore the most difficult element to analyze.

In general, the curriculum development element should function to gather information from the real world as to what behaviors are necessary for corpsmen to be successful on their future jobs (e.g., conduct job task analysis). It should also gather information from incoming corpsmen about the skills they currently possess (their entry level repertoire). This information should result in (a) the production of behavioral objectives for a course and (b) the production of course and lesson plans that will structure the corpsman's learning efforts so that he will successfully pass the behavioral objectives at the end of a learning experience. The major internal function ("internal" to the Curriculum Development Subsystem) of the curriculum development element (3.3) is to constantly compare the results of behavioral objective and milestone testing (2.2.1 and 2.2.2) to the course and lesson plans (2.1.1) to be sure that these three components are correctly coordinated. If a group of corpsmen fail to pass a set of behavioral objectives on schedule, for example, it indicates that consideration should be given to plan revisions.

The major external function of the curriculum development element (2.3) is to compare corpsman success after job placement with corpsman success on performance objective and milestone tests to be sure that the behavioral objectives of a course realistically and successfully approximate the behavioral demands of the real-world job situation.

It can be seen that a corpsman does not simply pass through the curriculum subsystem once. He is, rather, going back and forth from instruction to evaluation to instruction many times. Each day he takes part in center activities he goes through the curriculum subsystem again. Thus, the input of the curriculum subsystem is not the corpsman himself but rather "corpsman efforts" that are being constantly made by corpsmen. And it is these **efforts** and not, properly speaking, the corpsman that the reinforcement subsystem rewards.

Different elements of the curriculum subsystem change at different rates. For example, the evaluation element is the product of an analysis of the required outcomes of training (e.g., the behaviors needed by the corpsman to obtain and hold a job in the case of the vocational clusters). It is the standard of the curriculum subsystem, and consequently it changes very slowly. It does change, of course, for job requirements change, and sometimes we find we have set our standard too high or two low — but it doesn't change nearly as often as other elements of the curriculum subsystem.

The instructional element should change whenever results show that a significant number of corpsmen are not prepared, following the prescribed instruction, to pass the behavioral objectives. The instructional element in general changes relatively quickly when a course becomes developed to the point where it routinely succeeds in getting the corpsman to pass the behavioral objectives. Of course, specific instructional components may change with every corpsman. It is the great advantage of human instructors that they can easily vary the examples, tasks and practice exercises, depending upon the corpsman they are instructing.

Developing the corpsman advisory system

Once having analyzed the men's urban centers' programs and synthesized a model of the Corpsman Advisory System, the problem became one of first developing the components necessary for the system and then implementing the total system. This was obviously an extensive undertaking, since each of the men's urban centers had different programs, and it required a phased developmental approach.

The curriculum subsystem was selected as the object of the first development phase because it was the output from this subsystem that constituted the necessary inputs for all other subsystems. The critical component within the curriculum subsystem was the specification of behavioral objectives. Since the various men's urban centers offered in excess of 45 separate vocational programs, the specification of behavioral objectives for just the vocational programs constituted a tremendous challenge. The specification of behavioral objectives for social skills programs and for academic (basic) education programs was also challenging. The effort of specifying these objectives is now nearing completion, having taken almost two years of effort on the part of a great number of people, including almost all the senior vocational instructors and curriculum personnel in Job Corps Men's Urban Centers.

In the course of developing behavioral objectives, a staff training plan and a curriculum development document (how to write behavioral objectives) were produced for Job Corps Men's Urban Centers. Following this, conferences were convened, one after another, at which appropriate center curriculum and vocational (or social or academic) supervisory personnel met to determine Job Corps-wide standards. The conferences resulted in:

1. General agreement by the centers' representatives on the names of the clusters, the programs in the clusters and the modules within each program.
2. General agreement by the centers' representatives on the arrangement of the modules within each program and the arrangement of the milestone within each module.
3. Development of the component behavioral objective titles for all milestones (the complete behavioral objectives are currently being written by individual centers).
4. The physical output of each conference was a notebook incorporating all of the above which guided the centers in altering their programs to accommodate the national standards.

After each conference, a series of editing and revision cycles between the individual centers, Job Corps headquarters and the contractor assured the broadest possible acceptance of the standardized set of behavioral objectives.

The following clusters containing two or more programs each have been analyzed and standardized thus far:

1. The Food Service Cluster
2. The Automotive Cluster
3. The Transportation and Heavy Equipment Cluster
4. The Electrical/Electronics Cluster
5. The Building Trades Cluster
6. The Metal Trades Cluster
7. The Plastics Cluster
8. The Agriculture Cluster
9. The Business Skills Cluster
10. The Health Occupations Cluster
11. The Social Skills Cluster

The Academic Clusters are not included in this listing since they had been analyzed and formalized under a previous effort* and were incorporated into the urban centers' Corpsman Advisory System without changes.

The Job Corps has now begun a developmental effort that will result in a complete and consistent Data-Communications Subsystem. This effort requires 1) the development of sufficient software and 2) the acquisition by individual centers of certain new hardware. Various options are involved in this effort that have not yet been resolved.

Each of the individual centers is preparing an individual proposal regarding their proposed plan for implementing the Advisory Subsystem and the Reinforcement Subsystem.

Summary

The Corpsman Advisory System's current contribution to Job Corps is twofold. The system provides Job Corps with a model of how the Job Corps Men's Urban Centers' education process might work. And, by specifying behavioral objectives, the system allows Job Corps (and anyone else for that matter) to determine exactly what a corpsman should be learning in a given course of instruction.

The CAS Curriculum Subsystem model has already resulted in proposals for the development of cost-effectiveness techniques to rationalize the ongoing curriculum development efforts. And the existence of behavioral objectives has lead directly to the development of sophisticated audio-visual module tests that will allow for quality control over Job Corps graduates from all men's urban centers.

While the Corpsman Advisory System is far from completed, its success thus far has resulted in many new discoveries in the area of educational systems analysis and development. The Job Corps' commitment to the implementation of the total Corpsman Advisory System with all its educational, counseling and motivational (reinforcement) subsystems — perhaps the most comprehensive educational systems effort yet undertaken — seems likely to prove a rich source of new ideas and a "systems laboratory" for all educators for many years to come.

□

---

*As part of the conservation center CAS effort directed by Margulies, Speeth and Goldberg.

Instructional Systems Development: Cost and Content in College Courses

Robert M. Brown

An instructional systems development approach to education will have costs which are quite high, when it is prorated on some basis such as student-credit-hours or the cost of an instructional hour. Robert M. Morgan estimates the developmental costs at $30,000 per teaching hour.[1] The $30,000 is the developmental cost and does not include operating costs, but it does include the development of models, test construction, field testing and the like. If a course meets 45 times per semester, then the cost is $1,350,000 per course. Prorating this cost over five years (ten semesters) yields a cost of $135,000 per semester. The operating costs must be added, and if these are assumed to be 11 percent of the developmental costs, then the total cost is $135,000 + $14,850 = $149,850 rounded off to $150,000. This compares none too favorably with the cost of current instruction. The current type of course generally produces about 90 student-credit-hours at $75 per credit-hour. The instructionally-developed course would have to produce 2,000 student-credit-hours per semester to reach the "break-even" point and to be on a comparable basis.

The cost of instructional development is high when compared to current instruction. However, assume that 500,000 students are taking freshman English each year in colleges across the country for three credit-hours each; then the cost of producing 1,500,000 student-credit-hours by the current methods would be $112,500,000 per year.

The main point of the cost estimates is that the audience for instructionally-developed courses will have to be increased to pay the cost; of that *the results will be such that the extra money will be worth it.* Half of the students who enter college do not graduate for various reasons, and the remaining half do not get 100 percent in all their grades, so there is room for improvement on the college scene.

1. Morgan, Robert M. ES' 70—A Systematic Approach to Educational Change. *Educational Technology*, September, 1969, 9 (9), p. 53.

Robert M. Brown is professor of education, East Carolina University, Greenville, North Carolina.

A look at the current "content" of some college courses may help to explain part of the problem.

Two freshman courses were investigated in two modest studies, economics and biology. The purpose of the parts of the studies presented here was to determine what was being taught in each course. It was a simple survey situation with some follow-up interviews for clarification of certain points. No attempt was made to determine instructional strategies, objectives or any other aspect of instructional development; the intent was merely to find out the current situation. There was no attempt to take the current "content" and solidify it by using some of the principles of instructional development, when perhaps a completely different approach should have been used.

The faculty members in other instructional fields, although sympathetic to the aims of an instructional systems approach, do not necessarily believe in it. Many college faculty have some rather definite ideas of what should and should not be in a course, and who should have a say in its development. The ideas of fellow faculty may not necessarily agree with those of the various behaviorist schools, and the faculty members do not hesitate to express their valid opinions in these matters. It was not usually possible in a relatively short period of time to convince faculty members from other fields that instructional technology was as good a thing as some believe. This disclaimer is for the purpose of showing that there was an awareness about instructional systems development in these surveys, but it was not used in that context after several meetings with fellow faculty members.

The two small pilot studies on "content" generally followed the same approach. The tables of contents of the most popular textbooks were analyzed for commonality by graduate students in each field. Faculty members in each field were asked to comment on the appropriateness of the "content" topics. The topics in economics were also checked in the handbook of the American Economics Association. The respondents were asked to check whether they gave "heavy emphasis" — 3; "moderate" — 2; "some" — 1; or "none" — 0. These values were then converted into a percentage basis.

Sixteen topics were finally used in the economics questionnaire and the topics were stated in broad terms. A good response was obtained when, for example, the instructors were asked for the degree of emphasis they placed on "money, credit and banking." But when the broad term "money, credit and banking" was further defined as "that aspect of economics which . . . etc.," then *there was almost no agreement on topics.*

The study was limited in scope, but the direction of the agreement seemed to indicate that the divergence of opinion would have grown with more respondents.[2]

The next course checked was the basic biology course for freshmen taught in college. A catalogue survey indicated that only ten percent of the colleges

2. New York State Economics Council. *A Pilot Study of the Use of Instructional Materials in Economics.* New York State Economics Council, Albany, 1969. The report gives greater details of the questionnaire and methodology.

offered a biology course for non-science majors, whereas all of them offered a biology course for science majors. This small study concentrated on the course for science majors and was conducted by questionnaire and interview. It was felt that there would be more agreement on the topics of a natural science course, biology, than on a social science course, economics. But this did not happen, and the range of content, once again, was quite wide.

The purpose of presenting two "content" investigations was to give some basis to the belief that no two courses are the same on the college level. The wide variation in "content" and the need for large audiences, because of the cost of instructional development, pose a dilemma which is difficult to overcome. If other fields—such as history, art and mathematics—were investigated, the results also would probably show wide variations. College instructors generally do not like to use and will not use materials prepared or packaged by others—with the evident exception of the textbook.

The main conclusion tentatively drawn from the pilot study was that the economic instructors were attempting to get the students to look at problems the way a particular type of economist would look at them—that is, to think like an economist would think, to use an economic method, or at least to consider an economic side of problems—to appreciate an economic point of view.

The wide variety of "content" seems to point to a type of "methodology" goal where the content could vary widely. In fact, the more diverse the "content" the better, because an economic methodology or an economic way of thinking or looking at problems should be tried in many situations. The line between "content" and "methodology" was not too clear, and there appeared to be a considerable overlap.

The "content" of the biology field also varied widely, and it seemed pointed toward the same type of goals implied in the economic responses—a view or a way of looking at things rather than the mastery of particular bits of "content."

The reconciliation of cost and content is difficult at this stage of the art. Customary patterns of courses will probably change, but the change will not be too rapid unless "instructional development" finds something more than "behavioral objectives" as its goal. Just now, "behavioral objectives" on the college level seem to mean "content" objectives, which do not seem to be the "real" objectives of a college course.

Simple or complex methods of repackaging subject matter will not greatly enhance learning about a subject.

Instructional development must develop systems of approaches to "innate" methods of thinking about problems in a particular field or groups of fields, with the particular subject matter of a field as an almost insignificant variable—so that the end result is a system of thinking, approaching and appreciating within the learner from a discipline's point of view.

Instructional systems development can reach large audiences and economically justify its existence when it concentrates on new or implied goals for the various subject fields, instead of using new methods to reach old subject matter goals. □

Self-Shaping Training Systems and Flexible-Model Behavior, i.e., Sales Interviewing

Robert L. Morasky

Training in any setting usually requires a series of changes in student behavior. Without instructor control over the changes, a student's behavior can change randomly, incorrectly or, perhaps, not change at all. When the instructor is controlling the rate, order and type of behavior change occurring, the student can become like a machine, responding to stimuli only as contingencies direct. A compromise between these two positions would be a situation in which the rate, order and type of behavior changes were controlled by the student. Such a situation would logically be a "self-shaping" training system. A self-shaping training system would have to permit *and train* a student to control purposeful modifications in his behavior. Since 1966 an attempt has been made to develop and evaluate just such a system.* The purpose of this article is to illustrate the structure and rationale behind a self-shaping training system, and to summarize parts of the research evaluating it.

A training system must establish skills within a certain applied discipline in order to be optimally useful. In this case, sales interviewing was selected as terminal behavior because of the high utilitarian value, and the unique characteristics constraining such a system. Sales interviewing as a particular type of interviewing is unique, because a stable model for mastery performance does not exist. The salesman must plan and evaluate his interview style to determine what most often accomplishes his goal. The model for mastery performance must be flexible to accommodate the varying contingencies associated with the task of selling a product. This contrasts with behavior for which a stable model exists, that is, a situation in which mastery performance is predictable. It is not always possible to tell a novice salesman to follow X steps in Y order and always make a sale. This characteristic of sales interview training was one constraint on the training system developed. Other constraints arose as a result of assumptions and data concerning student behavior.

The Self-Shaping Sales Interview Training System (SSSITS) was based on two major assumptions: 1) A salesman normally does not accurately retain information about his interviews, and 2) a salesman can shape his interview behavior if he is given adequate feedback. Let us consider the validity of these two premises, and then consider some secondary questions associated with the system.

*A number of individuals and organizations have contributed to this development. Most notably among them were: Theodore Mallon of the National Life Insurance Company of Vermont, Richard Mentzer of the Equitable Life Assurance Society, and the International Textbook Company of Montreal.

Robert L. Morasky is assistant professor of psychology, State University College of Arts and Science, Plattsburgh, New York.

What is meant by the first assumption? Basically, it was assumed that an interviewer could not tell you in any accurate sense the type, sequence or amounts of certain behaviors which occurred in an interview, *even if he could recognize those behaviors at the time the interview was taking place.* In order to evaluate the first assumption, subjects conducted simulated sales interviews with clients provided by the experimenter. Immediately after completing the interviews, the subjects were asked if certain behaviors occurred, in what order they occurred and how often they occurred in terms of percent of the total interview. Afterwards, each subject completed an interaction analysis of his interview. In all cases significant differences were found between the immediate subjective evaluation and the interaction analysis data. The first assumption may be accepted as valid.

The important implication which follows from the first assumption is that if an interviewer cannot accurately recall what happened in an interview which he has just left, he cannot evaluate the behaviors which occurred in that interview. Therefore, it becomes imperative for him to have information about what happened in his interview.

At least two phases of the SSSITS are suggested by the first assumption and its implications. In one phase the student conducts a simulated interview attempting to achieve some objective. In the other or following phase he conducts an interaction analysis in order to receive feedback concerning his behaviors during the interview.

Most students must be taught how to complete an interaction analysis, so a training phase was necessary which accomplished that objective. In addition, interaction analysis required the use of specific behavior categories which the student must be able to discriminate. Therefore, two more phases can be added to the system; an interaction analysis training phase and a behavior category discrimination training phase.

Some explanation of "interaction analysis training" and "behavior category discrimination training" are probably necessary at this point. The interaction analysis technique used was similar to the system described by Amidon & Hough (1967). Basically, the person performing the interaction analysis identifies the type of behavior occurring at three-second intervals. It is possible to gather a variety of information from interaction analysis data; however, only four types of information were relevant to the self-shaping system: (1) the types of behavior which occurred, (2) the order in which the behaviors occurred, (3) the amount of each behavior which occurred and (4) the behavioral patterns which occurred.

Before a student could use the interaction analysis technique, he had to learn which behaviors or behavioral classes were relevant. This was accomplished in the behavior category discrimination training phase. Ten behavior types were identified by the researchers as a result of an interview task analysis. More will be said later regarding the validity and reliability of the behavior categories.

It should be noted here that the instruction in both of the training phases was accomplished through the use of self-instructional materials. The interaction analysis training materials could best be described as following a "mathetic" design (see Gilbert, 1962), whereas the discrimination materials employed a consistent "discrimination programming" design (see Smith, 1967).

The second assumption upon which the system is based suggests that if an interviewer is given information about what occurred in an interview, he can exert more control over subsequent interviews. In order to test this assumption, an augmented feedback mechanism was needed. Bertalanffy (1968) has suggested that feedback serves to make a system self-regulating and guarantees direction of action. The interaction analysis served this purpose.

In order for a student to demonstrate that he was exerting more control over an interview, it was necessary for him to

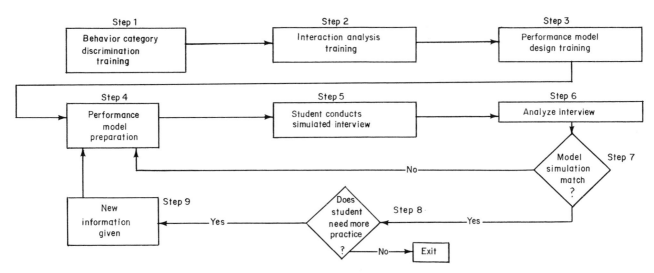

Figure 1
The Total Self-Shaping Sales
Interview Training System.

develop a model before the interview which he would attempt to match during the interview. It was found that subjects could not match their early simulated interviews to model interviews which they had previously developed, but model matching occurred with varying rapidity as more simulated interviews were conducted and feedback obtained. If feedback was not available, model matching did not increase in frequency. Control over the type of behaviors occurring in an interview was achieved most rapidly, although control over the sequence of behaviors was not difficult for subjects to achieve. Given a plus or minus five percent limit, the matching of model to simulated interview behavior percents required the greatest number of simulated interviews. The second assumption may also be accepted as valid. A sales interviewer can learn to control the interaction in an interview within the limits of the feedback available.

Three more phases should now be added to the system. In Figure 1 a "Performance Model Design Training" phase, a "Performance Model Preparation" phase and a "Model-Simulation Match?" decision phase are inserted in their proper positions. The self-shaping interview training system is now almost complete. Let us survey the total system:

Step 1: *Behavior Category Discrimination Training*
An instructional phase in which the student must learn to identify examples of the parts of mastery performance.
Step 2: *Interaction Analysis Training*
An instructional phase, the purpose of which is to give the student skills to objectively evaluate his attempts at mastery performance.
Step 3: *Performance Model Design Training*
An instructional phase in which the student either learns what the specifications for mastery performance are, or he must learn to construct a set of specifications for his behavior.
Step 4: *Performance Model Preparation*
An operation phase in which the student prepares a model of mastery performance.
Step 5: *Student Conducts Simulated Interview*
An operation phase in which the student attempts mastery performance to match his model.
Step 6: *Analyze Interview*
An operation phase in which the student must measure his performance and compare it to the model of mastery performance.

Step 7: *Model-Simulation Match?*
A decision phase in which the data from the interaction analysis is compared to the model. Options: A match allows the student to proceed to Step 8. A non-match recycles the student back to Step 4.
Step 8: *"Does Student Need More Practice?"*
An administrative phase in which instructor decides if the student has had sufficient opportunity to demonstrate his ability to control his behavior and behavior change.
Step 9: *New Information Given*
An operation phase which places the student who needs more practice back in the system.

Shaping of any behavior most often requires several approximations to a terminal behavior. In fact, it is the reinforcement of successive approximations which allows shaping to take place. Shaping or successive approximations to mastery performance are accounted for in the "shaping-loop" of the system, Steps 4 through 9.

Behavioral categories to be used in a system such as this one must meet certain criteria in order to function. In the SSSITS, ten behavior types were used. Five categories pertained to the salesman's behavior, while four involved customer behavior. One category was non-specific. As stated previously they were identified as a result of task analysis of actual interviews. They were not meant to be either extensive or detailed. They must, however, be sufficient in number and kind to provide meaningful feedback to a student.

Certain questions should be applied to behavior categories identified for use in any shaping system. Specifically, one might ask, are they sufficiently different to allow discrimination? It is obvious that fewer, broader categories will permit more gross discrimination, hence, greater reliability. For example, if only two categories—client responses and sales interviewer responses—were used, the identification of what is taking place is reasonably simple and highly reliable. On the other hand, with ten behavior categories, fine discriminations must be made, and reliability becomes a function of training and adequacy of category definitions. Comparisons of subject's interaction analysis data to experimenter's analysis data of the same interview showed a range of correlations between .76 and .93. The subjects evaluated for reliability had all completed the discrimination training phase of the SSSITS, and had completed from one to four simulated interviews. Hence, the categories appear to be sufficiently different to permit reliable discrimination.

115

Do the categories of behavior represent "important" events in a successful sales interview? Since the categories were derived as a result of observation of actual interviews, evaluation of selling strategies and discussions with subject matter experts, their validity as "important" behaviors is open to question. Early in the development of the system, experienced, successful sales managers were asked to evaluate video tapes of novice salesmen. These experts did the evaluation without having had training in recognition of the behaviors identified in the SSSITS. The significant aspects of the taped interviews identified by the experts were remarkably similar to the shortcomings and strong points identified by a nonsalesman using interaction analysis with the ten categories.

A further indication of the adequacy of any category system is its effectiveness at accounting for all the behaviors occurring in mastery performance. This particular system of categories had one "residue" or "non-specific" category into which any salesman or client behavior is placed that cannot easily be associated with one of the other categories. Obviously, if the percent of the total interview devoted to these non-specific categories was consistently and excessively great, say 30 percent, it would be necessary to examine (1) the discriminability of the other categories and (2) the possibility that a substantial behavior, yet unrecognized, is being placed in the non-specific category. Analysis of actual and simulated interviews using the SSSITS categories has yielded a mean of 19.4 percent for the use of the client and the salesman non-specific behavior categories. These findings suggest that the SSSITS categories can serve as a basis for interview analysis and feedback.

Other SSSITS studies completed have evaluated the need for individual system components and the effectiveness of the components developed. Future research will concentrate on the effectiveness of the system in an applied setting.

As mentioned earlier, a training system with this structure can successfully permit and train the student to make purposeful modifications in his behavior. Student behavior changes are accomplished with a minimum of instructor guidance and control. Feedback to the student does *not* come from an instructor, but, rather, is secured by the student through his use of an analysis technique. Success, or attainment of an objective via a controlled sequence of behaviors, can be evaluated and recognized by the student, independent of instructor involvement. The system does allow "shaping of the self."

Systems with components serving similar functions as the SSSITS are being used to teach a variety of skills such as printing, composition and classroom interaction. There is no reason to assume that the basic notion of a self-shaping system is applicable only to sales interviewing training. It could just as easily be applied to such areas as group and individual therapy training or cross-examination training for lawyers. A student's control over modifications in his behavior through the use of self-shaping systems might provide a closer approximation to self-selection and self-pacing in education. □

References

Amidon, E.J. & Hough, J.B., *Interaction Analysis: Theory, Research and Application.* Reading, Mass.: Addison-Wesley, 1967.

Bertalanffy, L.V. *General System Theory.* New York: George Braziller, Inc., 1968.

Gilbert, T.F. Mathetics: The Technology of Education. *Journal of Mathetics,* 1962, *1,* 7-74.

Smith, D.E.P. *On Discrimination Programming.* Ann Arbor: The University of Michigan Center for Research on Language and Language Behavior, 1967. (Mimeo.)

Applied Instructional Systems

Frederick G. Knirk and Castelle G. Gentry

A problem that has long plagued teachers and instructional technologists alike involves the determination of appropriate media for specific teaching purposes. Part of the problem has been the unfortunate view of media in isolation of the entire instructional system. Interestingly, two seemingly opposing views, the humanistic and the systematic, are currently keeping our attention on the contextual question.

Thanks to a number of researchers in several related disciplines, schemata for selecting appropriate media are beginning to emerge. This paper serves to briefly outline one such schema and to point up major weaknesses requiring attention before such a plan can be functional.

The system for developing instruction outlined below is a synthesis, an operational focusing of information from scattered places in the systems literature. Included are specific grouping of systems procedures and techniques resulting from our application of these ideas to several instructional problems. We are presently using the system to develop two basic courses in the area of instructional technology and to develop a "model" set of teaching procedures for the educabally retarded. Refinement has been guided by systems concepts despite the pressure of pragmatic concerns. This does not deny the eclectic nature of our present model.

Despite the constraint of linearity imposed by print, the system is highly dynamic, and can be expected to change through the continued insight that real-time experiment affords. We anticipate that the conciseness of this paper will be seen as valuable in that it gives sufficient detail of the workings of the system, while providing an overall view of a system for developing instruction.

From an instructional systems point of view, the schema depicted here consists of six com-

Frederick G. Knirk is associate professor, department of instructional technology, University of Southern California. **Castelle G. Gentry** is chairman of the department of instructional technology, University of Toledo.

ponents: goal determination, analysis, prescription, implementation, evaluation and revision. As in most systems, these components are controlled by planned feedback **(Figure 1)**. The system has a simplicity that is highly deceptive, implying that the reduction of a problem to a series of interrelated boxes, neatly labeled, represents a real solution. In fact, we have come a long way toward making this scheme work, but difficult theoretical and technical problems still oppose effective use of such a model. It is useful in our initial discussion to consider each of the components separately.

Goal determination

Determining the over-riding purposes of a system is a highly significant and direction-imposing part of a system, but it will be mentioned only briefly in this space.

In this article, the emphasis will be on implementing the goals without attempting to evaluate their worthiness. The goals are assumed to be valid, reliable and intrinsically valuable.

Task analysis

Task analysis (in various guises) has received a great deal of attention during the last few years, and this activity has served to strengthen the instructional systems concept. A careful examination of this component is useful in clarifying the instructional systems model presented here. The parameters for task analysis listed below are illustrated in detail in the succeeding pages:

1. reducing the goal to its several general objectives;
2. restating general objectives as terminal objectives and writing a criterion item for each terminal objective;
3. delineating the tasks that make up each general objective;

Figure 1

Planned Feedback

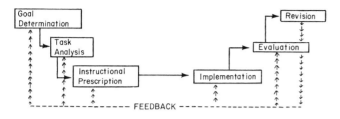

4. writing enabling objectives and criterion items for each of the tasks;
5. placing the objectives into a behavioral hierarchy;
6. balancing the objectives (taxonomic domains); and
7. sequencing the terminal objectives.

Reducing the goal to general objectives needs to be accomplished with some precision (**Figure 2**); otherwise, violation of important rules for behaviorizing objectives will result later in the system. A technique that has proven successful is to assume that a general objective has been written only when a **terminal objective**, specifying **one** behavior, can be written for it. As long as more than one behavior is required to satisfy a general objective, it should be considered to consist of more than one general objective. The breakdown should continue until one specific behavior satisfies the general objective (step 2). A major value of such a technique is that it provides a common reference point for others studying or developing similar instructional systems.

The criterion item written for the terminal objective serves to evaluate whether the general objective has been met or not, but it does not provide much instructional guidance. The third step of breaking the general objective down into tasks of the corresponding enabling objectives provides considerably more information for instructional guidance. The point needs to be emphasized that in this scheme a terminal objective is written for each general objective (G.O.1, G.O.2, G.O.3, etc.) and that each general objective is broken down into its logical tasks. Enabling objectives (E.O.) and their criterion items (C.I.) are then written for each task (T)

The third step involves delineating the tasks that make up each general objective. For example, given the general objective "to read the first grade level book," the tasks generated by such a general objective would include such tasks as: using the parts of speech, understanding punctuation, knowing how to construct sentences, using contextual clues, etc. If it should appear useful, it is relatively simple to continue the breakdown as illustrated in

Figure 2

Task Analysis

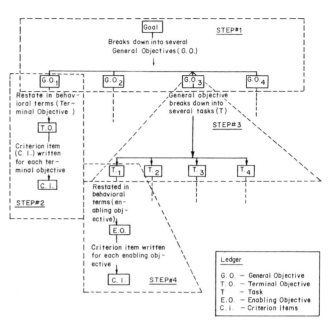

Figure 3. That is, tasks may be further subdivided into more specific kinds of knowledges, skills and/or values. Note also that it is important to continue the development of behavioral objectives and criterion items for each of the specifics. Each of these specific objectives is designed to assure that the enabling objective (written for the task) is met, just as each of the enabling objectives is designed to assure that the terminal objective is met. The analysis, as described here, generates a behavioral hierarchy (**Figure 4**), which serves to clarify the order in which the objectives should be learned. Usually the more specific objectives are dealt with first, then the enabling objectives, climaxing in the terminal objective.

Note that the scheme for breaking the goal down into its components (**Figure 2**) implies a more complicated sequencing problem. Since each of the general objectives of the instructional goal generates its own terminal objective, there still remains the task of sequencing the several terminal objectives of the behavioral hierarchies (**Figure 5**). Sequencing the objectives in this fashion makes a final ordering, or the developing of a critical path, much simpler. By inspection, it is now possible to determine, across the hierarchies, which objective logically precedes another and which of them can or should be accomplished concurrently. It is also useful at this point to determine if the various domains (cognitive, affective, psychomotor) have been covered satisfactorily. One way of making this determination is to match the objectives in the hierarchies with the categories developed by Bloom (Bloom, **et al.**, 1956), Krathwohl (Krathwohl, **et al.**, 1964), and Simpson (Simpson, **et al.**, 1966-67). The procedure usually points up to the systems designer those content areas not provided for in the initial planning.

Task prescription

The boundaries between Task Analysis and Task Prescription **(Figure 1)** are not clearly defined, so that, perhaps, it might be argued that the first stage of the prescription, as arbitrarily determined here, could well be included under Task Analysis.

Figure 3

Subdivision of Tasks

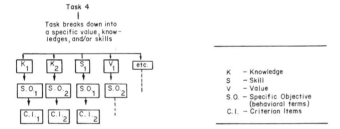

The Task Prescription stage is concerned with categorizing the objectives on the basis of learning types. Placement of the boundaries does not appear significant as long as the order of the stages is maintained. The journey from objective specification to the specification of instructional strategies and media is the core of a useful model. Unfortunately, this process is presently the most ill-defined part of instructional models. The most useful approach currently available is one described by Briggs (Briggs, **et al.**, 1967). Mager and Beach (1967) use a similar approach in presenting an instructional model dealing with vocational instruction. The approach uses a set of eight learning types explicated by Gagne (Gagne, 1965).

Briefly, Gagne contends that these eight learning categories encompass all possible behaviors. He has also described the essential conditions complementing learning behaviors in each of the eight categories. To oversimplify, if the objective can be placed in the appropriate learning category (problem-solving, principle, concept learning, multiple discrimination, etc.) then the learning conditions assigned to that particular learning category can be identified **(Figure 6)**. With these conditions stated, it would seem that the selection of a teaching/learning strategy and the selection of the right

media would be much simplified. But, in fact, this is not so. The problem of appropriate media selection is presently receiving considerable attention, as are problems of bridging between the conditions for learning and the selection of strategy. A major obstacle to media and strategy selection is that the learning conditions are too vague. The addition of a set of media characteristics which can be matched with the objectives, the learning conditions and the teaching strategy is a contribution to the selection process. It must be admitted that at this point practitioners using the model find themselves operating primarily at the art end of the instructional continuum. That is, they find it necessary to make decisions on an intuitive and expedient basis.

A major element of the systems approach that needs attention at the stage where objectives are translated into strategies is that of **determining alternative solutions** to the instructional problem. This notion is foreign to most educators, who often feel fortunate if they can generate one viable solution per problem. The usual procedures are to modify what is presently being done or has been done, and to consider all of the constraints before doing that. The idea of temporarily putting constraints aside and deliberately developing several alternatives smacks of inefficiency to the busy educator.

Figure 4

Behavioral Hierarchy

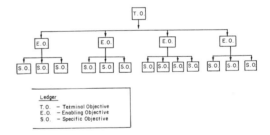

But there is some evidence that such an approach has a visible pay-off. First, the development of alternative strategies reduces the likelihood that a possible solution will be overlooked because some constraint such as money, time, or other resource makes viable consideration appear impossible at the time. Secondly, there is evidence that the process of evaluating alternatives often results in a synthesis of the best qualities of the several alternatives to produce one which is superior to any one of the original alternatives.

Prior to synthesis, it is important to look at the **expectations** and **constraints** relevant to the system. These evaluative criteria are used to select the best alternative, and to reject or change those which are not possible. At this point, the concept of **trade-off** has relevance; soft money (i.e., teacher time) versus hard money (i.e., cash), individualization vs. large group instruction, live teachers vs. mediated teachers, population to be served, entering behaviors,

Figure 5
Sequencing of Behavioral Hierarchies

Figure 6
Objective, Method, Media Match

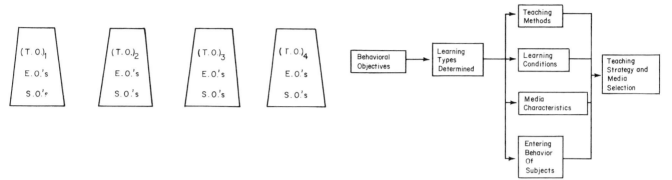

performance level are examples. Checklists of generalized expectations and constraints that can affect the operation of any system are available, but each instructional problem has constraints and expectations unique to itself, and are best discovered by those familiar with the environmental context of the problem. The willingness to ferret out the constraints and expectations and to state them in a finite manner pays high dividends for discovering solutions not easily perceived otherwise. Such criteria are also useful for evaluation of the system.

Despite apparent weaknesses, the proposed model does provide a testable strategy for attacking instructional problems.

Instructional implementation

Another factor which cannot be nicely catalogued has, arbitrarily, been placed within the implementation stage. This is the development of **feedback and control mechanisms** of the system. A condition providing mixed blessings is the self-perpetuating nature of organizations, or systems.

Almost immediately after the creation of a system, defenses designed to maintain a static condition begin to take form. Such defenses often reduce the usefulness of a system in terms of its original purpose. The questions are: how can feedback be provided for a system, and what controls are necessary to assure that the system will be modified on the basis of that feedback? The precise specification of behavioral objectives is one giant step in the right direction. Strangely, a capability that most instructional systems lack is a means for evaluating the product of the system. A question dealt with most superficially in our schools is: do our students learn the behaviors that our system was designed to teach? The responsibility of the feedback component in a system is to ensure that the question will be asked, and that corrective action will be taken when indicated by the feedback.

The shortage of viable feedback alternatives is a second major weakness in the proposed model. The discipline called cybernetics (Buckley, 1968), whose central theme is regulation and control, speaks to the problem, although at present most of its principles are too general for much practical use in instructional systems. Others, particularly decision theorists (Miller and Starr, 1967), are generating ideas and information that provide some direction for the feedback mechanisms. As examples: auditing by an outside group is one feedback technique that reduces the bias within a system; the establishment of a problem-finding group within the system is another. Finally, the applied behavioral scientists, with such techniques as T-grouping and sensitivity training are working to promote openness in societal groups so that feedback will not only be received, but will be acted on, as well.

The steps within the implementation component have uniqueness for current instructional systems, sadly enough, **only** in terms of discussion. It is expected that the media prescribed in the previous stage would be either available or produced, that logistical support would be organized, and that a sample of the target population would be contracted for purposes of running a pilot or a field test of the system. It is appropriate that we consider the value of field testing for a moment. The willingness to adopt concepts without adequate preliminary testing in the field seems a strange phenomenon to persons outside education. For example, an industrialist would regard as suicidal the flooding of the market with a product whose effectiveness and marketability had not been previously tested. What is not apparent to the uninitiated is that it doesn't matter what you do if you lack criteria for measuring the effects of what you do. This does not mean that educators do not apply criteria to their situations, but that the criteria applied are often only indirectly related to some behavioral change in students.

Within the boundaries of the "systems approach," field testing of the system usually takes place in two stages: (1) the individual components are checked out under the most realistic conditions possible, and (2) the entire system is tested with samples made up of students from the target population. The feedback from these two stages determine how many cycles are necessary. Many useful techniques have been rejected after premature introduction by teachers and administrators into the system, due to defects which could have been readily spotted and remedied if field testing had been carried out. When an older system is being encroached upon, it requires little justification for defending its boundaries. There is not thought of overcoming this defensive characteristic of systems entirely, for the loss of such a stabilizing factor could only result in chaos; but awareness of the tendency provides a more meaningful control of the rate of change in a system.

Evaluation of the system

As will have been noted, various factors relevant to the evaluation of a system are discussed in sections dealing with other components of the system. The earlier statements about feedback mechanisms has particular relevance for this component. It is under the Evaluation rubric that validation of the criterion instruments and other feedback mechanisms fit. Effective models for such validation (Stufflebeam, 1968) are available, and it would logically follow that instruments thus validated could in turn be used to validate the entire instructional system. Information or data from this component will prove most useful to the following Revision Component if the results are presented both in terms of individual components and in terms of the entire system. If the evaluative function becomes a continuing and on-going process (for each component), effective and replicable instructional systems should result. A major spin-off of such evaluation may be the encouragement of increased numbers of educators to move to a systems approach.

Revision or modification of the system

A systematic consideration of data is the first step in revising a system. The process of developing possible alternative solutions for each defective component is similar to that in the prescription stage. Again, the "best" alternative is selected and modified in light of the expectations and constraints which define the boundaries in which the system user operates. Changes are made based on the feedback data, and the system is again field tested prior to full implementation. It should be reiterated that the feedback mechanisms do provide a window through which we can pin-point malfunctioning or nonfunctioning parts of the system, but determination of new solutions moves from formula to the creative realm of individual and group artistry, to a process comprised of intuition, conjecture and experience. Lack of specific practicable means for ensuring that evaluative data will be acted upon, and that solutions forthcoming will be implemented, continue to be major weaknesses of instructional systems. The development of effective control mechanisms has the highest priority if a system following the proposed model is to operate successfully.

In conclusion, it is worth noting that the synthesis of findings across the sciences of communications, psychology, cybernetics, management and technology have promise for a developing science, or technology, of instruction. Practical problems, such as the shortage of teachers possessing skills for developing behavioral objectives, and distaste for developing such objectives due to the tedious and time-consuming nature of the task, are being overcome.

Such models as the one proposed give promise to a highly essential condition, that of producing **testable** instructional systems. The value of such systems is, of course, that they are subject to refinement and improvement in terms of student learning. □

References

Bloom, Benjamin S. et al. **Taxonomy of Educational Objectives, Handbook I: Cognitive Domain.** New York: David McKay Company, Inc., 1956.

Briggs, Leslie J. et al. **Instructional Media: A Procedure for the Design of Multi-Media Instruction.** Pittsburgh, Penn.: American Institutes for Research, 1967, pp. 28-52.

Buckley, Walter (Ed.) **Modern Systems Research for the Behavioral Scientist.** Chicago: Aldine Publishing Company, 1968.

Gagne, Robert M. **The Conditions of Learning.** New York: Holt, Rinehart and Winston, Inc., 1965, Chapter 2.

Krathwohl, David R. et al. **Taxonomy of Educational Objectives, Handbook II: Affective Domain.** New York: David McKay Company, Inc., 1964.

Mager, Robert F. & Beach, Kenneth M., Jr. **Developing Vocational Instruction.** Palo Alto: Fearon Publishers, 1967.

Miller, David W. & Starr, Martin K. **The Structure of Human Decisions.** Englewood Cliffs: Prentice-Hall, Inc., 1967, pp. 150-154.

Simpson, Elizabeth. The Classification of Educational Objectives: Psychomotor Domain. **Illinois Teacher of Home Economics Journal,** Vol. **10** (4) Winter 1966-67, pp. 110-144.

Stufflebeam, Daniel L. Toward a Science of Educational Evaluation. **Educational Technology,** July 30, 1968, pp. 5-12.

Structural Communication: An Interactive System for Teaching Understanding

Naomi Zeitlin and Albert L. Goldberg

"The implied completeness of some instructional packages may very well deny the spontaneity of a less-structured curriculum and inhibit participation by the student."

— John I. Goodlad

There are few discussions of multimedia which do not include, at some point, Webster's definition of "media." This definition now: "a means of effecting or conveying something." Add the suffix "multi," and the genii of hardware and gadgetry springs out from the magic lantern. But in the '70's, researchers in the field are able to consider Webster's definition objectively, and separate the magic from the lantern.

Medium and presentation

Tosti and Ball (1969) proposed a new system model whose significant feature lay in the separation of medium from presentation form. Westinghouse Learning Corporation is currently developing such a multimedia course for the Office of Education at the United States Naval Academy, Annapolis, Maryland.

Naomi Zeitlin is an analyst with Westinghouse Learning Corporation, supervising the application and development of Structural Communication materials.

Albert L. Goldberg is division manager and project director, Westinghouse Learning Corporation, Annapolis, Maryland.

The work described in this article is being carried out by Westinghouse Learning Corporation, Annapolis, Maryland, and Structural Communication Systems Ltd., Kingston-upon-Thames, Surrey, England, in conjunction with the United States Naval Academy and the United States Office of Education under Contract No. N00600-68-C-1525.

The course, INTRODUCTION TO PSYCHOLOGY AND LEADERSHIP, is an experimental design model that will yield data on the comparative impact of presentational forms. The model provides for isolation of major variables, in time and form, in the stimulus, response and management dimensions. A unique feature of the course, though not an intrinsic feature in the design, is the inclusion of programmed group discussion. This is done by the technique called STRUCTURAL COMMUNICATION™, which has been under development in England for the past four years, and is, as yet, relatively unknown on this side of the Atlantic.

As will be described in greater detail below, Structural Communication is generally allied to the WLC research design, in that it is a medium in the definitional sense — a form for effecting a (successful) communication. The central device in Structural Communication is the Study or Discussion Unit, (which is the equivalent of the "program" in P.I.) depending on whether the technique operates in the individual or group mode. Structural Communication Systems, Ltd. (Kingston-upon-Thames, England), which invented the technique, is developing eight such units for Westinghouse Learning, to be used as the enrichment segments of the USNA course. These are in the Discussion Unit mode, and provide a self-operational, controlled situation package for group discussion within the context of the subject matter.

A significant gap

The use of Structural Communication in a multi-media setting rectifies a serious defect in the average model. To date, there has been no "technological" means of bringing students into interaction with each other. The student interacts solely with the medium itself, so to speak. Le Baron, a "self-confessed" proponent of multimedia (in a paper prepared for the AAAS convention, "Communications and Multimedia in Education," Dallas, Texas, 1968), made the following point:

> "No mediated classroom so far has made provision for comfortable interaction of groups of students, or for direct student-to-student interaction within the context of the subject matter. Yet it appears that the true vitality of the new media rests on the ability to promote just such new and exciting modes of learning interaction, both among individual students and other persons, and between the individual student and the technological system."

Structural Communication fills these requirements. Outwardly, it bears the typical features of a P.I. technique. It is individualized and paced; it can be projected via hardware; and provides computer compatible data. Atypically, it does not provide a conditioning learning situation (stimulus control) in the domain of knowledge, and it does not proceed in a small-step linear sequence. It is, by nature, an integrative, synthesizing technique that puts the student into a situation where understanding is gained. The student gains insight into the topic as a whole system, and the mental process is in both the cognitive and affective domains. The student is generally forced into a realization of his own values or viewpoints by a challenge-response situation, so that the communication he is receiving is less colored and distorted by his ingrained assumptions. The unit provides optional situations for decision making. It is this openendedness that distinguishes Structural Communication from other programming techniques.

The communication of understanding

The art of communicating understanding consists in devising a means whereby the recipient of a message can reproduce or simulate the action by which the author reaches his own understanding. The author can be said to understand a topic when he has grasped the concept and principles that underly it, which are interwoven to form the whole. This necessitates a high degree of expertise on the part of the author, not just in the programming technique, but in the subject matter itself. Thus, "Structural Communication author" is a more appropriate title than program writer.

In the USNA Leadership Course, the student is taught principles of psychology and operational guidelines for military organization and management. In reality there is an almost untraceable merging of these elements. Structural Communication as a technique for communicating this reality helps the student

to distinguish the elements, and understand the dynamism that brings the elements together.

It is generally assumed that P.I. causes the student to learn in a conditioned way, and conditioning results in a reflexive response. Structural Communication provides the conditions for a student to learn by a simulated experience, and calls for a reflective response. In the linear program the communication is transmitted according to narrow and precise behavioral objectives. The control of the process is completely outside the student. Structural Communication on the other hand is broad-based and relies on the student's own controlling capacity.

The educational context of Structural Communication

Structural Communication is used where the aim is to educate the students into thinking about the patterns and judging the processes that bind the elements, i.e., looking into the wider relevance of what they are taught. In the WLC course at the USNA, for example, the midshipman is taught the principles and characteristics of individual psychology, group behavior, the military organizational set-up, military performance, and accepted behavior. How can he make sense of the reality? Structural Communication challenges the student to review "real life situations" (case studies) in terms of a dynamic web of these elements which he has learned in linear organization. This means an exercise in "synthetic" understanding, and judgment on how and where the operational or causal principles apply or lie so that he can use his knowledge for decision making.

In structuring the material, the author is concerned with two areas — subject matter, i.e., information and theme, though in reality they are not separable. The type of themes Structural Communication deals with are as follows (see **Systematics**, Dec., 1967):

(a) visible arrays: such as an animal body or man-made mechanism;
(b) situations or events, historical or hypothetical;
(c) subjective experiences, such as works of art and art appreciation;
(d) ideational systems, such as scientific hypotheses; and
(e) imperatives, i.e., instructions leading to action.

What is a Structural Communication?

The approach used in communicating such themes is that of Gestalt psychology. Structural Communication concerns itself with the communication

of a unified message, with the premise that the "whole is greater than the sum of its parts." Communication of such a simple "message" intact is a special art, and the technique that Structural Communication employs is similar to that of a successful dialogue. A speaker will only know at the time of speaking if the listener has understood him if he, the speaker, can verify this by asking specific questions, and get feedback which indicates that the recipient has understood.

It is this very simple procedure that Structural Communication reproduces, but without the physical presence of the author, through the Study Unit. The verification procedure consists of monitoring the significant points of the message. In education this offers a particular facility — that of monitoring the student's reception of a lesson for misconceptions, where misconceptions are known to occur in the teaching of a set of principles or operation of principles.

The procedural flow chart in Structural Communication is designed according to the structural principle: "Nature and all situations with which we have to deal are organized structures. They are neither atomic and random nor are they homogeneous and continuous. We recognize and understand situations to the extent that they have a well-defined structure. Human behavior is successful to the extent that it corresponds to the patterns of the situation, both internal and environmental." Thus, the process the author goes through in preparing the program — designing his communication — is one of mapping these inner and outer patterns, and the relationships between them, in terms of the dynamic components of time and space. From this "map" he will derive a matrix and set of problems which together form the core of the Study Unit. The matrix, usually 20-25 items, called the Response Indicator, is the device that enables the recipient to "talk back" to the author. The Response Indicator, therefore, acts as the communication interface. The items are usually statements of fact, concepts or operations. They act as semantic units, and as such may be used to discuss different dimensions of the theme (indicated in the problems) where the items vary in significance, value and interpretation. The response matrix, then, restates in a highly summarized and "structured" form the significant parts of the theme.

A simple analogy will serve to explain the above. Take the case of the elephant in the fable of the four blind men. Each man has a valid description of the elephant; that is, valid according to **his own** criteria. The sum of their viewpoints represent a theme: blind men and an elephant. But this, of course, is not the whole story; that is, the whole story of the elephant as a living, functioning entity in his particular environment. If we were to communicate an understanding of "the what," "the why" and "the how" of the elephant, we should have to start with the elephant himself. Appropriate items for a Structural Communication Response Indicator would be a summary of the parts of the elephant. To **understand** the beast, however, as the dynamic entity, in its particular environment, we would have to consider these parts as they appear not only to blind men, but to men like the hunter, the circus owner and the naturalist. The elephant's size would be significant to the circus owner as a source of humor in the ring; the huge tusks would be of interest to the hunter as a source of profit; and the huge feet would tell the naturalist something of the animal's unique ability to survive in rough terrain. A careful structuring of such factors, how they interrelate, and what their conjoint and diverse significance is, will gradually build up a complete and organic description. This then is the substance of a Structural Communication.

Feedback and diagnosis

The student's understanding is verified by discussion of the important dimensions of the theme. He registers his response to the three to five problems posed, and a diagnostic technique is incorporated into the study unit to analyze typical sets of combinations drawn from the response indicator. As this matrix contains items relevant to the theme as a whole, there are no "wrong" items, and hence no "wrong" answers, but merely **degrees of relevance.** Hence, Structural Communication provides a genuine device for open-ended, programmed instruction.

Obviously, a special set of criteria for diagnosis is called for. The following are examples of typical criteria by which the author designs the feedback system (see **Systematics,** December 1967):

(1) **"The Criterion of Misconception.** The inclusion of certain items as a response to a particular problem is found to correlate with the hypothesis that the student is approaching the problem with some notion incompatible with the solution. The student is routed to a comment that indirectly points out the possible difficulties that have arisen."

(2) **"The Criterion of Key Points.** The omission of certain items as a response to a particular problem is correlated with the student's failure to grasp essentials necessary to the approach to the problem. The student is routed to a comment which indirectly indicates features not noticed or not given sufficient importance by the student."

(3) **"The Criterion of Solution in Depth.** The inclusion of specific sets of items indicates an insight or deeper perception on the part of the student, and the comment is an encouragement to him to pursue this insight." The criterion may be taken a stage further and test for the recognition of internal contradiction between items — the conditional omission of certain items based on the set included.

The diagnostic and feedback technique thus serves not just as a verification of successful communication but as an instrument for revealing more complex aspects of the theme, once the basic intention is understood, to analyze the logic of a response and instruct the student in reasoning, and to reflect on the consequences of his decision. He is thus instructed in assessing the route by which he arrives at a particular solution or misconception — in plain language — not just **that** he has made a mistake or hit the right answer, but **how** he got there!

How is a study unit organized?

A Study Unit has six major sections:

1) **Intention** — This section briefly describes the theme the author intends to communicate, and its general or curricular context.

2) **Presentation** — This gives a carefully considered outline of the theme and any subsidiary themes. The student assimilates the primary content, which is to be discussed in greater detail in subsequent sections. The Presentation may be in textual form, or through other media such as a sound tape, film, or even physical objects. It may even be given as a lecture, or be derived from practical activities.

3) **Investigation** — In this section, the problems are posed which challenge the student's understanding of the primary message, and act both as a channel for further information and as a means whereby the author guides a student in his investigation of the topic in detail. The problems may be investigated on an individual basis, i.e., where the device is the Study Unit; or on a group basis, where the student investigates the theme by discussing the problems with his peers in terms of the Response Indicator, as well as with the author through the feedback system. It is at this stage that a teacher or instructor may become involved, too.

Figure 1

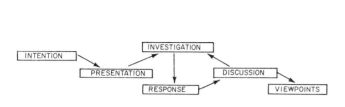

Figure 2

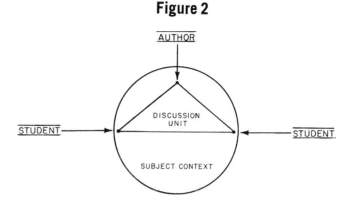

4) **Response Indicator** — Discussed above.

5) **Discussion** — This section falls into two parts: (a) the diagnostic tests which are designed to monitor the student's reception of the communication at strategic points; the student applies this test himself to the numerical array representing his selection from the response indicator to locate (b), the discussion comments.

6) **Viewpoints** — The treatment of any theme by any author always reflects a viewpoint. This may not be the only admissible one. There is, then, provision for an optional section, where the author will state his explicit viewpoint. In the Discussion Units the author states his own interpretation of the problems, which serves as a reinforcing element. It comes significantly after the student has done his own work in investigating the problems, and constructing a reasoned interpretation. By this stage the student will have developed his deeper understanding of the theme, and be able to consider the author's viewpoint from a position of strength.

Figure 1 illustrates the main pathway through a study unit.

Given the complexity of many "real-life" or natural situations, it is impossible to confront the student with every set of combinations. But, in working through a study unit, he will have experienced a **requisite** variety, given the contextual design, which will have exercised him adequately in appropriate judgmental processes and enable him to deal with analogous situations. The versatility of the technique is further demonstrated by the option, in the investigation stage, to use the unit either as an Individually Prescribed Instruction device or as part of a curricular package.

Interaction

It should now be clear to the reader how Structural Communication can fill the gap indicated by Le Baron — by providing an interaction device. The Study Unit acts as the medium through which the author (who equates with a teacher), the student, his

peer and the environment are brought into interaction. An interesting observation to report here from experiences at a field trial at the USNA was that the students interacted with each other not just within the semantic framework of the discussion unit, but also drew on their own individual experience to understand and instruct each other in understanding the theme. **Figure 2** illustrates this three-way interaction:

Some examples of Structural Communication

Structural Communication has a very wide field of application: in the sciences, humanities and management training*; also, it can be used from the elementary level to college level education. Though the services of the English company are being used within a one-course context by Westinghouse at the Naval Academy, the discussion units cover a wide range of contexts, and employ a variety of learning situations. In one such unit, "The Sociology of Discipline: The Organization," the student is asked to structure the particular discipline of three extreme instances — a penal prisoner, a monk and a diplomatic representative — in terms of inner acceptance or acquiescence, external conformity and organizational structure. However, before the student engages in investigating the problems, he is asked to draw up his own list of characteristics he associates with discipline. This means in effect that the student is confronted with his own value system. In the discussion that follows, when he uses the Response Indicator that gives the comprehensive survey of key characteristics of discipline relevant to the three polarized situations, he is made aware of the extent to which his selection diverges from the author's view because of his own value system. This enables him to distinguish whether the interpretation he gives of the problem may be unacceptable to the author based on miscomprehension or because of conflicting values.

*Applications of Stuctural Communication to Management Education are to be described in a forthcoming issue of the **Harvard Business Review** (tentatively, late 1970).

Figure 3

Response Indicator for Study Unit
"Problems in Individual Behavior"

the working of a primary drive is present	a learned drive is operating	powerful influence of the need for safety is present	the need for esteem is dominant	the need for belonging is operating
1	2	3	4	5
there has been a breakdown in reality testing	exaggerated anxiety reactions are manifest	responses are controlled by negative reinforcement	there is an aggressive response to conflict	a striving has failed to give rise to an appropriate instrumental behavior
6	7	8	9	10
a strong need for self-actualization is present	repression may be a significant factor here	double approach-avoidance conflict is evident	avoidance-avoidance conflict is shown	there has been extrinsic reinforcement
11	12	13	14	15
the activity itself is reinforcing	contradictory personality traits appear in different situations	there has been a negative transfer from prior learning	a matter of conflict between "self-image" and "social-image"	overt behavior is insufficient basis for interpretation
16	17	18	19	20
knowledge of antecedent conditions is inadequate for prediction	approach-approach conflict is evident	feedback is inadequate to permit adjustive behavior	ego gratification is impairing perception	normal social differential reinforcement has been inhibited
21	22	23	24	25

This exercise in identifying with another viewpoint to arrive at an objective understanding is taken a stage further in an accompanying unit. The second discussion of discipline, "The Sociology of Discipline: the Individual," deals with the breakdown of discipline in four significant situations, including the case of an American prisoner of war in North Korea who was susceptible to brainwashing. He is first asked, in this latter case, to adopt the hypothesis that discipline in the American army was seriously defective, and to analyze the defects by means of the matrix. He is then asked to consider the state of discipline in the camp from the Chinese point of view, to reach an understanding of how they were able to attempt brainwashing the individual. The case discussed occurred before the establishment of the Six-Point Code of Conduct, and the midshipman gains insight into the significance and importance of the six articles.

In another discussion unit, "Problems in Individual Behavior," the theme is quite different. It is concerned with the process of psychological observation and interpretation. We reproduce below the Response Indicator for this unit (Figure 3).

The objective of this unit is to give the midshipman an understanding of the value of psychological observation and interpretation itself, outside of an academic context, and an understanding how the various schools of psychology can explain a real life situation. The exercise, which integrates the fragmented examples of specific psychological phenomena he has learned, shows him the extent to which a system can describe behavior, where it falls short, overlaps or contradicts other systems.

We show in **Figure 4** a sample of the behavioral timetable the student follows. A case study is shown in **Figure 5**, which the student uses in conjunction

Figure 4
Extract from Behavioral Timetable for "Problems in Individual Behavior"

	INTERACTION ACTIVITY	TIME MINS.	DECISION MAKING ACTIVITY
	Individual Activity		
1	Study explanatory notes [text p. i]		
2	Read INTENTION [text p. 1]		
3	Read PRESENTATION [text p. 2]	20	Do PRELIMINARY EXERCISE using p.8 of this form [text p. 2]
4			
5	Study INVESTIGATION [text p. 4]		
6	Study the report for CASE STUDY ONE [text p. 5]		
7		10	Make **individual selection** from RESPONSE INDICATOR [text p. 38] for CASE STUDY ONE Response Items 1 2 3 4 5 6 7 8 9 10 11 12 13 14 15 16 17 18 19 20 21 22 23 24 25
	Group Activity		
8	Discuss CASE STUDY ONE in group		**1st group attempt** at CASE STUDY ONE Response Items 1 2 3 4 5 6 7 8 9 10 11 12 13 14 15 16 17 18 19 20 21 22 23 24 25
9			
10	Read appropriate DISCUS-SION comments [text p. 8] using diagnostic procedure [text p. vi] and discuss them	20	
11			**2nd group attempt** at CASE STUDY ONE Response Items 1 2 3 4 5 6 7 8 9 10 11 12 13 14 15 16 17 18 19 20 21 22 23 24 25
12	Read the CONCLUSION to CASE STUDY ONE [text p. 12] using p. 9 of this form to note the reference number of any comments you reread		

128

Figure 5

Case Study: Example from Discussion Unit "Problems in Individual Behavior"

The Place: A Subordinate Command in a Naval District.

The Report:

"I was personnel officer at a command where there were about 300 enlisted personnel. The service records of these personnel were maintained and administered by a support activity eight miles away. My chief responsibility therefore was to be liaison officer between the command and the personnel officer of the support activity.

"One day one of my men arrived in the office quite upset; thoroughly angry, he stated that he had gone to the support activity to re-enlist and had been told that they were much too busy to re-enlist him (he had not come to see me before going to the support activity). Fuming about the whole thing, he kept talking about writing to his Congressman.

"At this time the Navy had a big re-enlistment drive on, particularly for men with this man's rate.

What steps should I have taken to see that he re-enlisted and to change his attitude? How should I have dealt with the personnel officer at the support activity who was senior to me?"

The Problem

The Case of the Angry Seaman is typical of the many situations that arise in which an officer is confronted by a man angry or disturbed by the treatment he has received. The personnel officer is aware that all is not as it should be in communications between his command and support activity, but his immediate problem is to put the man straight.

You are asked to make a psychological description of the situation. The behavior of the man is reported by the personnel officer, who says nothing about his own behavior. You have to see through his words to the structure of the seaman's behavior. In doing so, you may find it necessary to refer to the personnel officer himself as an element intrinsic of the behavior of the man.

Figure 6

Examples of Feedback Comments from "Problems in Individual Behavior"

Comment: If you have omitted response items #4 and #9, read the following:

"The relevance of these terms should be pretty obvious. The man is exhibiting an emotional response to the conflict in his experience in the form of hostility towards the source of his frustration. By stimulus generalization, this hostility is spreading to take in the whole Navy as its object.

"With the fracturing of his self-image, the man becomes activated in his need for esteem. He talks of writing to his Congressman in order to regain a feeling of position and power."

Comment: If you have included item #21, read the following:

Even though we introduced this item right at the beginning in a positive light, we have to recognize three things:

1) The officer can always get more information (call the support activity to check on the man's story).
2) In a real situation you cannot have all the information you might like.
3) Something can be understood and brought into action on the information at hand.

Comment: If you have included item #15, or omitted item #16, read the following:

"A lot will depend on the resolution of the situation. As soon as the officer reacts, opens his mouth, or simply begins to listen, he begins to influence the behavior of his man.

"The man is full of righteous anger. If the officer sides with him and promises he will complain to the personnel officer at the support activity, the man will feel justified. His response will then be **extrinsically reinforced.** Whether he calms down or not depends on the **kind of need** that is dominating him.

"If the officer tries to calm him down directly and questions him about the actual events, **intrinsic reinforcement** will go on: the anger directed at the support activity may spread to the Navy itself **(stimulus generalization)."**

with the matrix of psychological descriptions shown **(Figure 3)**. Some sample comments are shown in **Figure 6**.

The Behavioral Timetable shows a Preliminary Exercise. As in the discussion unit on Discipline, the student is confronted with the extent of his own understanding before entering into the discussion. He is asked to write a behavioral description on a given topic. After completion of the discussion unit, he is asked to write another description on the same topic, and compares it with his first; thus, he is provided with a tool for self-evaluation. To bring the whole exercise "home," the student is asked to use the Response Indicator to analyze the behavior of the group during the discussion period.

The timetable shows the degree to which the student interacts with the materials and his peers, and the significant points for decision-making activities. It is common in a tutorial or discussion situation that a student has no firm ideas to contribute. By using Structural Communication, the student is guided into a chain of ideas up to a point where he has developed sufficient understanding of his own reasoning to be able to engage in fruitful discussion.

Another interesting feature of the process is that the student is asked to make his selection of response items according to specific criteria of relevance. Not only does this force him into a more precise act of discrimination, but it provides him with a stronger base for articulating his analysis. One student, for example, working with the materials asked for an explanation of the criteria "peripheral." He received the explanation with uncertainty. Nevertheless, ten minutes later he had assimilated the word into his own vocabulary, and used it in arguing a point with a fellow student.

Production of a finished Structural Communication Study Unit requires an extended period of field trials. WLC and Structural Communication Systems will be collaborating on an ongoing basis in developing and testing at the USNA. The data collection is aimed at ascertaining suitability for the student population in terms of clear semantic and ideational communication, and verifying that appropriate diagnostic and feedback features have been incorporated into the materials. This requires data samples from more than 100 students, with intervening revision where needed. To evaluate the materials, simple scanning is not sufficient. A new type of learning experience is provided. There is no other way to experience Structural Communication than to **experience** it — to do a study unit. This applies to the outside observer as well as to those involved in production, who need data based on student experience of the materials.

This article has briefly described an innovative technique embraced by the broad definition of "multimedia." Its application to a developmental course in Psychology and Leadership at the U. S. Naval Academy is being studied and validated in conjunction with other media and elements of the substance of the course. Thus far, modest gains with a small sample of midshipmen have been realized, and it can be reported as a "promising" approach to stimulating students to interact with students. The yield of such interactions has already suggested for the instructor a potential role as director of more meaningful dialogues with students.

Additionally, Westinghouse Learning Corporation is currently studying the application of prototype machine configurations employing Structural Communication where trade-offs can be projected for a group-machine mode while maintaining and capitalizing on the thrust of student interaction capability. The engineering of such a system is in its initial stages. □

References

Brudner, Harvey J. Computer-Managed Instruction. **Science,** November, 1968, 970-976.
Heinich, Robert Mediated Instruction: an Alternative to Classroom Instruction. **Theory Into Practice,** October, 1968, 146-148.
Le Baron, Walter. In Defense of Multi-media. Santa Monica, California, Systems Development Corporation (SP-3241), February, 1969.
Morgan, Robert M. A Systematic Approach to Educational Change. **Educational Technology,** September, 1969, 49-54 (a treatment of the conceptual base of the United States Office of Education ES '70 program — the context for the United States Naval Academy program, among others.)
Systematics (The Journal of the Institute for the Comparative Study of History, Philosophy and the Sciences) (Eng.) December, 1967. Entire Issue (see also, A. M. Hodgson, Structural Programming in Education, **Systematics,** March, 1967, 346-370.
Tosti, Donald T. & John R. Ball. A Behavioral Approach to Instructional Design and Media Selection. **A V Communication** Review, Spring, 1969, 5-25.

General Articles About Education Technology at the United States Naval Academy

Chemical and Engineering News, July 29, 1968.
Conord, Albert E. Educational Applications of Time Sharing at the United States Naval Academy. **Journal of the Association for Educational Data Systems,** December, 1969, 37-49.
Cray, Douglas W. Knowledge Industry Trains Guns on Annapolis. **New York Times,** October 15, 1967.
Koontz, Jesse L. Multimedia Course Development. No. PC-1168-9 Annapolis, Maryland, **Academic Computing Center, U. S. Naval Academy,** December, 1968.

Training System Evaluation Using Mathematical Models

Carl N. Brooks

This paper applies mathematical modeling techniques to the pre-design evaluation of the performance of an automotive mechanics training system. First, the method of deriving the model will be demonstrated in three stages:

1. derive the flowchart model of the system as it should operate
2. convert flowchart functions into mathematical form
3. derive the equations describing the system performance

Second, the mathematical model will be applied in **predicting** the system performance. This application demonstrates the economic advantages of using the mathematical modeling approach.

Origin

The U.S. Department of Transportation, the Federal Highway Administration, recently published an RFP (Request for Proposal) to produce a standard program of instruction and lesson plans for a course of study for automotive mechanics at the entry level classification.[1] This was predicated on Highway Safety Program Standard 4.4.1 dealing with periodic inspection of all registered vehicles.[2] The Standard provides, as a minimum, that: ". . .the inspection is performed by competent personnel specifically trained to perform their duties and certified by the State. . . ." Consequently, the proposal invited by the RFP requests a solution to a **real-life** problem and, for this reason, it was selected as a conceptual exercise in the Designing Education and Training System course conducted by Education and Training Consultants Company.[3]

Carl N. Brooks is vice president, Educational Systems Division, Education and Training Consultants Company, Los Angeles.

Training system

Figure 1 represents the process required to design the Automotive Mechanics Training System. This was produced by one of the regularly scheduled ETC classes by the end of the fourth day of activity. The system was conceptualized as seven subsystems: PERFORM JOB ANALYSIS (1.0), ESTABLISH STANDARD FOR TERMINAL PERFORMANCE (2.0), ESTABLISH TRAINEE SELECTION METHOD (3.0), DEVELOP CURRICULUM (4.0), CONDUCT PILOT STUDY (5.0), EVALUATE COURSE EFFECTIVENESS (6.0) and CONDUCT PROGRAM (7.0). It was refined to the fourth level of detail, but this was a limitation of time allocated in the course rather than a paucity of methods or facts.

Need for the pre-design performance evaluation

With this overview of the characteristics desired in the Automotive Mechanics Training System and the process necessary to design that system, we now examine the need for **pre-design** evaluation.

The process of designing and testing this system requires a **large investment** of manpower and money. Evaluation of the performance of the system **before** design will examine the validity of the investment in two ways:

1. Are the desired system characteristics mutually compatible and also compatible with the environment?

2. Will the investment yield the desired results in producing automotive mechanics?

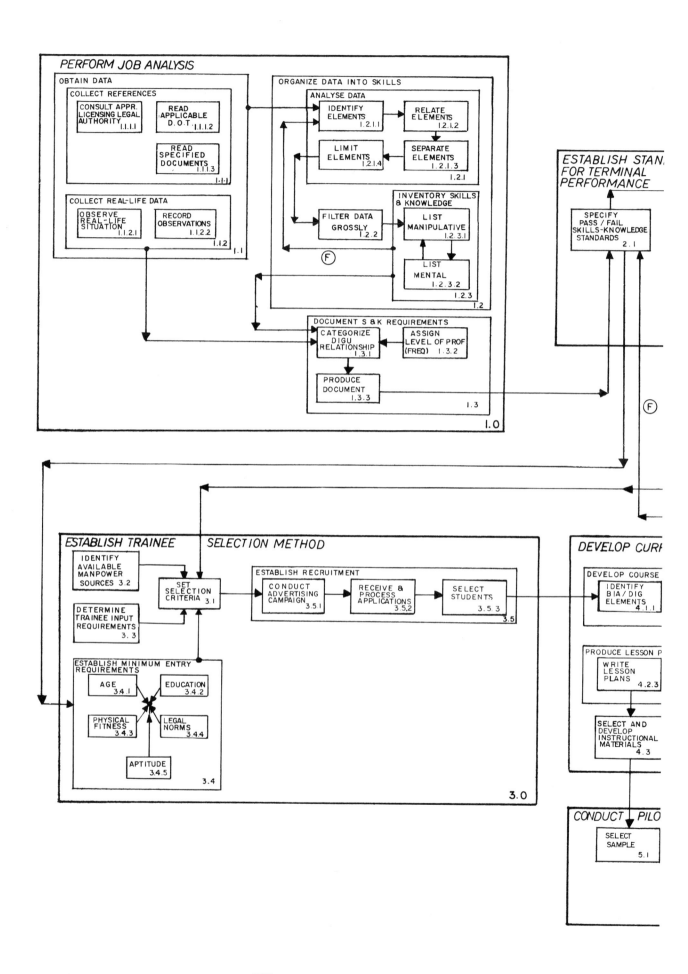

PERFORM JOB ANALYSIS

OBTAIN DATA

COLLECT REFERENCES

CONSULT APPR. LICENSING LEGAL AUTHORITY 1.1.1.1

READ APPLICABLE D.O.T. 1.1.1.2

READ SPECIFIED DOCUMENTS 1.1.1.3

1.1.1

COLLECT REAL-LIFE DATA

OBSERVE REAL-LIFE SITUATION 1.1.2.1

RECORD OBSERVATIONS 1.1.2.2

1.1.2

1.1

ORGANIZE DATA INTO SKILLS

ANALYSE DATA

IDENTIFY ELEMENTS 1.2.1.1

RELATE ELEMENTS 1.2.1.2

LIMIT ELEMENTS 1.2.1.4

SEPARATE ELEMENTS 1.2.1.3

1.2.1

FILTER DATA GROSSLY 1.2.2

INVENTORY SKILLS & KNOWLEDGE

LIST MANIPULATIVE 1.2.3.1

LIST MENTAL 1.2.3.2

1.2.3

(F)

1.2

DOCUMENT S & K REQUIREMENTS

CATEGORIZE DIGU RELATIONSHIP 1.3.1

ASSIGN LEVEL OF PROF (FREQ) 1.3.2

PRODUCE DOCUMENT 1.3.3

1.3

1.0

ESTABLISH STAN... FOR TERMINAL PERFORMANCE

SPECIFY PASS / FAIL SKILLS-KNOWLEDGE STANDARDS 2.1

(F)

ESTABLISH TRAINEE SELECTION METHOD

IDENTIFY AVAILABLE MANPOWER SOURCES 3.2

DETERMINE TRAINEE INPUT REQUIREMENTS 3.3

SET SELECTION CRITERIA 3.1

ESTABLISH RECRUITMENT

CONDUCT ADVERTISING CAMPAIGN 3.5.1

RECEIVE & PROCESS APPLICATIONS 3.5.2

SELECT STUDENTS 3.5.3

3.5

ESTABLISH MINIMUM ENTRY REQUIREMENTS

AGE 3.4.1

EDUCATION 3.4.2

PHYSICAL FITNESS 3.4.3

LEGAL NORMS 3.4.4

APTITUDE 3.4.5

3.4

3.0

DEVELOP CURR...

DEVELOP COURSE

IDENTIFY BIA / DIG ELEMENTS 4.1.1

PRODUCE LESSON P...

WRITE LESSON PLANS 4.2.3

SELECT AND DEVELOP INSTRUCTIONAL MATERIALS 4.3

CONDUCT PILO...

SELECT SAMPLE 5.1

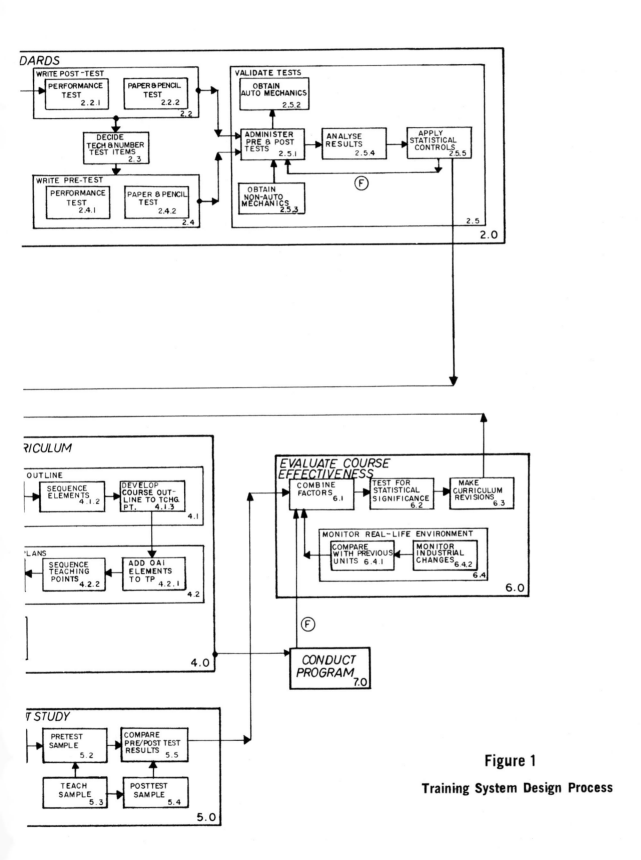

Figure 1

Training System Design Process

133

An affirmative answer to **both** questions insures that the training system is realizable as specified, and the expenditure should produce the desired results. On the other hand, negative answers indicate that the system is ill-conceived or cannot meet its goals. In this latter case, the characteristics and goals may be **modified** and these modifications simply substituted in the evaluation model until a realizable set is obtained. Of course, it may be found that the initially identified goals just cannot be reached. The project would then be abandoned **without** the large expenditure of money and manpower required to reach the **same conclusion** using the designing-and-testing approach.

Performance evaluation model

Introduction · The first step in pre-design evaluation is to construct a model of the training system, describing its interrelationship to the environment within which it will operate. The automotive mechanics course will be one of the functions interrelating within the real world. Operation of the course calls for a combination of instructors, teaching facilities and groups of trainees coming from the general population. Hence, we must model the ways in which the course is expected to bring them together and their influences upon one another. The first step is to create a **graphic** picture of these **relationships.** This is followed by quantification of the words or descriptors in this graphic picture.

Flowchart · We start modeling by picturing the functions and their interrelationships in a flowchart. This development follows in the time-honored tradition set forth by Silvern[4] and is exemplified in the preceding papers in this issue. The flowchart model of the Automotive Mechanics Training System in operation is shown in **Figure 2.** The codes in each rectangle of this model identify the corresponding rectangle and function in **Figure 1.**

In **Figure 2,** the relationship of the course to the target population and trainees is represented by the upper closed loop. The relationship to instructional methods and instructors is given by the lower closed loop.

Now, we will discuss **Figure 2,** which interrelates the **operational** blocks of **Figure 1.** Brackets [] will be used for the descriptors in the **Figure 2** model while parentheses () will be used for the descriptors in **Figure 1** for more precise communication. The target population from which the trainees are to be drawn is defined in the IDENTIFY TARGET POPULATION [3.1] rectangle. This identity is established in (3.1) of **Figure 1.** The training system will next DETERMINE AVAILABLE AND QUALIFIED TRAINEES [3.5.2] to take the course. The real-life data for this is obtained in (3.5.2) of **Figure 1.** From this

group [3.5.2], and knowing how many trainees the course will accommodate [5.0], the system will SELECT TRAINEES [3.5.3]. Then the TRAINEES TAKE COURSE [7.0] and this results in two states: GRADUATE TRAINEES [7.0] or DROPOUT TRAINEES [7.0]. The experience of the trainees in taking the course, and finding and holding jobs subsequently is fed back to the target population pool [3.5.2] through CHANGE POPULATION PROPENSITY [3.5.1] to take the course.

The lower loop depicts the relationship of the instruction. The design must IDENTIFY METHODS OF INSTRUCTION [4.2.3] to be used. This corresponds to WRITE LESSON PLANS (4.2.3) in **Figure 1.** From these methods, we will CALCULATE COURSE CAPACITY (TRAINEE) [5.0]. This is implicit in CONDUCT PILOT STUDY (5.0) of **Figure 1.** We SELECT TRAINEES [3.5.3] and the TRAINEES TAKE COURSE [7.0]. From this interaction, ways to IMPROVE COURSE EFFICIENCY [6.3] appear as **feedback.** This corresponds to MAKE CURRICULUM REVISIONS (6.3) in **Figure 1.**

Functional Block Mathematics · **Figure 2** provides a flowchart model or "block diagram" of the Automotive Mechanics course in operation which is quite similar to the flowcharts derived in the other papers in this issue. Now, we embark upon the next quantum step of **refinement** in the logical structure of these flowcharts. We will convert the word descriptions within the rectangles, the **descriptors,** to **mathematical symbols and equations.**

Let us define

$y(t)$ = number graduating at time t

$x(t)$ = number starting course at time t

ρ_D = percent dropping out of course

τ = length of time course takes

Then, immediately the number graduating is seen as

$$y(t) = x(t - \tau)[1 - \rho_D] \qquad (1)$$

and the number dropping out is $x(t - \tau)\rho_D$. These are entered into the appropriate rectangles, replacing descriptors of **Figure 2** as shown in **Figure 3.** Now let

$P_A(t)$ = population available and qualified

$S_A(t)$ = course capacity available

Then, at any time, either there will be enough available capacity to handle **all** the available trainees, or else the number of trainees will be **limited** by the capacity. Thus, the number of trainees entering the course is always the smaller of those available and those that can be accommodated, or

$$x(t) = \text{Min}\{P_A(t), S_A(t)\} \qquad (2)$$

Now, let us examine the characteristics of the available population. The two major candidate groups are high school students and unemployed individuals. We define

P_H = high school population

$\rho_u P_T$ = unemployed population

where

P_T = total population of U.S.

ρ_u = percent unemployed

The percent of each group interested in taking the course is the **propensity** defined as

$\rho_{AH}(t)$ = percent available from high school population

$\rho_{AU}(t)$ = percent available from unemployed population

Then, the total available population is sum of individuals available from high schools and from ranks of the unemployed

$$P_A = \rho_{AH}P_H + \rho_{AU}\rho_u P_T \qquad (3)$$

These replace the appropriate descriptors of **Figure 2** in **Figure 3.**

Various methods of instruction may be used. To **each** method of instruction we assign an identifying index, i. Then we define

U_i = number of units of i th method of instruction

S_i = trainee capacity of each of the i th units

The total trainee capacity of the i th method is just the product of the number of i th units and the capacity of each, or $U_i S_i$. The total trainee capacity of the system is the sum of the capacity of each method.

$$S_A = \sum_i U_i S_i \qquad (4)$$

This completes the mathematical model of the Automotive Mechanics Training System in operation as shown in **Figure 2.**

Performance simulation

Approach · The next step is to convert the flowchart of **Figure 2** into a group of equations to describe the course in operation. Because the graphic model contains two loops, it will take a set of two equations to convert the flowchart of **Figure 2** to **Figure 3**. From equation (2), we notice that x(t) is a **nonlinear function**. This indicates that the describing set of equations will be nonlinear, making numerical evaluation of the equations complicated. Hence, we will replace the **exact** equations by an **approximate** pair that are simpler to evaluate. This is accomplished by noting that the **minimum** selection of equation (2) means that at any given time

the whole system is **controlled** either by the available population or the available capacity. It may be stated: the system behaves either as if it is **population limited** or **capacity limited.**

Population Limited · When the system is **population** limited, the lower loop in **Figures 2** and **3** has no effect on system performance. Then system performance is described by an equation for the upper or population loop. Using the linear approximations for propensities

$$\rho_{AH} = ky + c \qquad (5)$$

$$\rho_{AU} = ky + c \qquad (6)$$

the equation for system performance in the population limited case is

$$y(n\tau) = [1-\rho_D]\{k[1-\rho_D][P_H+\rho_u P_T]P_A((n-2)\tau) \\ +[P_H+\rho_u P_T]c\} \qquad (7)$$

This equation tells how many automotive mechanics would graduate from the program if there were sufficient instructors, etc., to handle all candidates who applied and were qualified to take the course. The number of graduates (output) would then be represented by the curve in **Figure 4,** which is just the plot of equation (7).

Capacity Limited · At the other extreme, when system performance is determined by the lower loop in **Figures 2** and **3,** the system is **capacity** limited. Assuming that only human-instruction and computer-assisted instruction (CAI) are used in the training system, and assuming an efficiency improvement factor of the form

$$1-e^{\frac{(n-1)\tau}{\alpha}}$$

for human-instruction, the number of graduates from the capacity limited system is

$$y(n\tau) = [1-\rho_D] [U_1 30(1-e^{\frac{(n-1)\tau}{\alpha}}) + U_2 M] \qquad (8)$$

where

U_1 = number of human instructors

U_2 = number of computers

M = number of trainees per computer

The curve of equation (8) is plotted in **Figure 5.** It shows the number of graduates if the training system is only controlled by the lower loop.

Performance prediction

Total System · The two system equations, above, were simplified by assuming that first one and then the other loop was controlling the output.

Figure 2
Flowchart Model of Automotive Mechanics Training System in Operation

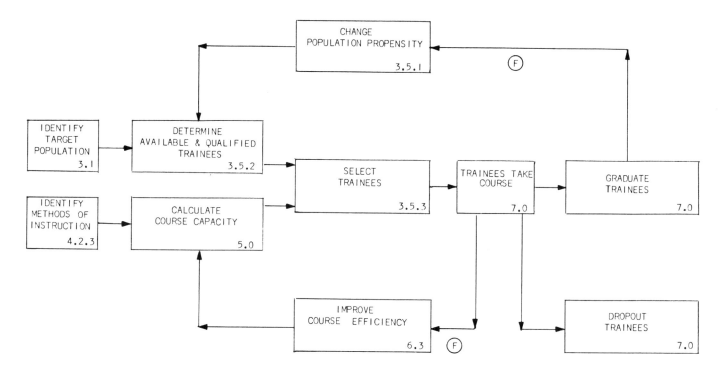

Figure 3
Mathematical Model of Automotive Mechanics Training System in Operation

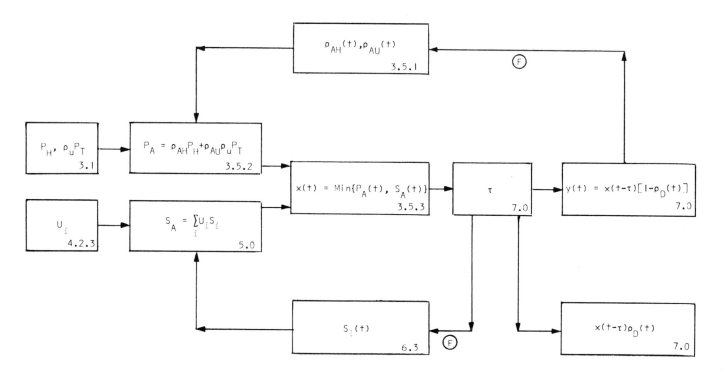

Figure 4

Output of Graduates When Automotive Mechanics Training System is Always Population Limited

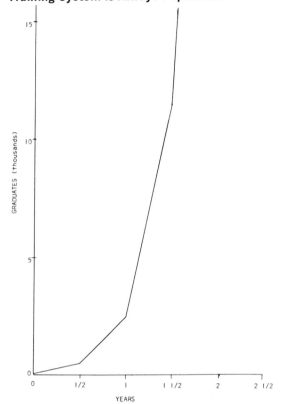

Figure 5

Output of Graduates When Automotive Mechanics Training System is Always Capacity Limited

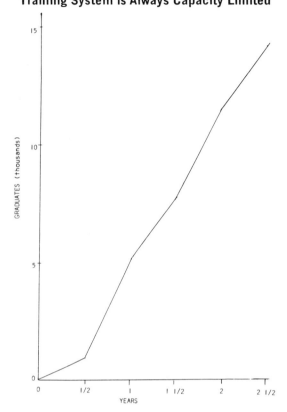

However, we are interested in **predicting the real-life performance or output of the total system.** The real-life situation is **not** modeled using just **one** loop as we observe in **Figures 1** and **2.** In the real world, control may change from one loop to the other. Now, we will use a graphical plotting technique to estimate overall system performance.

Equations (7) and (8) have been replotted in **Figure 6.** Equation (7) produces the curve labeled POPULATION LIMITED and equation (8) produces the curve labeled CAPACITY LIMITED. Notice that during the first year of operation, the population limited curve provides **fewer** graduates than the capacity limited curve. The interpretation is that the number of candidates available and qualified is **less** than the number that can be taught. However, as the system continues to operate, after 1½ years the number that can be taught is **less** than those available and qualified, and the control has shifted. Thus, where the curves **crossover** between 1 and 1½ years the system changes from too few **trainees** to too little **instructional** capacity. At any time, the number of trainees which can be graduated by the training system is determined by which curve is lower on the graph in **Figure 6.** This is emphasized by cross-hatching the area below the curves. The cross-hatched area represents the predicted system **output.**

The Automotive Mechanics System has the design objective of graduating 50,000 automotive mechanics per year (1). It is clear from **Figure 5** that the system evaluated here is not going to reach that output very quickly. Also, observe that the **ultimate** stumbling block is **capacity** and not population. The natural thought is to increase the **capacity.**

Varying Capacity • The real power of a mathematical model in studying a system **before** it is designed is about to be demonstrated using a **simulation** technique. We will examine what happens to the system output (number of graduates) as the capacity is varied. This is called a **parametric study** because a parameter is varied.

In this case, the parameter is the number of instructors. The curves in **Figures 4, 5,** and **6** were calculated for 1000 instructors. The system capacity is plotted in **Figure 7** for 500, 1000 and 2000 instructors. At first glance, it appears from **Figure 7** that 2000 instructors will permit the system to produce 50,000 graduates per year by the end of 2½ years. However, it may not be possible to immediately acquire 2000 instructors on a full-time basis qualified to teach the automotive mechanics course. Faced with that, other alternatives can be evaluated by simulating on the mathematical model.

Figure 6

Graphical Estimation of System Output

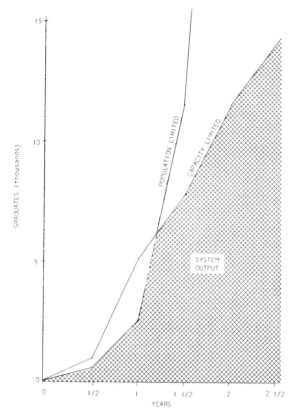

Figure 7

System Capacity as a Function of Number of Instructors

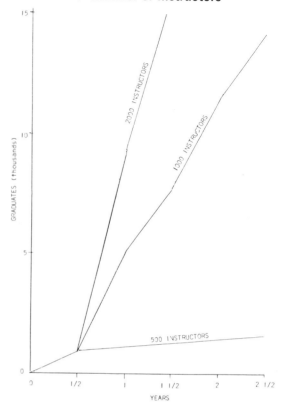

This paper has described the process of deriving a **closed-loop** mathematical model from the **closed-loop** flowchart model. The power of modeling and simulation has been demonstrated in evaluating the Automotive Mechanics Training System by simulation **before** it is designed.

In the case cited, a serious question has been raised regarding the design of an adequate training system.

Open-loop instructional systems have been modeled and simulation performed using even less sophisticated techniques.[5] This ability to evaluate alternatives and to prevent false starts and bad designs demonstrates the economic advantage of mathematical modeling in the pre-design stage. □

Appendix

The numerical values used in calculating **Figures 4, 5, 6** and **7** are:

$$k = 10^{-6}$$
$$\rho_D = 0.10$$
$$P_{II} = 2.5 \times 10^{6}$$
$$\rho_u = 0.01$$
$$P_T = 250 \times 10^{6}$$
$$c = 10^{-4}$$

$U_1 = 1000$ (varied in **Figure 7** — see text)
$\alpha = 3$
$U_2 = 10$
$M = 100$
$\tau = \frac{1}{2}$ year

References

1. Request for Proposal, "Motor Vehicle Repairs and Inspection Personnel — Manpower Development Program," National Highway Safety Bureau, Federal Highway Administration, U.S. Department of Transportation; May, 1968.

2. "Periodic Motor Vehicle Inspection, "Highway Safety Program Standard 4.4.1, National Highway Safety Bureau, Federal Highway Administration, U. S. Department of Transportation, Washington D.C.; 27 June, 1967.

3. Course Outline, "Designing Education and Training Systems," Education and Training Consultants Co., Los Angeles, California; November, 1968.

4. L. C. Silvern, "LOGOS: A System Language for Flowchart Modeling;" this issue.

5. L. C. Silvern, **Systems Engineering of Education IV: System Analysis and Synthesis Applied Quantitatively to Create an Instructional System.** Los Angeles: Education and Training Consultants Co., 1969.